T0305876

The CISO Playbook

A CISO is the ultimate guardian of an organization's digital assets. As a cybersecurity leader, a CISO must possess a unique balance of executive leadership, technical knowledge, strategic vision, and effective communication skills. The ever-evolving cyberthreat landscape demands a resilient, proactive approach coupled with a keen ability to anticipate attack angles and implement protective security mechanisms. Simultaneously, a cybersecurity leader must navigate the complexities of balancing security requirements with business objectives, fostering a culture of cybersecurity awareness, and ensuring compliance with regulatory frameworks.

The CISO Playbook aims to provide nothing but real-world advice and perspectives to both up-and-coming cybersecurity leaders as well as existing ones looking to grow. The book does not approach cybersecurity leadership from the perspective of the academic, or what it should be, but more from that which it really is. Moreover, it focuses on the many things a cybersecurity leader needs to "be" given that the role is dynamic and ever-evolving, requiring a high level of adaptability.

A CISO's career is touched from many differing angles, by many different people and roles. A healthy selection of these entities, from executive recruiters to salespeople to venture capitalists, is included to provide real-world value to the reader. To augment these, the book covers many areas that a cybersecurity leader needs to understand – from the pre-interview stage to the first quarter and from security operations to the softer skills such as storytelling and communications.

The book wraps up with a focus on techniques and knowledge areas, such as financial literacy, that are essential for a CISO to be effective. Other important areas, such as understanding the adversaries' mindset and self-preservation, are covered as well. A credo is provided as an example of the documented commitment a cybersecurity leader must make and remain true to.

Andres Andreu, the Deputy Chief Information Security Officer (CISO) at Hearst and a renowned cybersecurity leader, holds prestigious credentials including CISSP and ISSAP and is a Boardroom Certified Qualified Technology Expert (QTE). With a diverse career traversing federal government, corporate sectors, and entrepreneurial ventures in cybersecurity, he is a mentor, startup advisor, and an acclaimed author.

Security, Audit and Leadership Series

Series Editor: Dan Swanson, Dan Swanson and Associates, Ltd., Winnipeg, Manitoba, Canada.

The *Security, Audit and Leadership Series* publishes leading-edge books on critical subjects facing security and audit executives as well as business leaders. Key topics addressed include Leadership, Cybersecurity, Security Leadership, Privacy, Strategic Risk Management, Auditing IT, Audit Management and Leadership

Why CISOs Fail (Second Edition)
Barak Engel

Riding the Wave
Applying Project Management Science in the Field of Emergency Management
Andrew Boyarsky

The Shortest Hour
An Applied Approach to Boardroom Governance of Cybersecurity
Lee Parrish

Global Audit Leadership
A Practical Approach to Leading a Global Internal Audit (GIA) Function in a Constantly Changing Internal and External Landscape
Audley L. Bell

Construction Audit
Building a Solid Foundation
Denise Cicchella

Continuous Auditing with AI in the Public Sector
Lourens Erasmus and Sezer Bozkus Kahyaoglu

Ironwill 360° Leadership
Moving Forward: Unlock Twelve Emerging Trends for Forward Thinking Leaders
Douglas P. Pflug

The CISO Playbook
Andres Andreu

Leveraging Blockchain Technology
Governance, Risk, Compliance, Security, and Benevolent Use Cases
Shaun Aghili

For more information about this series, please visit: www.routledge.com/Internal-Audit-and-IT-Audit/book-series/CRCINTAUDITA

The CISO Playbook

Andres Andreu

CRC Press
Taylor & Francis Group
Boca Raton London New York

CRC Press is an imprint of the
Taylor & Francis Group, an **informa** business

Designed cover image: © Shutterstock

First edition published 2025
by CRC Press
2385 NW Executive Center Drive, Suite 320, Boca Raton FL 33431

and by CRC Press
4 Park Square, Milton Park, Abingdon, Oxon, OX14 4RN

CRC Press is an imprint of Taylor & Francis Group, LLC

© 2025 Andres Andreu

ISBN: 978-1-032-75796-4 (hbk)
ISBN: 978-1-032-76207-4 (pbk)
ISBN: 978-1-003-47755-6 (ebk)

DOI: 10.1201/9781003477556

Typeset in Times
by Apex CoVantage, LLC

For my wife, Sharon and four children, Christopher, Kenneth, Caleb, and Rebecca. To my children, take this book as an example of that which can be achieved with motivation, discipline, and by living in a free country. Cherish that, don't let it go to waste and don't ever let it be taken from you.

For the unsung, and sometimes unseen, guardians of the digital realm – Chief Information Security Officers and their security teams worldwide. Your tireless vigilance weaves the invisible armor that shields us all, securing the foundations upon which our future world relies. This book honors your silent dedication and relentless pursuit of digital protection, in every byte and beyond. May you find resilience and continued excellence in every challenge you face.

Contents

Foreword

PRUDENT GUIDANCE FOR PRESENT AND FUTURE CISOS

When Andres showed me the new book that he was developing for CISOs, I was immediately excited. I loved the idea of helping them develop skills in the many, many roles they are asked today to fill. Unlike more traditional professions, the role of CISO is obviously new – and we can all benefit from some career guidance.

The idea Andres includes in his chapter on "being a student of the business", for example, is easier said than done. I can tell you that it took me nearly three decades to learn the business of telecommunications. And without this knowledge, I'm not sure how managing security would have been possible. Too many CISOs skip this step.

The challenge of "being a builder" also resonates strongly with me, especially given the fact that so many CISOs are being asked to reinvent their programs. I don't know how this would be possible without creative skills and Andres has wonderful advice in this regard. Building programs is the essence of well-organized security management.

Developing "risk management skills" is also addressed in this fine book, and while this might seem obvious, it always amazes me how many CISOs have such a thin understanding of risk and how it is managed but never removed. Risk management is truly the fundamental basis for managing security and one can never learn enough in this area.

"Team leadership and executive leadership" are also addressed in this book, and I can tell you from personal experience that these can be opposite skills. Navigating the various pitfalls is tough, and I'm glad Andres included these topics. So many of my advisory clients struggle so much with these skills. I can't wait to hand them this book.

I especially liked that "communications skill" is addressed, since my observation is that the best CISOs are also the best at connecting with people. There seems to be a direct correlation between good communication skills and success in the position. This involves both oral, written, and even unspoken communications.

"Vendor management" is also addressed in the book, especially from the perspective of negotiating deals and contracts. This is a skill that few technical people have, so CISOs with such background will truly benefit from the discussion. I know that this is one of my own weaker skills.

I could go on and on here, but perhaps it makes more sense for you to just turn the page and get started with this fine book. Learning the skills of being a great CISO is not easy, but the investment of time is well worth it. I'm so glad that you've picked up a copy of this excellent work.

And I hope that you enjoy and benefit from this fine contribution from Andres.

By Dr. Edward Amoroso
Chief Executive Officer, TAG Infosphere, Inc.
Research Professor, NYU

Preface

The concept of leadership has existed throughout history. The concept of protecting sensitive elements of information has existed throughout history. The coupling of the two isn't in its infancy, but it doesn't have a terribly long legacy either. The specific fields of cyber and information security and the need for dedicated leadership within either of those domains have emerged as a relatively recent development. It is a response to the global increase of usage and reliance on digital technologies. With all of the amazing developments that make digital technologies useful and appealing comes the growing threat of nefarious action. Cyber attacks seem like a normal thing at this point. They are proof of the fact that a subset of the human race will continuously figure out ways to misuse that which was intended for some legitimate use. In the same way that law enforcement was invented to try and combat crime, the need for specialized digital security practices has emerged in response to the unique challenges raised by the digital age.

The digital age commenced with standalone computing devices, and this was focused on business, government, and military environments. In a relatively short span of time, this expanded into advancements of information technology and permeated the consumer space. Another major dynamic of this expansion is the proliferation of interconnectivity. Within the realm of interconnectivity, there have been waves of evolution from proprietary networking to the Internet as it exists today. There was a time that a physical penetration of a target facility was a required element for a digital attack. The rise of the internet, the widespread use of computers and mobile devices, and the digitization of traditionally closed environments, such as critical infrastructure, have brought about new challenges and risks that require dedicated attention, expertise, and leadership.

Parallel to all this evolution and transformation are the respective threats. Most agree that this started with Creeper in 1971, albeit within a controlled network (not in the wild). The first elements of digital malware emerged around this time, in the 1970s and 1980s, with the first known virus (Elk Cloner) found in the wild in 1982. This is a general demarcation of the beginning of the cybersecurity field. Later in the 1990s and early 2000s, information security leadership started to show signs of importance in response to all of this activity. This started as a pure technology play and evolved into cybersecurity as a parallel realm. While the differences can be many and subtle, at a high level Information Security (infosec) focuses mainly on protection of information by way of enforcing authorized access. It is an overarching term covering systems and policies intended to protect information. Cybersecurity covers a wider scope, touching just about everything relevant to electronic systems and related communications. Within cybersecurity, there are subcategories such as Application Security (appsec), cloud, network, and critical infrastructure security. Irrespective of the differences cyber and/or information security leadership has gained prominence and recognition as digital attacks have become more impactful, sophisticated, and prevalent.

Cyber and information security leadership have organically evolved to address the need for dedicated attention to the ever-changing landscape of threats. The fact that this has gone through an evolution alludes to the fact that at some point in the past this responsibility was placed on people as simply part of their job, not entirely being the job. Governments, companies, and organizations have recognized the need for dedicated security leadership in an effort to protect resources from bad actors. Today cybersecurity leadership, in particular, has expanded to encompass a wide range of roles and responsibilities beyond exclusively being a protector. These include being a strategist, being a responder (as in incident management and response), being an assessor (conducting risk assessments), and being an evangelist by championing a culture awareness and pushing for security-first thinking.

Cybersecurity leadership is established as a necessity at this point. It covers a vital space providing protection for individuals and organizations alike from the growing, and ever changing, landscape of cyber threats. At a high level, the importance of cybersecurity leadership can be gleaned within the following areas:

- Evolution – The digital landscape is constantly evolving, and with it, the landscape that makes up cyber threats. Complexity and sophistication of threats, and the malware that comprises key areas of those threats, continue to rise. Cybercriminals are generally sophisticated, and what was once considered nation-state-level sophistication is now common. Effective cybersecurity leadership is crucial to evolve state toward a proactive one, as opposed to the tradition of reactiveness.
- Protection – The reliance on technology, especially innovative technology, is obvious and now part of modern-day life. Expecting people to go backward for the sake of security is ridiculous. Humans have proved their general willingness to give away their data. It is our reality. Cybersecurity leadership is essential to pursue the best possible level of confidentiality, integrity, and availability of this data.
- Scope – In addition to protecting personal and corporate entities, cybersecurity leadership plays a critical role in safeguarding national security interests. Nation-states and nefarious actors often target sensitive resources and this is evolving to the cyber-physical domain. Critical infrastructure attacks, for instance, can negatively impact human life. This goes beyond the realm of protecting data. A strong comprehensive cybersecurity strategy is in demand. It must foster collaboration between government and private sector entities in order to collectively combat cyber threats that could potentially impact economic stability and public safety.
- Innovation – As more and more organizations embrace innovations such as digital transformation, cloud computing, Internet of Things (IoT), attack surfaces dynamically expand. Cybersecurity leadership plays an essential role in enabling all of this innovation by ensuring security by design. Another way of looking at this is the difference between facilitating business as opposed to facilitating safe business. A CISO needs to seek out that balance between the benefits of innovations and a security-first mindset within an organization.

- Resilience – Cyber resilience represents an organization's ability to respond to and recover from the impact of threats. A cyber-resilient organization should be able to adapt and overcome crises and adversities. Cybersecurity leaders are responsible for developing and testing incident management programs and plans, conducting continuous risk assessments, and implementing security controls. This also encompasses organizational culture aspects such that employees are synchronized in mission and the protection of the organization's reputation.
- Interconnectedness – The interconnected nature of the digital space means that a cyber attack on one entity can negatively impact other entities. Cybersecurity leaders must promote domestic and international cooperation, information sharing, and collaboration to combat cyber threats collectively. This field is too complex to effectively operate in isolation.
- Regulations – Governments worldwide are enacting stringent cybersecurity regulations to address growing cyber threats and the lack of corporate response. Organizations must comply with these regulations to avoid legal penalties and reputational damage. Cybersecurity leaders are responsible for being intimate with and implementing these requirements.

On this last point, it should be noted that many in the cyber and/or information security industry frown on government involvement in this space. But, too many companies have displayed a lack of giving this space the necessary importance. From a pragmatic perspective, this disregard has prompted the need for regulatory involvement. Regulators are positively helping put cybersecurity on the forefront of an organization's focus. This spans the C-Suite and reaches the boardroom. Among global regulatory entities increasing pressure toward cyber resilience are:

- United States of America (USA) – Multiple regulatory entities are involved in cybersecurity oversight:
  - The Cybersecurity and Infrastructure Security Agency (CISA) is the national coordinator for critical infrastructure security and resilience. They also play a key role in fostering collaboration and partnership between government and relevant non-government entities.
  - The National Institute of Standards and Technology (NIST) provides well-known and popular cybersecurity frameworks and guidelines.
  - The Securities and Exchange Commission (SEC) is pushing for many advancements in this space. In particular, they are pushing for the requirement that public companies disclose directors' cyber security expertise. The push is to give cybersecurity the same level of board attention that financial elements are now given at that level.
  - The Federal Trade Commission (FTC) generally enforces cybersecurity regulations for financial institutions.
- European Union (EU) – The European Union has taken significant steps to enhance cyber resilience and protect its member states' critical infrastructure and data. General Data Protection Regulation (GDPR) establishes data protection requirements and imposes substantial penalties for

non-compliance. Another directive, the Network and Information Security Directive (NIS Directive) mandates cybersecurity and incident reporting requirements for operators of critical services.

- United Kingdom (UK) – The United Kingdom has taken its own steps to enhance cyber resilience. The National Cyber Security Centre (NCSC) provides guidance, best practices, and incident response support for both public and private sectors. The UK government has also introduced the Cyber Essentials, and Cyber Essentials Plus, certifications which offer a framework to help organizations understand how they fare against common cyber threats.
- Singapore – The Singapore government has established the Cyber Security Agency (CSA) to oversee national cybersecurity efforts. It works with critical infrastructure sectors, businesses, and individuals alike to enhance cyber resilience. Singapore has also introduced the Cybersecurity Act, which provides a legally enforceable framework for the regulation and protection of critical infrastructure.
- Australia – The Australian government has implemented several initiatives to enhance cyber resilience. The Australian Cyber Security Centre (ACSC) provides guidance, threat intelligence, and incident response support. The government has also introduced the Notifiable Data Breaches (NDB) scheme, which mandates organizations to report certain data breaches to impacted individuals and the Office of the Australian Information Commissioner (OAIC).
- International – Several international organizations are also promoting cyber resilience:
  - The International Organization for Standardization (ISO) provides standards such as ISO 27001 for information security management systems.
  - The Financial Stability Board (FSB) and the International Monetary Fund (IMF) actively encourage cybersecurity measures in the financial sector.

These examples highlight some of the efforts from regulators globally to address cyber resilience. It's important to note that this landscape is dynamic, new regulations and initiatives are being actively worked on to keep up with cybersecurity landscape evolutions.

It should be noted that throughout this book the title of Chief Information Security Officer (CISO) will be used. It has become a commonly used title in the industry. Here it is reflective of, and equivalent to, that role that has the last word on cyber and/or information security matters within a given company or organization.

The mindset of a CISO is the biggest asset/weapon this person has. To be clear, and not do anyone a disservice, being a CISO is not for the faint at heart; nor is it for those who expect fair play. The cybersecurity field is not even close to a level playing field. A CISO candidate, or really anyone looking to operate in this field, must understand, and accept, this reality before going in. In particular, a CISO, being fully aware of the challenges, is still willing to take on this unfair fight. Attackers have, and most likely will for the foreseeable future, the advantage. Period. A CISO fears not.

Ultimately, a CISO represents the entity to bring cybersecurity leadership to the forefront of today's business world. By way of reality, the business world has somewhat morphed into a modern digital battlefield. As a CISO, facing down evolving cyber threat landscapes, protecting sensitive data, pursuing cyber resilience, protecting human life, adhering to compliance and regulatory requirements, enabling digital transformation and innovation, and supporting safe global interconnectedness will become part of your normal workdays. While a CISO will most likely not live in the trenches, the teams they guide and direct will look to them for direction and leadership. Strong and effective leadership will require a CISO to provide informed guidance. As such, there are many things a CISO should, and will need to, "be".

About the Author

Andres Andreu, the Deputy Chief Information Security Officer (CISO) at Hearst and a renowned cybersecurity leader, holds prestigious credentials including CISSP and ISSAP, and is a Boardroom Certified Qualified Technology Expert (QTE). With a diverse career traversing federal government, corporate sectors, and entrepreneurial ventures in cybersecurity, he is a mentor, startup advisor, and acclaimed author.

His government tenure includes a significant impact in lawful intercept technology within federal law enforcement, earning three US Department of Justice awards for his contributions to drug law enforcement. Transitioning to the corporate realm, Andres made a mark at Ogilvy and Mather as a partner and Chief Application Architect, later consulting for high-profile entities like the United Nations. As a founding member and key executive at Bayshore Networks (acquired by Opswat in 2021), and former CISO at 2U, Inc./edX, his expertise has been pivotal in shaping cybersecurity landscapes.

Andreu's leadership and innovative approaches have garnered him accolades such as a Top 100 CISO (C100) by Security Current, Top 50 Information Security Professional, and recognition in leading industry publications. His experience encompasses both offensive and defensive cybersecurity strategies, underpinned by a philosophy that balances executive and employee objectives.

Author of *Professional Pen Testing Web Applications* (Wiley, 2006 – ISBN: 978-0-471-78966-6), contributor to *97 Things Every Application Security Professional Should Know* (O'Reilly Media, 2024 – ISBN: 978-1-098-15217-8), and articles with various magazines, his work extends beyond writing to inventing, with patents in cybersecurity innovations (WO2020069367A1, US20200193035A1). He advises the Forgepoint Capital Cybersecurity Advisory Council and serves on multiple advisory boards.

A Cuban immigrant and proud American citizen, Andres balances his professional achievements with a happy marriage and four wonderful kids. He is an international-level certified Judo coach with USA Judo and an artist. Andreu's multifaceted career and personal achievements highlight his profound impact on the cybersecurity field and beyond.

Special Contributors

Rod Aday
Chief Information Security Officer,
Bank of China, USA.

Yuri Aguiar
Chief Enterprise Data Officer, WPP

Rubi Arbel
Chief Executive Officer and co-founder,
Scribe Security

Brian Arellanes
Independent Board Director, CEO, and
founder, ITSourceTEK

Felix Asare
Deputy Chief Information Security
Officer, Putnam Investments

Anik Bose
Managing Partner, BGV

Vlad Brodsky
Chief Information Officer and Chief
Information Security Officer, OTC
Markets Group

Chris Castaldo
Chief Information Security Officer,
Crossbeam

Jamey Cummings
Partner, JM Search

Dan Elliott
Principal for Cyber Security Risk
Advisory, Zurich Resilience
Solutions (ZRS) Canada

Douglas Gotay
Co-founder, Satellite Growth Services

Billy Gouveia
Chief Executive Officer and founder,
Surefire Cyber, Inc.

Maria Graham
Account Executive, Nuspire

Paul J. Guerra
Chief Information Security Officer,
StockX

Carlos Guerrero
Senior Compliance Executive, 360
Advanced

Ross Haleliuk
Head of Product, LimaCharlie

Patrick Hayes
Chief Product Officer, Third Wave
Innovations

Brandon Hoe
Founder and Executive Producer,
ClearSketch

Terence D. Jackson
Chief Security Advisor, Microsoft

James Kenigsberg
Entrepreneur and Technology Evangelist

Geoffrey Kerr
Executive consultant, Cyber Security
Resiliency Consultancy

Mike Krass
Owner/visionary, MKG Marketing

Adam Lahav
Major Accounts Executive, Wiz

Surinder Lall
Senior Vice President of Information
  Security Risk Management,
  Paramount Global

Ramin Lamei
Founder, TechCompass

Nia Luckey
CIO Advisory Services Sr. Consultant,
  Infosys

Casey Marquette
Chief Executive Officer, Covenant
  Technologies

Jesse Meadors
Founder, Tutela Talent

Jason Ossler
Director of Advisory and Response,
  Surefire Cyber Inc.

Dennis Partridge
Vice President of Cybersecurity, 2U/edX

Aric Perminter
Founder and Chairman, Lynx
  Technology Partners, LLC

Michael Piacente
Managing Partner and cofounder, Hitch
  Partners

Arti Raman
Chief Executive Officer and founder,
  Portal26

Jose Alejandro Guinea Rivera
Global Architect and Offensive
  Security Manager, Corporacion
  Mutli-Inversiones

Cristian Rodriguez
Field CTO for the Americas, CrowdStrike

Robert D. Rodriguez
Chairman and founder, SINET

Neil Saltman
Author of Cybersecurity Sales: A
  Buyer's and Seller's Perspective

Kevin Senator
Chief Executive Officer, Constella
  Intelligence

Stuart Seymour
Group Chief Security Officer (Group
  CISO and CSO), Virgin Media O2

Alvaro Soneiro
Team Lead, Vulnerability Management
  and Red Team, United Nations

Seth Spergel
Managing Partner, Merlin Ventures

Susan Peterson Sturm
Sr. Director of Security Business
  Development and Strategic
  Partnerships, Wabtec

Christine Tornabene
Senior Director, Cloud Security,
  2U/edX

Lisa Xu
Chief Executive Officer, NopSec

Aleksandr Yampolskiy
Chief Executive Officer and
  co-Founder, SecurityScorecard

Alberto Yépez
Co-Founder and Managing Director,
  Forgepoint Capital

Bob Zukis
Chief Executive Officer, Digital
  Directors Network

CHAPTER 1 – Be the Candidate

Type	Author	Page
Expert Advice	James Kenigsberg	18
Expert Advice	Surinder Lall	19
Expert Advice	Casey Marquette	20
Expert Advice	Jesse Meadors	20
Expert Advice	Michael Piacente	21
Real World Perspective	Casey Marquette	24
Real World Perspective	Jamey Cummings	25

CHAPTER 2 – Be a Student of the Business

Type	Author	Page
Expert Advice	Chris Castaldo	43
Real World Perspective	Vlad Brodsky	44
Real World Perspective	Dan Elliott	44
Real World Perspective	Arti Raman	45
Real World Perspective	Lisa Xu	45

CHAPTER 3 – Be a Builder

Type	Author	Page
Real World Perspective	Brian Arellanes	86
Real World Perspective	Cristian Rodriguez	87
Real World Perspective	Robert D. Rodriguez	87

CHAPTER 4 – Be a Risk Manager

Type	Author	Page
Expert Advice	Rod Aday	107
Expert Advice	Terence D. Jackson	108
Real World Perspective	Dan Elliott	108

CHAPTER 5 – Be an Operator

Type	Author	Page
Expert Advice	Felix Kyei Asare	120
Expert Advice	Patrick Hayes	122

CHAPTER 6 – Be a First Responder

CHAPTER 7 – Be a Team Lead

CHAPTER 8 – Be an Executive Leader

CHAPTER 9 – Be a Governance, Risk, and Compliance (GRC) Advocate

CHAPTER 10 – Be a Measurer

CHAPTER 11 – Be a Communicator

CHAPTER 12 – Be a Vendor Manager/Negotiator

Acknowledgments

Those who have authored books know the dedication and discipline necessary to do so, much respect to you. Beyond my effort, this endeavor was molded by many others with much greater expertise than me, the feedback and guidance from the following have been invaluable:

- Vlad Brodsky
- Christopher Castaldo
- Chris Gates
- Casey Marquette
- Yonesy Nuñez
- Michael Piacente
- Ira Winkler

Beyond them the following deserve acknowledgement:

- Every member of every team I have ever managed. My years in leadership run deep, but they would not matter if it wasn't for each and every one of you who tested me, pushed me, challenged me, and elevated me. Thank you for the opportunity to work and grow together, I do cherish all of those memories, good and bad.
- My wife, Sharon, for supporting me through all of my ideas, goals, and accomplishments.
- My parents, Jose and Gladys, who sacrificed everything in the name of getting my sister and me to a land where we could live free from tyranny.
- My children, Christopher, Kenneth, Caleb, and Rebecca, for being a major motivating factor in me always pushing myself to do more. It is now your turn to outdo me.
- Dan Swanson for sparking this idea and helping me along the journey.
- The teams at CRC Press for bringing this all together.
- My loyal, beloved, and fiercely protective Rhodesian Ridgeback, Gunner, I miss you dearly. Rest in peace.

1 Be the Candidate

You have embarked on the journey toward getting the job. You have decided to make a move into a new CISO role, or maybe you are pursuing your first CISO role. Given this context, you are the CISO candidate. In either case, there are some areas a CISO candidate needs to consider during the process when they are interviewed and when they are considering if a particular company is a good fit. This last point matters, you, the candidate, must be a good fit for a CISO role; but the role and company must also be a good fit for you.

To be clear, this is not a chapter on interview preparation (i.e., covering questions interviewers will be asking you), it is focused on the questions a CISO candidate should ask the interviewer(s). These are questions and principles crafted to give a CISO candidate a strong sense of what they could be getting into.

The CISO role is not for everyone. The role requires a certain mindset and attitude. A CISO candidate must accept certain realities. The main reality is that the business world, as we have come to know it, is always in a state of flux. Whether based on perception or not, gone are the days when business had a sense of certainty and stability. This United States Army describes these types of environments with an acronym that is very relevant to what a CISO will face. The acronym is "VUCA", which stands for "Volatile", "Uncertain", "Complex", and "Ambiguous".

- Volatile – change will be rapid and unpredictable, especially in its extent and detectability.
- Uncertain – the present is unclear, and the future is uncertain.
- Complex – your ecosystem will be made up of many disparate, interconnected entities, with the potential to create chaotic conditions.
- Ambiguous – there is simply a lack of clarity or awareness about certain situations.

Any CISO with experience, especially in facing major incidents, can attest to the relevance of this acronym. VUCA represents a set of challenges that CISOs and their team(s) will have to face at some point, maybe often depending on the environment. Individually, each of the elements in the acronym can be significant, but in combination, they make up a formidable force. VUCA environments can be tricky because they:

- Create anxiety and destabilize people.
- Can be demotivational and overwhelming.
- Can create situations where bad decisions are made or worse, indecision takes over.
- Can take a long time to detect and combat.

DOI: 10.1201/9781003477556-1

In order to make yourself successful and effective in a VUCA environment you must divide and conquer, and break down VUCA components into solvable elements. Each one will have its own root cause and solutions. Strategically, create your own version of meaning for each element in the acronym. Bob Johansen addressed this best with his framework called "VUCA Prime", presented in his 2009 book "Leaders Make the Future". Consider the following summary:

- Establish a clear vision for yourself – this starts with eliminating resistance on your part, accepting the volatility, and embracing the reality of constant change. Then set a clear vision for you and your team(s). The vision, and execution model of your team(s), must be one rooted in flexibility so that there is a general modus operandi of adaptation and overcoming.
- Create your own culture of understanding – become a student of your environment. Aim to gain an intimate understanding of the business you are protecting. This can help you develop new ways of thinking that are rooted in competitive business intelligence and not just security for the sake of security. A major part of your learning will come from continuous reading to stay in tune with macro events. Another part will be from communicating with customers to be in tune with their needs, concerns, and expectations. Simulations will help develop your contextual understanding. Perform simulations and/or tabletop exercises to anticipate and devise responses to scenarios.
- Seek clarity – clear communications and healthy collaboration will help, especially given situations that are often complex. Fostering a culture where disparate teams can come together and work effectively in fast-paced and chaotic situations will be of great value to you as a CISO.
- Pursue agility – you need to lead but get out of the way so your team members can shine. Part of this requires an embracing of different ideas and approaches. Be a leader and not a dictator. As you lead, keep an eye out for those moments when you can really introduce, and promote flexibility and agility. As conditions change during an incident flexibility will play a key role in how well the team handles things.

At the heart of all this is a CISO that is positive no matter what conditions are at hand. Assuming you accept this reality of chaos, have the right mindset, and can navigate successfully within VUCA environments, you are in a good place to start this journey. Come to terms early, you will pursue continuous improvement but getting to a state where your organization is "fully secure" will prove elusive. Don't ever work from a position of fear, discipline yourself to be positive and just constantly learn and improve.

A CISO must face difficult situations. They need to handle these in a fearless fashion, and you start showing that side of you at this early stage in the journey toward a job. Ask bold questions (you are about to get many examples), show you are a confident leader, and that you can think both operationally and strategically. You are interviewing the interviewer as much as they are interviewing you.

THE COMPANY OR ORGANIZATION

Your inquisition will begin with seeking out information about the hiring company, or organization. Ask questions about the culture of the company. Probe to see if the company has a security-first culture or even a technology-first culture. Try to get a sense of whether security is important to the company, and its employees, or is security seen as a burden. A CISO role in a company that hires one because a regulatory body is forcing them to will be very different from one where they organically decide things need to improve.

You want to get a good read on the hiring organization before you make any decisions. One key factor to dig into is the actual business model of the organization. On the business front, find out if the organization's financial health is positive. Also, query for some details about the level of employee turnover. Trying to get a sense of cybersecurity comes into play given the business model and the culture of the company.

Company culture will be a major factor for a CISO. It would be wise to dig into this aspect hard. This reconnaissance starts before the interview, that homework is on you by way of leveraging any publicly available intelligence. A good CISO candidate aims to extract a lot of intelligence about the organization, its mission, goals, and culture from both public sources as well as from the interviewer(s).

In the spirit of understanding as much as you can before taking on the role, here are some questions to consider:

- Is the company public, private, or is it a non-profit?
  - If public, are there focused resources set aside for handling areas like governmental regulations?
- How many business units does the company have?
  - If multiple, how autonomous are they?
    - Do they have their own cybersecurity teams?
- How many employees does the company have?
- Is the company funded (venture capital, investments, etc.) or is it generating revenue?
- Are financials available for review (typically only applies to a publicly held company)?
- How does the company generate revenue?
- What sectors does the company operate in?
  - Are they heavily regulated?
- What is the company's reliance on external entities (outsourcing, third-party ecosystem, etc.)?
- Is my cell phone going to be this organization's incident response plan or is it more mature than that?

Having some understanding of some of these points is important since you want to work with a company where the stakeholders will support you, so that you can, in turn, support the business. Knowing some of this information will help you understand if this is a supportive organization, one that will work with you to align your security goals with the larger organization-wide goals. On this point of a supportive organization:

- Has there been an external review of the organization's security?
  - If so:
    - When was it performed?
    - Was it requested by the board or the Chief Executive Officer (CEO)?
    - What were the results?
  - If not:
    - Is the organization willing to perform one as a first step when this role gets filled?
    - Warning flag – it is not a great sign if, at this stage, an organization has never had their security scrutinized by an objective external entity. Either they can't afford one, don't want to face a negative truth, don't care about security, or are just immature, relevant to cybersecurity and its role in modern-day business.
- How do you see cybersecurity fitting into the organization's strategic goals?
  - If this answer is fuzzy, this is a warning flag as this CISO role may be fighting an uphill battle.
- Who does the C-Suite believe is accountable when cybersecurity outcomes are negative?
  - If the answer is exclusively the CISO, then in this job the title stands for "Chief Information Scapegoat Officer".
- Can you give me your personal perspective on cybersecurity and how it should be factored into daily and larger strategic, business functions?
  - How does this vision of "how it should be" differ from reality at this organization?
- What types of initiatives do you feel are missing in cybersecurity?
  - Are those missing in this organization in particular?
- When was the last time you specifically supported a cybersecurity initiative?
  - What was it?
  - What exactly did you contribute?

THE POSITION

Simply put, regarding the position itself you want to understand, as best you can, exactly what you are potentially getting yourself into. Try to get a sense of how this role is perceived in the organization. Some questions to start with:

- Is the role purely seen as a function of IT?
- Is the role seen as a member of the executive team?
- Is the role an executive role (C-Suite) or is it a vice president (VP, SVP, EVP, AVP, etc.) level role?
- Is this role consulted when corporate decisions (Mergers and Acquisitions (M&A), major investments, etc.) are being made?

Is the company a product (customer-facing web application, etc.) company? If it is:

- Does this role own and/or oversee product security?
- Is the security function consulted for product security matters?

One key point to query is whether this is a new position in the organization. If it is:

- Why was there no formal security leadership to this point?
- What is now driving the creation of this position within the organization?
- Who (senior executive, board member, etc.) is sponsoring, and calling for, this position?
- Has someone determined the success criteria for this role? If so, who? If so, ask to see the success criteria.

If this is not a new position:

- How many CISOs or security leaders has the organization had?
- What has been the average tenure of each previous security leader?
- Tell me more about the previous security leaders, what did they do right and wrong from the company perspective?
- Why did each of them leave the organization?
- Were any of the previous security leaders terminated after a security incident? If so, get the details.
- I would like to speak with some of the previous leaders. Are there any legal or NDA restrictions in place? Are company executives ok with me reaching out to these folks?

Regarding the greenfield level of this role in this organization, the answers require some analysis. You will need to correlate these data points to your appetite for tackling challenges from scratch or expecting certain mechanisms in place. Generally speaking, the early security leaders of an organization face tougher uphill battles. They will pave the path for subsequent leaders, this is just reality. For your own sake make sure you are comfortable with this organization's maturity in their security journey.

Find out if any existing employees (internal candidates) applied for this position. If so, are they still being considered? This is important to know. If you end up getting the job these people will be working for/with you. This could make for some contentious feelings, so you need to go in aware.

Type of CISO

Dig into expectations regarding the type of CISO the organization is looking for. This may not seem important at first but is a critical factor in reference to the possibility of success and/or job satisfaction. The goal is to ensure you are a good fit for the role and the role is a good fit for you. When there is a mismatch in terms of fit, the possibility of job dissatisfaction becomes very real, even if there is success from a productivity perspective. Typical types of CISO roles are:

- Operational – operational CISOs tend to be tactical and come from the ranks of the practitioners. They tend to be doers and are action-oriented, analytical, adaptable, and decisive. Since they have lived in the trenches, tactical and operational CISOs generally handle operational disruptions calmly and bring a practical perspective to technical challenges. In some organizations, this type of CISO is found in the "Deputy CISO" role.
- Compliance/Risk-focused – the compliance and risk-focused CISO often has a less technical background. They come to the job with expertise in risk management, regulatory requirements, privacy, and compliance auditing. This type of CISO leadership style is not so action-oriented, instead, taking a risk management approach, and angles of compliance. They tend to be methodical, disciplined, organized, chaos-averse. They typically bring a focus on rigorous processes and thorough documentation.
- Steady State – steady state CISOs are best suited to organizations with established and/or mature programs. The aim for this type of CISO is to maintain the existing security posture and pursue slow and steady improvements over time. They generally bring a calm demeanor and an ability to advocate for conservative investments in a security program.
- Transformational – transformational CISOs generally come from information technology or business backgrounds and enjoy dynamic, fast-paced environments. The transformational nature of this type of role can take different forms, such as transforming a technology-centric program into one more aligned with the business or taking on the journey of migrating from on-premise environments to those that are cloud-hosting-based.
- Post Breach – this type of CISO enters an organization after a major breach and aims to mitigate the fallout from the event. They tend to be very cool-headed under pressure and enjoy the large challenges this type of situation brings with it. For this type of person, there is satisfaction in helping during times of crisis.
- Field – field CISOs generally enjoy interacting with external entities, such as customers and the public. They are sometimes seen as evangelists. They are typically confident and charismatic, thriving in fast-paced environments. Often, they come from an application development or product management background. These types of CISO roles are often found in the cybersecurity vendor companies. In those spaces they focus on helping customers operationalize the use of specific products, providing executive-level guidance, and acting as a liaison.

REPORTING STRUCTURE

As a CISO candidate, you will want to understand the organizational hierarchy at hand. To have any real chance of success you will need to have a voice with some authority. Putting aside crisis situations, a lot of what a CISO brings to the table may not be welcome. It may quietly be perceived as counter to progress. This means that if this role is, for instance, shoved into an IT function the likelihood of being heard at executive decision-making levels is low. Of course, given a crisis, you will be fully heard and supported. Structural questions to consider:

- What role does the CISO role report into?
  - How many other direct reports does this role have?
    - Pay attention to the answer. You don't want your voice to be lost in a sea of other voices by reporting to someone with too many people reporting to them. This role is too business-critical for you to be struggling for a voice or face time.
- Does this role report to the board?
  - If it does:
    - How often?
    - Is there a review process of the cyber security board report before submission?
      - If so, how are differences managed?
      - If your original data is manipulated in any way, this is a major red flag because this can easily become a censorship layer presenting an inaccurate reality to the board. More importantly, this is done in your name. The board thinks they are hearing from you, the CISO.
    - Is there someone on the board skilled in cyber security?
    - Is there executive support for one-on-one direct communications between individual board members and the CISO?
  - If the role does not report to the board:
    - Why not?
    - Have any previous security leaders (if applicable) reported to the board?
      - If so, did something go wrong?
    - Are there security updates provided to the board via some proxy (legal representative, etc.)?
      - Are these updates put through a censorship process before being passed on to the board?
      - If yes, this may be a major red flag because this can mean that an inaccurate reality is being presented to the board, again in your name.
- Does the CISO actually meet with the CEO and their direct reports?
  - If so, on what cadence? Or is it just based on need?
  - If not, this is a warning flag as a CEO that is not engaged could be a problem. Even worse, is a CEO that prefers not to know things so they can claim plausible deniability.
- Is the CEO willing to meet with me as part of this interview process?
  - If this answer is no, this may be a warning flag as the CEO may not consider this hire important enough to be part of the hiring process. While organizational culture plays an important role here, cybersecurity has

reached a level of corporate importance that a CEO should be directly involved.
- As part of my interview process can I also speak with:
  - Chief Privacy Officer
  - Chief Legal Officer/General Counsel
  - Chief Risk Officer
- Is there a cyber security steering committee?
  - If yes:
    - How often does it meet?
    - Who is on the committee?
    - Does it have a subset of members that have voting rights?
    - Is it a committee in its own right or a subcommittee?
      - If a subcommittee, what is the overseeing committee?

LEVEL

There are generally two strings you should concern yourself with regarding leveling, "Position" (sometimes called "Position Title") and "Business Title". You may start with these being equal strings, something like "SVP, Cybersecurity" where "SVP" equals Senior Vice President. That position string sets your level at the SVP level, this will dictate your package. But your business title may be, or eventually become, "Chief Information Security Officer". Considering the role level, be aware that this may not make you part of that organization's executive team.

AUTHORITY

Understanding the relevant reporting structure, and level set up, for the target CISO role is relevant to the subject of the position's authority. The structural point will have a significant impact on the CISO's ability to influence. Of equal importance, it will have an impact on who the CISO will have direct access to. For a CISO to be effective the role needs to have access to the right people (stakeholders, decision-makers, CFO, etc.) and enough influence to drive cultural change and attitudes toward cybersecurity. If this CISO role is tucked away in IT, if it is structurally multiple levels away from the C-Suite, the reality of the matter is that the role will most likely not wield the authority, and in turn influence, to make culturally impactful changes.

The CISO role is no longer a purely technical one. It's important that the role has the independence and authority to drive cybersecurity change, and growth, in the organization. One dimension here is that of checks and balances. The CISO role is exactly that to entities like IT. This, then, begs the question about the soundness of those structures that have the CISO role within IT, particularly as IT's goals and objectives often end up at odds with those of cybersecurity. If you pick up on this authority status you may want to take this as a warning flag. These setups say a lot about the organization's attitude, and this is often a good indicator of the relevant state of cybersecurity maturity.

None of this is to say that there are not IT leaders that are supportive of cybersecurity. They may even be advocates, but often the pressures they themselves face will become the source of conflicting interests. Barring a negative security incident, this unfortunately means that IT priorities will mostly take precedence (at least that is the historical pattern). There is also the human dynamic where it is difficult to objectively perform a check and balance function of the very people who are your bosses. These are a few of the reasons why security mature organizations now have their CISO's reporting into roles that are outside of IT; the CEO, Chief Operating Officer (COO), Chief Risk Officer (CRO), or Chief Legal Officer.

BUDGET

While it may seem early to be probing into budget-related questions some are very telling at this early stage. One angle here is that you need to understand what kind of resource (budget, humans, etc.) support your program could receive. The other angle is to extract a sense of the maturity perception tied to this role within this specific organization. Simply put, if the CISO is not trusted with their own budget then this organization probably doesn't sit at a strong security maturity level, and they probably don't see the CISO as a mature part of the executive team.

- Is there a cybersecurity budget or is it factored into some other larger budget, like IT?
    - If is part of IT's budget:
        - What is the overall IT budget?
        - What percentage of that budget is dedicated to security?
- Who controls the cybersecurity budget?
    - If the answer is, not "the CISO", then who is it?
    - If the answer is not "the CISO", this may be a warning flag as this organization probably doesn't see the CISO role as mature or business critical.
- What has been the cybersecurity budget for the past N years?
    - During those N years has there been growth, or has it been year-on-year flat?
- How is the budget split between Capital Expenditure (CAPEX) and Operating Expenditure (OPEX)?
    - CAPEX refers to the money a company spends to buy, upgrade, or improve assets used for business purposes. This includes software solutions, technology infrastructure, equipment, hardware, facilities, etc. These assets will have a useful life and value for more than one financial cycle (annual budget, accounting period, etc.). Common examples for a tech company would be:
        - Constructing new office buildings
        - Purchasing automation tools and equipment for manufacturing facilities
    - OPEX refers to ongoing expenditures required for the day-to-day operations of the business. These are expenses tied to normal business activities and consumed within a financial cycle. Some examples include:
        - Employee salaries and benefits

- Software license subscriptions
- SaaS tools
- Cloud computing services
- The key difference is that CAPEX adds to the asset base of the company and adds benefits over multiple years. OPEX is spending that supports existing operations and must be continually incurred to run the business on a periodic basis.
- Ask to see a sanitized version of the budget.
  - If possible, construct a list of the security products they already use. If that is not possible from the budget document, ask for that list.
    - The list is important because it can expose weaknesses in their strategy to date. Those are weaknesses the incoming CISO will have to contend with.
      - Example: The list of used products reveals that there has been a focus on internal resources (endpoints, laptops, email, etc.). But the company hosts multiple data-driven customer-facing resources (web applications, mobile applications, etc.). You see nothing on the list that can actively protect those elements (database, web application, etc.). This should prompt you to probe into this and understand if this is by design or if the organizational culture is such that the security program has no say regarding customer-facing resources (this happens!). Further questions should cover liability, if the security program cannot improve the security of customer-facing resources, who is responsible if a breach takes place on that side of the business?

Package

The terms "salary" and "package" are often, mistakenly, used interchangeably. But as you reach the ranks where many CISO roles sit, you need to be aware of the distinctions.

- Salary – salary, or base salary, refers to the fixed amount of money paid to an employee on some regular basis. At the CISO level, this is most likely a fixed amount earned on an annual basis. This is a subset, or one component, of a "package". Sometimes it is expressed as a monthly amount and it usually represents a gross amount of money before the withholding of deductions (taxes, benefits, etc.). Unless there is some extreme circumstance, the salary component of an employee's package is usually one that is steady and does not vary.
- Package – a compensation package, sometimes referred to as a total rewards package, refers to the combination of salary and other elements that comprise overall compensation. It includes not only the base salary but also other monetary and non-monetary components. But these additional elements can vary widely and can be arbitrarily ceased at the organization's discretion.

Salary is not everything, ultimately make sure a role/job is a good bi-directional fit. When coming up the ranks we generally fixate on salary because that is all we get. But that isn't the case at the CISO level. Often, you will hear of a large number that makes up the package an individual has. The actual salary component of that overall package is most likely not the source of the bulk in the numerical figure. Non-salary elements, often referred to as executive benefits, are the additional components that aim to attract, retain, and incentivize top-level leaders and/or executives. These elements can take various forms but generally include:

- Bonus – in the CISO role you may be eligible for performance-based bonuses, such as annual or quarterly bonuses. These are generally tied to achieving specific financial or strategic goals. These bonuses are often structured as a percentage of the relevant base salary.
- Equity – equity-based compensation grants you ownership or rights to the company's stock. This may include Restricted Stock Units (RSU), Performance Based Stock Units (PSU), and/or stock options. The dollar value of these equity grants depends on the company's stock price or performance over time. Also, pay attention to the vesting schedule. Getting shares granted to you does not mean you can cash them out. You must wait until you are vested in shares before you can turn them into cash.
  - When a company grants shares to an employee, it technically means that the employee is given ownership over, or the right to own, a certain number of shares. Vesting, on the other hand, refers to the process by which that employee gains full ownership of those granted shares and, in turn, can sell them.
  - The specifics of equity grants in public and private companies can vary. Unlike public companies where there are clear market prices for stock, the valuation of equity in private companies can be more complex. Private companies may establish internal valuation methods, or leverage external experts, to determine an estimated fair value of their equity. Additionally, private companies may have restrictions on the selling of stock. Try to get these details up front if they apply to the role you are pursuing.
  - RSU – RSUs represent a promise to grant company stock to an employee. Generally, at a future date even though some transactions are negotiable. When an employee receives RSUs they do not immediately own the underlying stock. The RSUs in question will vest over some predetermined time period, typically subject to certain conditions (current employment, achievement of goals, etc.). Once some RSUs vest, the employee receives the company's stock equivalent of the cash value of the vested RSUs. RSUs are often valued based on the market value of the stock at the time of vesting.
  - PSU – PSUs are also a promise to grant company stock to an employee. But PSU grants are entirely contingent upon achieving some specific goals. The number of PSUs that ultimately vest depends on the degree to which the performance targets are met. This means you are not

guaranteed a 100% vest and this could be due to things outside of your control.

- Stock options – stock options give employees the right to buy a specific number of company shares at some predetermined price. This is known as the exercise price or strike price. The employee is not obligated to exercise the options but has the opportunity to do so within a specified 'time frame. The exercise (buy) price is typically set at the fair market value of the company's stock at the time of grant. If the company's stock price rises above the exercise price, the employee can purchase at the predetermined price, making a profit.
- Retirement and/or pension plans – some packages contain enhanced retirement benefits, such as contributions to a defined contribution plan (e.g., 401(k)). These plans can provide you with savings toward retirement at no extra effort on your part.
- Health and insurance benefits – standard packages also include comprehensive health insurance coverage, including medical, dental, and vision plans. Some also include life insurance coverage.

The specific elements (perks, deferred compensation, etc.) and structure of packages vary across companies, industries, and jurisdictions. From an awareness perspective, the non-salary elements can form a significant portion of your overall compensation. If your pursuit of this role is taking place via a qualified and competent recruiting expert they will guide and advise you along the way.

PROTECTION

As part of your security programs, you will build incident management programs that come to life in the face of a crisis. Parallel to them you must build your own crisis handling program as a form of self-preservation. CISO personal liability is a real concern. While it is not a rampant problem you should take some precautions. As the person responsible for overseeing an organization's cybersecurity program you may one day be held accountable for relevant incidents, outcomes, breaches, and/or regulatory non-compliance. These are some factors to consider regarding CISO personal liability:

- Duty of care – CISOs owe a duty of care to their organization. They are expected to responsibly act in the best interests of the organization and its customers. If a CISOs actions, or decisions, are deemed negligent, they may be held personally liable for damages and/or losses.
  - Digging in a little, cybersecurity duty of care refers to the legal and ethical obligation of individuals to take reasonable measures to protect data, systems, and networks from unauthorized access or other cybersecurity threats. It encompasses the responsibility to set forth a best effort to prevent, detect, and respond to security incidents in a proactive and diligent manner.
- Legal and regulatory – CISOs operate in a complex legal and regulatory landscape. Depending on the applicable laws and/or regulations, CISOs

may have legal responsibilities related to data protection, privacy, cyber-security controls, incident management, and compliance. Failure to fulfill these obligations may result in personal liability.

- In the event of a material incident, CISOs may face legal actions, including shareholder lawsuits or regulatory enforcement actions. These actions can stretch allegations into the realms of negligence and failure to implement industry best practices. CISOs may be named individually in such lawsuits, leading to personal liability.
- Indemnification and insurance – CISOs often seek some protection through indemnification provisions which specify that the organization will cover legal expenses, judgments, or settlements resulting from their actions. The coverage is most likely subject to the CISO proving they acted in good faith and in the best interests of the company. Additionally, Directors and Officers (D&O) insurance, and golden parachute clauses, may provide coverage for CISOs in certain situations.

Dig into this last section (indemnification and insurance) with specific questions, such as:

- Is the CISO granted "Right of Defense"?
- Is the CISO covered under the company D&O insurance policy?
- Does the company provide the CISO with a "golden parachute" clause?

Here are some relevant points that are helpful:

The "Right of Defense" provision would require the employer to provide a CISO with a broad right of defense. This means that if the CISO becomes involved in any legal situation, or claim, arising from their work-related duties, the company will be required to provide legal representation and cover all reasonable legal expenses.

D&O insurance is a type of liability insurance designed to personally protect company directors and officers from legal claims, and expenses, that may arise from actions or decisions made while performing their duties. It is not a cybersecurity-centric mechanism and covers company directors and officers. The definition of what constitutes a "director" or "officer" is subjective to the organization. The policies generally provide financial coverage for defense attorney costs, settlements, or judgments resulting from lawsuits. Some key points about D&O insurance:

- Coverage scope – D&O insurance policies offer liability coverage for company directors and officers to protect them from claims which may arise based on operational decisions made and/or actions taken as part of their duties. These policies typically cover claims related to alleged breach of fiduciary duty, negligence, misrepresentation, errors in judgment, or failure to comply with laws or regulations.
- Coverage variations – D&O policies vary in terms of coverage limits, policy exclusions, and specific terms and conditions. They can be tailored to the needs of different organizations and are typically purchased by the company for the benefit of its directors and officers.

- Coverage parts – D&O insurance policies often consist of three main coverage parts:
  - Side A coverage – Protects individual directors and officers when the company cannot indemnify them (e.g., bankruptcy). At risk here are the personal assets of the individual officer and the policy would pay claims on behalf of that officer.
  - Side B coverage – Reimburses the company when it indemnifies directors and officers for covered claims. At risk here are corporate assets and the policy would pay claims on behalf of the company.
  - Side C coverage – Covers claims made against the company itself as a separate entity. At risk here are corporate assets and the policy would pay claims on behalf of the company.
- Risk management – D&O insurance is a part of an organization's risk management strategy. This is especially so for organizations with a board of directors. It represents one incentivizing factor for officers to partake on a board and today's increasingly complex business landscape means most organizations face a heightened possibility of liabilities and litigations. Hence, coverage of this sort is just sound practice.

As a CISO you are not guaranteed this type of coverage. This is entirely up to the organization at hand. At this stage, all you can do is ask. You could also try to negotiate this into your package. But there are ways to handle this later as well, once you are in a CISO role you can pursue this further and that is covered in Chapter 13.

A golden parachute clause is another provision that is not cybersecurity-centric but can be very important to a CISO. It is a contractual provision typically included in employment agreements of executives. It is designed to provide benefits to executives in the event they are terminated as a result of a merger or acquisition. These benefits can include:

- Severance payments – this is a lump sum payment that is made to the employee when they are terminated. Golden parachute clauses often stipulate that if the executive's employment is terminated due to a triggering event, they will be entitled to receive a substantial severance package.
- Bonuses – these are additional payments that are made to the employee in addition to their severance payments. The clause may specify that the executive is entitled to receive additional bonuses, retention bonuses, or continuation of certain benefits, such as healthcare coverage or retirement benefits, even after the termination of employment.
- Equity vesting – if the executive holds RSUs or other equity-based compensation, the golden parachute clause may include provisions that accelerate the vesting of these equity awards upon the triggering event. This allows the executive to gain immediate ownership of these equity holdings.
- Non-Compete waivers – in some cases, a golden parachute clause may include provisions that waive non-compete agreements that are in place.

In the realm of cybersecurity, there will most likely be added provisions that address the protection from threats and response to cybersecurity incidents. One example is a cybersecurity incident response or breach notification clause. This clause outlines the responsibilities and actions to be taken by a CISO and team in the event of a security incident. Additionally, some agreements may include provisions related to confidentiality and Non-Disclosure Agreements (NDA) to protect customer data, intellectual property, and/or trade secrets. Failure to meet those requirements could nullify the protection afforded by the clause.

It's important to note that the terms and conditions of golden parachute clauses can vary widely depending on many factors (company policy, applicable laws in different jurisdictions, etc.). It should also be noted that these benefits are not to be treated like "get out of jail free" cards. Conduct yourself like a professional with integrity and character and hopefully, you should not have to tap into any of these for protection. Also, remember that insurance companies have their investigative arms. If an insurance company finds wrongdoing on your part, they may have grounds for legitimately not providing you coverage.

RISK

Risk management is tricky. A point of clarity is that risk comes down to dealing with uncertainty. Uncertainty means there is a lack of data points to factor into a decision-making process. This uncertainty makes predicting and quantifying the probability and impact of risks difficult. But mature organizations formalize this as much as possible. Try to get a sense of where this organization ranks from a maturity perspective:

- Who in the organization accepts or rejects risk?
  - Assuming someone does, what process is followed when addressing risk?
- Does the company have an Enterprise Risk Management (ERM) committee?
  - If so, how often do they meet?
- Does the company maintain an enterprise risk register?
  - If so, are cybersecurity risks documented in it?
    - Are risk acceptance or rejections documented in this register?
  - If not, does cybersecurity have their own risk register?
- How often are cybersecurity risks reviewed?

INCIDENT MANAGEMENT

The likelihood of the CISO overseeing some negative event or incident is high. It's just part of the job. But it would be helpful to try and get a sense of how the company has managed incidents to date. How a company responds says a lot about its maturity, organizational culture, and integrity. Understanding this, even if only partially, should give you a good sense of the work facing you in terms of building a capable incident management program.

- Does the organization have a formal, well-defined incident management program?
  - If so, does it consist of one incident handling plan or multiple?

- Has the organization experienced any impactful cybersecurity events?
  - If so:
    - How long ago was the last one?
    - How did the organization respond?
    - Was there a relevant incident handling plan and did it work smoothly?
    - Was there a postmortem conducted?
      - If so, does the organization make improvements based on the findings?
- Who takes the lead in incident response, the CISO or Chief Legal Officer/ General Counsel?
  - If it is the CISO, what role does the Chief Legal Officer/General Counsel play during incident handling?
- How were the customers and partners communicated with?
- Does the organization use external entities with incident-handling expertise?
  - If so:
    - Are they on retainer?
    - What is the threshold that must be met to engage with these external experts?

THE TEAMS UP AND DOWN

A strong factor in the success or failure of CISO is the team. "The team" is a relative term, in reality, there are multiple teams that make up your team as a CISO. There is a team above (CISO reports to) and a team below (reporting to the CISO). There are also peers of course. Regarding the team below you need to ask some probing questions:

- In respect to key players (from the interviewer's perspective), how long have they been in their roles?
- Are there any current open roles?
- How many full-timers versus contractors make up the team?
- What are the skill sets of the team members, especially the full-timers?
- Do you know of anyone on the team that is actively looking to leave?
- Has the team grown or shrunk as of late?
- Are there any missing skills on the team?
- Does the CISO have the authority to directly address poor performers?

If the team is heavier on the contractor side, you may want to dig into that and get a sense as to why that is the case. Typically, contractors are brought in as staff augmentation or to address a niche skill missing on the full-time team. Teams that are too heavy on the contractor side generally are bound to that model because the domain expertise lies with those outsiders. So long as you keep paying them that model continues to function. But this could impact your ability to drive positive change as a new CISO.

Looking up the tier of folks the CISO will report into:

- In respect to key players (from the interviewer's perspective), how long have they been in their roles?
- How is the cybersecurity team viewed by those at this executive level?

You want to get a good sense for how much damage control you would have to do. If the cybersecurity team has been reduced to a powerless formality that sits quietly in a corner, then you need to know that. In that case, the warning flag is the uphill battle of turning executive perceptions around regarding the cybersecurity team. Another warning sign you need to pay attention to is the fact that you could be walking into a cybersecurity team with low morale, a nightmare situation.

A CISO is not a one-dimensional being. This role calls for a balance of many skills, including soft ones. Outside of the day job, a good CISO stays engaged and needs to be supported by the organization.

- Does the organization provide a career and/or executive coach?
- Does the organization support community engagement (writing blogs, speaking at conferences, getting interviewed on podcasts, participation in CISO forums, and advisory board positions)?
  - If you plan on being a public speaker, make sure you get an up-front understanding of the organization's corporate communications policies. If there is a conflict between the policy and your personal goals, address that early.

If you see too many warning flags, please consider walking away and continuing your search. This role is by default stressful, and burnout is a real phenomenon. The right fit is out there.

OFFER LETTER

If you are feeling like you have a good fit and get an offer letter, carefully review it. Here are some important things to look for:

- Position and responsibilities – verify that the offer letter specifies the correct job title, department, and the key responsibilities and duties associated with the position. Ensure that the letter accurately reflects the role you discussed during the hiring process.
- Start date and employment type – confirm the start date, as well as the correct status (full-time, part-time, contract). Ensure that the letter accurately reflects the terms you agreed upon, including the duration of any fixed-term contracts or probationary periods.
- Compensation – pay close attention to the details of your compensation package. Look for information on your base salary, bonus, equity grants (if applicable), and any other agreed-upon benefits. Review how and when your salary will be paid, such as monthly or biweekly, and ensure that it aligns with your expectations.

- Benefits – assess the offered benefits package, including health insurance, retirement plans, vacation time, sick leave, and other perks. Make sure any waiting period or eligibility criteria, are as agreed upon. Also, pay attention to the extent of coverage.
- Termination – pay close attention to the terms related to termination, including the notice period required from both parties. This is a high-risk role, and things happen that can end in a resignation or termination. Make sure you are comfortable with any conditions under which your employment can be terminated and the potential impact on severance pay and/or benefits.
- Non-Disclosure – look for clauses related to confidentiality and non-disclosure of proprietary information or trade secrets. Understand your obligations to protect sensitive company information during and after your employment. Especially pay attention to these sections if you plan on being a public figure at an industry level.
- Non-Compete – take note of any non-compete, or non-solicitation, clauses that restrict your ability to work for a competitor or solicit organization team members. Evaluate the duration of these restrictions considering potential impact on your future opportunities.
- Governing laws – understand the jurisdiction under which any disputes would be resolved. Carefully review any provisions related to arbitration, mediation, or other dispute resolution mechanisms.
- Conditions – assess if the offer letter includes any conditions that need to be met before your employment can commence, such as background checks, prior art declarations, intellectual property declarations, or the need to sign certain agreements.
- Timeline for acceptance – take note of the deadline by which you need to accept or decline this offer. Obviously, make sure to meet the deadline.

An offer letter is a legally binding agreement between you and your employer. As such, it's crucial to carefully review and fully understand its contents. Make sure you are comfortable with everything in that document. If you have any questions or concerns about the offer, consider seeking clarification from the hiring manager or consulting with a legal professional.

EXPERT ADVICE

In the realm of contemporary business, the role of a CISO stands as a linchpin in safeguarding digital assets against an array of evolving threats. From the vantage point of a seasoned Chief Technology Officer (CTO), the quest for an exemplary CISO transcends mere technical acumen; it demands a nuanced understanding of cybersecurity strategy, regulatory compliance, and agile incident response. The ideal candidate embodies a blend of visionary leadership and tactical prowess, capable of orchestrating a symphony of security measures tailored to the company's unique landscape.

A hallmark of effective leadership lies in self-awareness, and for the CTO, this manifests in a candid acknowledgment of personal knowledge gaps. Recognizing the intricate nature of cybersecurity, the astute CTO seeks a CISO whose expertise fills these voids, creating a symbiotic partnership that strengthens the organization's defense posture. Whether it's navigating complex compliance frameworks or devising proactive strategies to mitigate emerging threats, the collaborative synergy between the CTO and CISO forms the bedrock of a resilient cybersecurity infrastructure.

Moreover, beyond technical proficiency, lies the imperative of aligning cybersecurity initiatives with the company's overarching goals and values. By fostering a culture that champions proactive security measures over fear-driven tactics, the CTO and CISO cultivate an environment where cybersecurity becomes ingrained in the company's DNA. Empowering employees to embrace their roles as stewards of security not only bolsters defense mechanisms but also fosters a sense of collective ownership in safeguarding the company's digital assets.

In this symbiotic relationship, the CTO and CISO emerge as strategic partners, navigating the complex terrain of cybersecurity with a shared vision of fortifying the company's digital resilience. By synergizing technical expertise with strategic alignment, they propel the organization towards sustainable growth and success in an ever-evolving threat landscape.

– James Kenigsberg, Technologist, Futurist, and advisor, recovering CTO.

Aspiring cybersecurity professionals must exhibit an unwavering commitment to excellence and a readiness to go the extra mile. In a sector plagued by a pronounced scarcity of skilled candidates, complacency is simply not an option for those serious about securing a position. To distinguish yourself in this competitive landscape, adopting a proactive mindset is paramount. This means not just applying for jobs but making yourself a standout candidate: familiarize yourself with potential employers, gain a deep understanding of the roles you're applying for, meticulously tailor your CV, continuously update your skillset, and remain abreast of the ever-evolving cybersecurity domain. The advent of artificial intelligence has only accelerated these changes, underscoring the necessity for constant learning and adaptability. The old adage that failing to prepare is preparing to fail.

Networking, often overlooked by job seekers, is crucial in setting yourself apart from the competition. Your capacity to forge meaningful connections coupled with an eagerness to learn from others, can be a significant differentiator. Additionally, honing your interpersonal skills such as mastering the art of conversation, understanding basic body language, and learning to present yourself confidently can greatly enhance your appeal to potential employers. Staying informed about the latest trends and developments in the cybersecurity industry is also essential. Remember, stepping out of your comfort zone is the first step toward growth; while comfort zones may be appealing, they are barren grounds for personal and professional development.

– Surinder Lall, SVP Global Information Security Risk Management, Paramount

In the dynamic landscape of job hunting, diversifying your network to include multiple recruiters is a strategic move that can dramatically widen your access to opportunities. While it's tempting to rely on a single recruiter, embracing a broader network offers distinct advantages.

- Access to a wider range of opportunities: No single recruiter has access to all job openings. Different recruiters specialize in various industries, roles, and geographic locations. Expanding your network ensures you don't miss out on diverse opportunities.
- Increased market visibility: Multiple recruiters advocating for you increase your visibility in the job market. This can lead to more interviews and, ultimately, better job offers.
- Benefit from varied expertise and insights: Different recruiters bring different insights and advice, enhancing your job search strategy. Their varied experiences can provide you with a richer understanding of the job market.
- Building long-term professional relationships: Networking is about building genuine relationships, not just transactional interactions. Developing connections with various recruiters can yield long-term career benefits.
- Enhanced negotiating power: Having multiple offers or opportunities can improve your negotiating position. It provides you with options and leverage, which can be beneficial in discussions about salary and benefits.

In conclusion, while it's essential to have a trusted recruiter, relying solely on one limits your potential. Networking with a range of recruiters not only maximizes your exposure to various job opportunities but also enriches your professional journey with diverse insights and relationships.

– Casey Marquette, CEO, Covenant Technologies

CRAFTING YOUR BRAND AS A SECURITY LEADER

Essential advice for aspiring heads of security and CISOs – As a seasoned recruiter specializing in the cybersecurity domain, I have had the privilege of assisting numerous professionals in securing their first roles as Head of Security or CISO. From this vantage point, I offer a key piece of advice to aspirants in today's competitive market: Establish a distinct personal brand.

Identifying your unique strengths – What elevates you as a security leader? Reflect on one or two standout qualities or "superpowers" you possess that have consistently yielded positive outcomes for the organizations you've served. This introspection is critical in distinguishing yourself in the field.

Experience as a narrative – Your career journey narrates your brand. Whether you've spearheaded a security program from scratch in a fast-paced startup environment or navigated the challenges of revamping a faltering security system in a mid-sized company, these experiences define your capabilities. Notably, experience managing a security breach is invaluable, akin to a litigator with courtroom experience or a soldier tested in battle. Articulate these experiences compellingly, highlighting your resilience and problem-solving acumen.

Understanding your career trajectory – Equally important is clarity about where you aim to steer your career next. For instance, transitioning from a startup to a large enterprise requires demonstrating your ability to adapt your entrepreneurial skills to more structured environments. Conversely, moving from an established enterprise to a startup demands showcasing your readiness to thrive in a dynamic, unstructured setting.

I refer to this reflective process as "career matching". It's a vital exercise to undertake before embarking on job applications or networking. By clearly understanding and articulating your unique brand and career trajectory, you not only position yourself as a compelling candidate but also chart a course that aligns with your professional aspirations and strengths.

– Jesse Meadors, Managing Director, Tutela Talent

OPTIONS FOR CISOS WHEN CONSIDERING NEXT STEPS OR FUTURE OPTIONS

The process of looking for a new role is not comfortable or natural for any executive. For the CISO specifically, they have enjoyed 9–11 years of rapid personal growth, scope expansion, and no shortage of qualified opportunities in what we are calling the "era of plenty". This is no longer the case, and with today's market more accurately described as a severely down market; with a greater supply of actively searching CISOs and significantly less demand (or quality) for the position. Over the past decade, many CISOs have seamlessly moved from one opportunity to another, whereas today CISOs find themselves actively searching for 6–9 months for a new role and it is often the first time in their career or in a long time that they have looked for a job. Frankly, CISOs stink at finding new jobs, and that's ok. Given their rapid ascent it is no surprise that CISOs sometimes struggle mightily in the recruitment process, and no one should expect them to be good at the job search process.

While there are no silver bullets or easy buttons, there are a few things that CISOs can do to enhance their search process for stronger outcomes.

First, ensure that you are thoroughly and strategically using your network. Fully utilizing your network is the most effective way to increase referral situations. Using a baseball analogy, your network is the path that will lead to the most "quality at-bats" – you will see more pitches and have more swings at the plate. Take the time to create a project plan around how you plan to manage your varied network. Avoid just thinking of a few people to call on one by one but instead figure out how to leverage the majority of your network at once. The network should be divided into those that can be direct influencers (i.e., executives within interesting companies that you may want to be part of), those that can be indirect influencers (first-line connections that can make direct referrals), and those who can influence the ecosystem (i.e., vendors, consultants, HR professionals, executive recruiters, etc.). Today, CISOs spend less time developing their own network and more time using LinkedIn and other job boards to create activity. This has been proven not to be a good use of your time and energy. When applying for an online job for a CISO or leadership position, the probability for a positive outcome is considerably low. In addition, you are going to experience a variety of quality and communication issues. Focusing on identifying who in your network will be able to help you achieve quality connections and outcomes is a stronger use of your time.

Next, identify, embrace, and enhance your personal brand. First, you need to identify and embrace your superpowers. When identifying, be honest with yourself and be as specific as possible. If you are a former software engineer turned security executive with the ability to speak the language of software/ product engineering at a code level, then that should be your superpower. If you are a business-focused executive turned CISO with a deep compliance background with multiple acquisitions in a public company, then that should be your superpower. These are highly differentiated skill sets and experiences that will separate you from the majority of CISOs who will become your competition. Claiming that you are a CISO who has the ability to speak to both technical leaders and business leaders is not a superpower, that is a must-have for the modern CISO and that does not separate you from the pack.

After identifying your highly-specific superpowers it is time to enhance your messaging so that the community can associate with your superpower.

Your brand is enhanced by talking, writing, presenting, and narrating on topics that you are the most familiar with. Pick topics that most would agree you fall into the expert category. As a widely considered subject matter expert, find ways to start a conversation around these topics. Start a blog, webinar, podcast, join a panel, create a paper, present at a conference, position yourself to provide a quote in an article, join a CISO community, join an open-source initiative, etc. There are no wrong or right answers with regard to building your personal brand. Find the pace and method that works best for you and your style.

I would offer to try several approaches and start with a smaller audience. Too many CISOs stick to one narrow theme and either get burned out or they run out of creative content to talk about. In addition, many CISOs try to get their message out to the whole community. Start with a local or highly defined portion of the community. Set an initial goal to acquire 100 followers for these topics within a specific community or region and build from there. Your most dedicated followers will seek out opportunities for you. Furthermore, don't worry about getting it right at first; just get it out there. Artifacts will be needed to build your brand. They are all not going to be perfect. Remember, these are also your swings at the plate; if it feels uncomfortable then you are probably doing something right and making an impact.

One note of warning from my experience. Too many CISOs spend too much time tweaking their resumes; trying to make that perfect document which captures who you were and what you've done, who you are and what you are doing, and who you will be and what you expect to achieve next. That's a lot to produce. I believe ample time should be spent on building and honing a resume, but more time should be spent getting to know the content on your resume. Not surprising but CISOs are excellent at recording results but they are not excellent at narrating results and achievements. Time to accelerate your storytelling skills; every bullet point on your resume should be accompanied by a story and anecdote that goes along with the achievement. Furthermore, I suggest having multiple examples ready to go and prepared to narrate in a succinct, clear story. Ninety percent of the CISO role will be storytelling; knowing what to say, how to say it to impact change and create action with a particular audience.

Finally, take time to add to your skills arsenal. Adding skills through training, certifications, courses, and even going back to school for an IS-focused MBA are wonderful additions to your arsenal of skills and experiences. Whether you have a passion around learning how to prepare organizations on GenAI best practices; you have a focus around preparing and presenting budgets; or you want to focus on developing your board-level presentation skills, finding the learning vehicle to participate in is a strong way to further prepare for the candidate experience.

– Michael Piacente, Hitch Partners

NEGOTIATING THE FINER POINTS OF AN OFFER LETTER

As with many technical positions, CISOs are not naturally strong at negotiating the finer points of compensation and personal protection; and that's ok. The one superpower that most CISOs possess is to approach problem-solving with curiosity. CISOs should harness this curiosity when negotiating for themselves. Knowing what questions to ask and keeping an open mind when negotiating on your own behalf will take you most of the way there. Working with a partner (i.e., executive search partner, trusted industry expert) will also provide a sounding board for evaluating decisions. If you are not sure of a term, language, or just require more clarity around complex concepts such as calculating equity value or bonus calculations, ask the company to define it and get it in writing.

Private companies often leverage equity as a significant portion of the CISO's compensation (upwards of 70% in some cases). That said, private companies, overall, struggle to provide clear explanations about CISO (and other executive) compensation making the process more onerous than it needs to be. In fact, we find that the majority of private companies (seven out of ten) are unable to effectively articulate the value of their equity over the long term; this should not be a guessing game as there is a clear calculation based on market factors and valuation that affect the value. Candidates should be prepared to ask for guidance and a walk-through of the equity calculation. Companies should provide a worksheet that clearly depicts the long-term value of your offer. In addition, they should provide examples of companies within their industry and/or company trajectory to provide context around what the expected equity will be. The same often applies for public companies who offer overly complex bonus payout structures.

– Michael Piacente, Hitch Partners

REAL-WORLD PERSPECTIVE

In the fast-paced world of recruitment, your resume is more than just a document; it's your personal billboard. To make it effective, you need to ensure it doesn't just describe your job role – it should highlight your unique contributions and achievements. The key? Quantification. Imagine a hiring manager sifting through stacks of resumes. They're not just looking for someone who "managed a team" or "led a project". They're searching for tangible, measurable results. This is where quantifying your achievements makes a profound difference. Take for example, the statement, "I led the vulnerability management program". While it shows responsibility, it lacks specificity and impact. Now reframe this with the quantification: "Achieved a 60% decrease in high-risk vulnerabilities by leading the vulnerability management program". This not only shows that you lead a team but also demonstrates the significant impact of your leadership.

This method serves two purposes. First, it captures the attention of the reader immediately. By placing the tangible outcome at the beginning of the bullet point, you ensure that the most impactful information is seen first, especially crucial when resumes are often reviewed in mere seconds. Second, it differentiates you from other candidates who may have held similar roles. It's no longer about what you did; it's about how well you did it and the value you brought to the organization.

In conclusion, a resume that reads like a list of job descriptions is a missed opportunity. Transform your resume into a powerful tool that showcases your value by quantifying your achievements. It's not just about stating your responsibilities; it's about highlighting the real, measurable impact you've made.

– Casey Marquette, CEO, Covenant Technologies

The CISO role has risen significantly in prominence over the last 15 years, and in conjunction with the higher visibility, the expectations of CISOs and their teams have continued to expand as well. As will be laid out by Andres in this chapter, the nature and priorities of various CISO roles will differ for a host of reasons, but one consistent theme in the ongoing evolution of the CISO role is the need to have a broad leadership skill set that goes well beyond technical acumen.

Cybersecurity is no longer the sole purview of CISOs and their teams. Today proactively identifying and addressing cybersecurity risks is a critical part of a broader enterprise risk management program. The most effective modern CISOs are those who can deftly navigate their evolving role while championing broader organizational influence and improving cybersecurity awareness throughout the organization.

Today's CISOs understand the need to collaborate with a wide range of departments to align broader security efforts with the organization's overall strategy. By building strong relationships with these key stakeholders, the CISO can ensure that security is considered in decision-making processes and integrated into various functions outside of their traditional sphere of influence. The intangibles are critical; CISOs who are effective communicators and influencers will be best positioned to help build a strong foundation for cybersecurity in their organizations.

– Jamey Cummings, Partner at JM Search

2 Be a Student of the Business

The first three months as a CISO are critical by way of setting pace and precedents. Moreover, it is the time for the CISO to become a true student of the business. This initial month, as well as the next two, will be a bit of a sprint but that will settle into more of a marathon pace. At a high level, the CISO needs to figure out a business' organizational culture as this will dictate rules of engagement and working norms. During this same compact period, a CISO must pursue a few other strategic initiatives.

Some level of current security maturity needs to be established as this will start identifying the areas where focus and budget are needed. A three- to five-year plan will need to be created with the goal of presenting this to the board and/or C-Suite. This will comprise the general blueprint that will guide the strategic objectives for the security program being built or expanded. The human side must also be factored in, and one must establish key relationships with privacy, legal, information technology (IT), the C-Suite, and, depending on structure, possibly the board of directors as well. The CISO must make themselves known, and available to the key players on all the aforementioned teams.

The learning of an organization's culture actually started during the hiring interview and bi-directional courting process. During the interview(s) a good CISO candidate must extract a lot of intelligence about the organization, its mission, goals, and culture from the interviewer(s). That must be tactfully achieved while the other side vets the candidate. The CISO candidate should have been in full reconnaissance mode while considering taking on the role. Arming themselves with anything publicly available is a must in order to make an educated decision in terms of moving forward. Obviously, if a candidate has contacts inside the organization, they could provide invaluable intelligence.

You are on site, or virtual, irrespective of being day one and time to hit the ground running. Objective one is to commence collecting information from those with domain expertise, the current employees. The goal is to gain in-depth knowledge of the business, its priorities, its norms, the good, the bad; you need to get as much as possible. As a new CISO, it is easy to put people on the defensive since the title represents a position of authority. As such, this requires some tactful interview and interrogation skills. Conversations will need to be conducted with employees, peers, mid-level business leaders, and external customers. Notice the tactic is to conduct conversations as opposed to interrogations or interviews. Realistically, you will be interviewing those folks, but this needs to be done tactfully, preferably as tactful conversations.

The objective is to get a sense of all points of strength, pain points, identification of key players and/or stakeholders, the existence of a security-first mindset, and how mature the cybersecurity culture is within the organization. One element of data to

DOI: 10.1201/9781003477556-2

try and hone in on is the identification of the unofficial trusted advisors. Oftentimes the title these folks have does not reflect their unofficial status of a trusted advisor but they exist in most organizations and they will become key partners over time. Be gentle in your interrogations to ferret out who they are. Sometimes external entities such as suppliers, vendors, and partners may be the best source of these data points. This human-centric process will prove valuable over time with established relationships, open lines of communication, and invaluable gems of culture (e.g., areas of toxicity, interpersonal battles, etc.); all of this will become ammunition needed to build the ultimate three- to five-year plan and overall security program road map.

Here are a couple of key points to try and extract from your conversations:

- Regarding senior leaders and/or the C-Suite, get a sense of their perception and/or understanding of the current cybersecurity team(s). The information you glean from this may be very telling in terms of areas you need to focus on. For instance, if you hear things like "I really don't know what those folks do", then you have a lot of work to do by way of establishing the operational and reputational value of the team.
- Meeting with your rank-and-file cyber and/or information security team members to get a sense of these types of data points:
  - Can they explain to you how the company makes money? Or in the case of a non-profit can they articulate the mission?
  - How do they perceive their actual role in protecting the business?
  - Can they articulate the direction of the company as projected for some time frame (N years)?
  - How do they think they're perceived by the rest of the company?
- Meet with legal and get a sense of how comfortable they are talking you through what happens, or what is supposed to happen, in the face of a security event or incident. Legal executives and senior legal staff should be 100% in tune with these processes. Pay attention to this because if they are not, you have to spend time resolving this.
- Meet with privacy and try to ascertain if cybersecurity is adding value to privacy initiatives.

How each of these entities responds will shed light on where you, your team, and your program really stand. The responses will also start pointing you in the direction where immediate attention is needed. A CISO's role is very much founded in relationship building and these answers will lay out some relevant paths.

Here are some recommendations of tactics to use when "not interrogating", or "not interviewing" people but having conversations with the goal of information extraction (Note – "across the table" is used loosely and applies to video-based conversations as well):

- Establish a level of comfort. Many elements come into play here.
  - The person across the table should not see you as a person in a position of authority. If they do, there will be protective and/or defensive layers that get instantly raised.

- Your demeanor is important in establishing a level of comfort. If you instantly establish a parent-child dynamic, the end result may not be a good one.
- Attire matters, if you show up in a business suit and the other person is in a t-shirt the dynamic may not make for a truly relaxed environment.
- People generally speak more openly and truthfully when comfortable and relaxed.

- Use icebreakers. Food is a great generic subject that everyone can relate to. An example could be "Are you a coffee drinker? If so, can I treat you to a cup? Do you like the strong stuff"? This type of dialogue is effective in establishing a level of comfort and possibly creating a small bond. Most people speak comfortably about food or coffee and the types of answers they give expose information about that person's lifestyle.
- Use compliments. To be safe, stick to things like clothing. An example is something like "That is a great shirt, the color is so powerful. If I may ask, where did you get it"? This presents a generic, but direct complement to the other person. Most times this will ease stress levels and commence creating a comfortable setting. A piece of advice, pay close attention to the way the person answers, not so much the answer itself. The way the other person answers will probably give away many queues by way of what you are working with.
- Be 100% present. If you want a candid and open dialogue, then be present. Make sure the other person in the conversation knows you are invested in what they have to share. Put away all distracting devices and engage.
- Make a connection. A human connection in a conversation is obvious and leads to deeper engagement and sharing of information. The opposite, a dry and unconnected conversation, is also obvious and is never a positive experience. A CISO looking to establish legitimate relationships and glean valuable information from them must establish connections when engaging with others.
  - Reconnaissance is essential here because the more you know about the other person the more you can connect and engage. Moreover, coming to the table with data points puts you in a position where it becomes very possible to identify if the other person is genuine and honest. Lead the conversation in the direction where the relevant subject comes up and read the demeanor, the body cues. There are plenty of open-source intelligence (OSINT) data sources (social media sites, etc.) that facilitate the gathering of detailed information about people.
- Feed into the strengths of the other person. If the conversational dynamic starts to revolve around an area of pride and/or strength for the other person then there is a high chance information will flow. The key here is that the information flowing in your direction is probably not something that would have surfaced otherwise.
- Let it flow. The trick is to establish a bi-directional dialogue. But you need to be sensitive to the flow, listen way more than you speak. Get people talking and let it flow. Engage as needed, being very conscious of the fact that the stage belongs to the other person.

- Use your emotional intelligence (otherwise known as Emotional Quotient or EQ). You give nothing away by being genuinely empathetic, warm, kind, and a down-to-earth human version of yourself. This must be done with control though. This will work toward your credibility with the other person, this interpersonal dynamic can lead to trust. Trust in turn is the essential component for establishing and maintaining a relationship with this person.

All this seeking of information is pursued in order to deepen a CISOs knowledge of an organization's culture. The importance of this understanding cannot be overstated. It is the one single element that if missing will lead to the failure of a CISO's efforts. Here is one example illustrating the concept: It is standard, and sound, practice to have regular security awareness training for employees. You, as CISO, feel that a regular cadence is necessary for the effectiveness of said training program. You aim to implement a monthly cadence. But, the organization strongly frowns upon anything perceived as counterproductive to an employee base hyper-focused on revenue generation. Employees get wind of your upcoming proposed monthly cadence and commence complaining to senior leaders. This causes friction for you and the likelihood of your monthly cadence starts to diminish. A good understanding of this organization's culture could have steered you in a different direction and avoided the friction (there will be plenty of other opportunities for friction given this role).

Ultimately, regarding organizational culture, three types of relationships will hold great value:

- The leadership culture, which consists of executives and senior business leaders.
- The user culture, which consists of customers, partners, employees, and end users.
- The security culture, which consists of the rank and file of the security team(s).

The importance of learning an organization's culture should be evident by now. This may become a longer-term process due to availability for those one-on-one conversations. Don't lose sight of this much-needed information. But there is so much more to gather in the first 30 days. To start off, let's set a clear goal for the end of the first month on the job: You must figure out what is important to the business.

Once your bearings are settled it's time to go head down and figure out what's important to the business. The "Business" can mean different things and context matters. For example, is the business a for-profit (e.g., revenue-generating) or non-profit entity? If you are the CISO for a non-profit organization, then you must understand that the mission is the most important thing to the organization. Funding comes from memberships, donations, and grants. The CISO may be expected to become part of that fund-seeking ecosystem by way of interacting with benefactors and ensuring them that the organization is safe. This is a different experience than working at a for-profit where revenue generation is of paramount importance. In this case, it is imperative for a CISO to quickly learn how the company generates revenue. Most of the CISO's efforts in this scenario will revolve around facilitating the generation of revenue and then protecting it.

Once this understanding and familiarity are in place, the CISO can align security efforts accordingly. Beyond alignment, prioritization starts to become possible based on this newly gained knowledge. Prioritization will require continuous attention given the pace of modern-day business and many other factors such as global events. A global pandemic, or large-scale conflict, will surely derail existing efforts and require flexibility on your part by way of re-prioritization of efforts. The COVID-19 pandemic which started in approximately late December 2019, is a classic example. Many CISOs had to fast track, or first implement, support for employees to work from home en masse. This was a survival exercise from a business continuity perspective and derailed many efforts that were already underway. Prioritization, combined with business alignment, will help you determine where to spend your budgetary resources as well as what is actually possible with the resources and skill sets at your disposal.

It is important to be careful at this stage because natural protective instinct will drive one toward wanting to be aggressive in action. Overengineering solutions is one area to be conscious of. Another one is the age-old notion of boiling the ocean, aiming to divide and conquer into small solvable problems. Little wins will go a long way in the beginning of this kind of journey. The bigger problems will get attention later.

To be clear, this does not mean that you don't face problems head-on. A certain focus and perspective are necessary at this stage. You need to find a way to map initiatives to what's important to the business. Show value early on. This way business leaders start seeing you as a partner, ally, and a source of value-add. At that point, you can start having meaningful conversations with business leaders that will lead to a positive impact on the business. The last thing you want to be seen as is a hindrance or the "department of NO".

FIRST 30 DAYS

These are some concrete areas that you will want to consider during this early phase:

- Crown Jewel Analysis.
- Attack Surface.
- The Basics.
- Metrics.
- Security as a Business function.
- Trust.
- Plan Development.

CROWN JEWEL ANALYSIS

It is imperative that you simply figure out what is business critical. Be aware that this may be different than what is critical to the business. Since "the business" is made up of people you may get different answers when trying to establish a crown jewel mapping. Ultimately, what is business critical is what needs initial attention. Determine which data and systems comprise what is critical to the company. The focus should be on what makes up the organization's strategic initiatives, revenue-generating model (if applicable), mission and core competencies, intellectual property, and business differentiators. These crown jewels are the digital assets that are most likely to be targeted by nefarious actors and thus must get immediate attention in terms of determining levels of protection. This data then has to be coupled with related risk appetite. At this stage you may not have a keen understanding of said appetite so tap into some of the relationships you have established for information. Then you can analyze if existing security strategies suffice. If they don't, or if they don't exist, then you can pursue implementation accordingly.

ATTACK SURFACE

The attack surface refers to the overall set of points where a nefarious actor can target anything you are responsible for. This could consist of systems, network ingress points, or Layer 7 egress points (software, applications, Application Programming Interface (API), etc.). The dataset that represents your attack surface will point you to areas that can be targeted, exploited, or compromised by bad actors. It represents the vulnerabilities and ingress points through which attackers will try to gain unauthorized access to data or disrupt business-critical services.

The management of your attack surface will be a continuous effort. But, a baseline will be necessary at this early stage. If there is one, analyze it so that you get a sense of the ecosystem you are now responsible for. If there isn't one, consider this in your plan and longer term set of initiatives. Chapter 3 covers this in more detail.

COVER THE BASICS

Ensuring that basic technology hygiene is in place is just sound practice. Securing modern-day organizations is a complex endeavor. As such, many technologies and products may be in place. Integration mileage varies depending on these product choices. Complexities aside, there are a few must-haves that should be implemented for good general coverage. If they are not in place or need improvements, you will need to consider this in your plans. These are some basic areas to consider:

- Zero Trust (ZT) solutions.
- Identity and Access Management (IAM).
- Software Bill of Materials (SBOM) across all applications, especially anything custom or written in-house.
- Attack Surface Management (holistic – external, internal, non-standard computing devices).
- Application Security (AppSec) (Web Application Firewall (WAF), Static application security testing (SAST), Dynamic Application Security Testing (DAST), etc.).
- API security.
- Cloud Security (configurations, etc.).
- Container Security.
- Penetration Testing (continuous, breach simulation, etc.).

- Data protection (encryption, disinformation, sharding, etc.).
- Security Incident and Event Monitoring (SIEM)/Security Orchestration, Automation, and Response (SOAR).
- Ransomware Resilience (prevention, detection, recovery).
- Threat and vulnerability management.
- Endpoint protection (anti-malware, detection, and response, etc.).
- Server, Container, VM protection.
- Multi-factor authentication.
- Application whitelisting.
- 24/7 security monitoring.
- File integrity monitoring.
- Privileged access management.
- Network security and segmentation.
- Intrusion Detection System (IDS)/Intrusion Prevention System (IPS).
- Remote Access (Virtual Private Networking (VPN), Browser-based solutions, etc.).
- Data loss prevention.
- Patching strategies.
- Security Awareness/Training.
- ICS/OT Security (if applicable).

IMPLEMENT BASIC METRICS

Implementing, extending, and maintaining a metrics program will be another important area for your attention. Focusing on metrics that subjectively matter to your target audience will be a factor that either feeds or detracts from your success. The value of metrics is that they act as proof of the value of security programs, objectives, plans, processes, and technologies. A typical list of target audiences includes the C-Suite, senior executives, and possibly members of the board.

Beyond proof of value, metrics can impact the ability to make informed business decisions, in particular, decisions that affect the organization's security programs. Quantifiable metrics, including what data and assets are at higher levels of risk, and details of prior events and incidents, can add a lot of value. That information helps decision-makers prioritize technology and security investments, and direct decisions based on real risk. Correlation across multiple entities in the respective ecosystem becomes critical in painting a good picture for decision-makers. Security teams should be able to correlate risk data with other risk indicators (known vulnerabilities, known deficiencies, threat hunting results, threat intelligence, etc.) to score, benchmark, and trend over time an organization's cyber risk.

SECURITY IS A BUSINESS CONCERN

If an organization is already security-first in its mindset, you are ahead of the curve. If it is not, it is on you as the final executive word regarding security matters to ensure that stakeholders and senior leaders see and treat, security as a business concern. A negative security event, or incident, can have an adverse impact on a business. When this adverse impact reaches the C-Suite and/or the board it is typically met with a reactive process. When security is seen as an actual factor in business-related processes, especially decision-making processes, the reactive impact can be reduced. You want the key businesspeople to understand that a strong security posture and program, can help the business succeed in a safe fashion. This is why it's imperative that cyber and information security teams always get, and continuously remain, integrated with the generally non-technical side of the organization, "the business". Creating a culture of open communication, and collaboration, between executive leaders, the board, senior leaders, and the security leadership will go a long way in getting security acknowledged as a business concern. When management understands that cybersecurity risk translates cleanly to business risk, they'll be more apt to be supportive, provide attention and resources, and participate in security efforts.

BUILD TRUST UP AND DOWN

As if the first 30 days were not packed enough, everything recommended thus far must be pursued while establishing credibility. This applies to peers, superiors, and direct reports, making up the "up and down" part of your human ecosystem. The last thing a CISO wants to be seen as is a dishonest politician or a used car salesman. Moreover, you don't want to come across as crass or rude because you want to build relationships and develop allies. Listen way more than you talk. The key people in your ecosystem, both up and down, need to genuinely feel like you've listened to their input and are there to help them succeed.

DEVELOP A PLAN

Factoring in all gathered data points (identified assets and crown jewels) it is time to develop a written risk management plan. The CISO becomes a central point of data collection and reporting here. The management plan can have checklists for deliverables and other simple-to-digest data points. Assuming the central point of control, communication between key internal and external stakeholders becomes important. On this point, the CISO must always act as an objective, neutral information broker and as a partner to all key organizational decision-makers. One effective way to accomplish this is using some of the conversational, and relationship-building, points that have already been covered. This objective stance, coupled with effective communication can move the organization forward in strategic fashion.

At the end of the first 30 days, it is recommended that you:

• Have gained perspective.
• Developed partnerships.

Perspective

• What matters to this business?
• What matters to the business leaders?

- Are the answers to the first two points the same, in range, or totally in different zones?
- Is this organization focused on itself, the employees, partners, or customers?
- How does this company generate revenue, or how does the organization pursue its mission?
- What is your role in helping them succeed with safe business?

Partnerships

- Who are the internal leaders you need to work with?
- Who are the external leaders you need to work with?
- Who do you need to be aligned with to help pursue success on a business level?
- Do you need to influence, negotiate, or both?
- Does the current perception of your team need to change?

Perspective and partnerships can largely be addressed in your first 30 days as a CISO.

FIRST 60 DAYS

Days 30–60 will be spent continuing what you started in the first 30 days. Please do not expect any of what is recommended here to simply be smooth sailing. Time buffers are factored in so that you figure out how to navigate your new environment, especially the human elements. Adding to what you have commenced in the first 30 days, you will be expanding your understanding of what you are now responsible for. Simply put, you will seek out an understanding of the resources you are working with in order to protect your new environment, the ecosystem. In essence, this is an exercise in developing an inventory of:

- Resources
- Ecosystem

INVENTORY YOUR RESOURCES

This is where you start gaining more intimacy with the resources you are now working with. Take inventory of what you have, what you don't have, and the delta, what is missing. This applies to your security team, organizational policies, organizational processes, and existing technology stacks. It also extends beyond the cyber and/or information security teams. General areas to take inventory of:

- Policies.
- Protective mechanisms.
- Security team.
- Broader team.

Policies are essential for setting operational guardrails, guiding organizations' security practices, and promoting awareness. They provide a foundation for implementing security controls, ensuring compliance, and establishing a proactive and robust security posture. Here is a general list of standard policies most organizations have:

- Acceptable Use Policy (AUP) – Defines acceptable and prohibited uses of organizational resources (applications, data, systems, networks, etc.). It should cover employee responsibilities and restrictions on unauthorized activities. Consequences for policy violations should also be included in this document.
- Privileged Rights Acceptable Use Policy – Given the context of escalated, or privileged, access levels, defines acceptable and prohibited uses of organizational resources (applications, data, systems, networks, etc.). It should cover employee administrative responsibilities and restrictions based on such elevated privileges. Consequences for policy violations should also be included in this document.
- Acceptable use of Artificial Intelligence (AI) Policy – Defines acceptable use of organizational resources as they relate to AI systems. It should cover data considerations, risks, and preventative measures that can be taken when interacting with AI systems. It should also cover employee responsibilities and restrictions on data exposure to AI engines. Consequences for policy violations should also be included in this document.
- Information Security Policy – Provides an overarching set of guidelines for managing information security across the organization. It should outline management's commitment, roles and responsibilities, risk management, and high-level security objectives.
- Incident Response Policy – Defines the organization's approach to detecting, responding, and recovering from security incidents. It should outline roles, responsibilities, and procedures for incident detection, reporting, containment, investigation, and recovery. It should also outline incident classification, escalation procedures, communication protocols, and coordination with relevant stakeholders.
- Public Disclosure Policy – Defines the organization's criteria for when an element of data can be disclosed to the public. It should outline the thresholds to qualify for public release, the approval process for a disclosure and then the approved mechanisms to use for the actual release of information.
- Password Policy – Sets requirements for creating, managing, and protecting passwords. It should cover complexity, length, expiration, reuse guidelines, and may also cover requirements for multi-factor authentication.
- Security and Endpoint Management Policy – Establishes security controls and configurations for the organization's endpoint devices. It should outline required security software components, monitoring, and encryption requirements and should also include guidelines for connected peripheral devices (USB-based storage, etc.).
- Mobile Device Security Policy – Defines security requirements and controls for mobile devices used for work purposes. It should cover device encryption, authentication, mobile application usage, mobile device security configurations, remote wiping, and measures to prevent unauthorized access or data leakage.

- Bring Your Own Device (BYOD) Policy – Set guidelines for employees who choose to use their personal devices to access organizational resources. It should address security requirements, device registration, remote data wiping, and acceptable use of personal devices.
- Network Security Policy – Establishes security controls and configurations for the organization's network infrastructure, including firewalls, routers, switches, wireless networking, and remote access devices. It should outline network segmentation, monitoring, and encryption requirements and should also include guidelines for firewall configurations, network intrusion detection systems, and access controls.
- Patch Management Policy – Establishes procedures for timely and effective patching of software (e.g., libraries, applications, etc.) and operating systems. It should address patch testing prior to deployment, deployment processes, and management and/or maintenance of patch management systems.
- Access Control Policy – Outlines the procedures and mechanisms for managing user access to data, systems, and network resources. It should cover organizational authentication, authorization, and access standards and/or practices.
- Remote Access Policy – Establishes guidelines for secure remote access to the organization's networks and other resources (applications DBs, systems, etc.). It should include authentication requirements and usage restrictions for remote connections.
- Physical Security Policy – Addresses physical security controls and measures to protect the organization's employees, premises, equipment, and data. It should cover access controls, visitor management, surveillance, theft protection, event playbooks (e.g., active shooter, etc.), and natural disaster responses.
- Background Check and Reporting Policy – Defines the fact that employees and/or contractors will undergo background checks as a condition of employment. For the safety of all other employees, this document should mandate that the person being investigated must report prior convictions. It should also address the contacting of references and guidelines about convictions once an employee. Consequences for policy violations should also be included in this document.
- Payment Card Data Security Policy – Defines secure design, implementation, and operation of processes and systems related to payment card data. It should also cover relevant roles, scoping, monitoring, logging, incident management, data storage and processing, access control, system maintenance, training, and testing. Consequences for policy violations should be included in this document along with exception criteria.
- Social Media Usage Policy – Establishes guidelines for employees' use of social media platforms as it relates to company information. It should address privacy considerations, protection of confidential information, appropriate use of corporate branding, and general social media best practices.
- Technology Safeguards While Traveling Internationally – Defines the organization's stance on the use of its assets while traveling internationally.

It should address rules of engagement before, during, and after a trip. Guidelines and practical advice should be included so the document is useful to the traveler. Embassy addresses, emergency phone numbers, and procedures should also be included along with a list of high-risk countries.

- Electronic Communications Policy – Defines the organization's stance on the use of communication technology (email, chat, etc.). It should address rules of engagement, proper digital conduct, protection of confidential information, personal use of work accounts, recordings of calls and/or video chat sessions, and possibly the use of specific capabilities within specific tools (e.g., shared channels with external vendors, communication with contractors, etc.).
- Corporate Electronic Communications Retention Policy – Defines the organization's stance on data deletion as it pertains to communications (email, chat, etc.). It should address contractual obligations with partners, timeframe not to be surpassed, and exceptions, if any, to this policy where data can be kept past the normal deletion cycle.
- Data Classification and Handling Policy – Provides guidelines for classifying and handling sensitive data based on its sensitivity and possible regulatory requirements. It outlines data access controls, retention guidelines, storage requirements, transmission protocols, and disposal procedures.
- Data Encryption Policy – Specifies the requirements for encryption of sensitive data in transit and at rest. It outlines algorithmic standards, key management, and controls for protecting data confidentiality and integrity.
- Data Breach Response Policy – Specifies the actions that should be taken in the event of a data breach. It should include incident reporting, containment, steps for mitigating the impact of the breach, and disclosures and notifications.
- Data Backup and Recovery Policy – Defines procedures for regular data backups, type of storage to use (e.g., immutable, etc.), multiple site storage, off-site storage, and data recovery processes. It should include backup frequency, retention periods, testing procedures, and restoration guidelines.
- Data Privacy Policy – Defines the organization's approach to protecting personal and/or sensitive information. The subjects of complying with applicable data protection laws and relevant regulations need to be covered in this document. It should also address consent, data subject rights, and data breach notification requirements.
- Security Awareness and Training Policy – Establishes guidelines for promoting cybersecurity awareness. It should outline the requirements for regularly scheduled training, the use of unscheduled social engineering tests, awareness campaigns, phishing simulations, and dissemination of security best practices. There should also be coverage (it may be in a separate policy) of awareness and/or handling of social engineering attacks. These will include phishing, pretexting (manipulation technique that tricks victims into divulging information), and impersonation (especially executive impersonation). This should cover industry and/or company best practices for identifying and responding to social engineering attempts.

- Vendor and Third-Party Risk Management Policy – Establishes guidelines and/or processes for assessing and managing risks associated with vendors, suppliers, and third-party service providers. It should cover due diligence, contract clauses, contractual obligations, data protection requirements, and ongoing monitoring of third-party security practices.

It's important to note that information security policies should be tailored to the specific needs, risk profile, and regulatory requirements of each organization. These policies serve as a foundation for implementing effective security controls and practices and should promote a culture of security awareness and compliance within the organization.

Policies are not an end all be all, so these are some of the questions (per policy) you should seek answers to as a CISO:

- Can this policy be enforced, or is adherence to this policy based solely on the honor system?
  - If it can be enforced, how?
  - If not, can something be put in place to enforce said policy?
- Is the policy easily accessible to all employees?
  - If it is not, then how can we make it accessible?

Regarding existing protective mechanisms, what is in place? And more importantly, is there a way to gauge the effectiveness of these mechanisms? Taking the cyber resilience angle, these mechanisms must be scrutinized such that you can either have a sense of confidence in them, or not. Generally, these are some things to look for:

- Any zero-trust solutions.
- Layer 7 protective mechanisms:
  - WAFs:
    - The rulesets matter.
    - Who manages the rulesets?
    - Are all ingress and egress points properly routed through these chokepoints?
  - API Gateways.
  - Is there a granular access control set up between tiers?
    - For example, will a Database (DB) server accept sockets/connections from any arbitrary host?
- Data protective mechanisms:
  - Is all DB access at least password-protected, and communication stream protected via Transport Layer Security (TLS)?
  - If a relational model, is there column-level encryption covering sensitive data?
  - Is the data effectively being backed?
  - Are data backups regularly tested so that restoration is known to work?
  - Is there sensitive data stored in files?
    - Where are files stored?
    - Are they encrypted at rest (not the volume, the actual files)?

- Intrusion Prevention Systems (IPS).
- Automations:
  - Are automated components taking autonomous action to tell other devices to act (e.g., block traffic, etc.)?
- Firewalls:
  - Have the configuration(s) been reviewed by experts?
- Network segmentation.
- Micro-segmentation.

Regarding your team, how complete is it? A great cybersecurity team comprises various roles that collectively work toward organizational protection. The specific roles may vary depending on the organization's structure, size, industry, and actual needs. Team building and roles are covered in Chapter 7.

Mature programs may also have Blue Team and Red Team setups. Some organizations just outsource these practices to expert consultants. The Blue Team handles the defensive side of the cybersecurity equation. They are responsible for testing, and validating, the effectiveness of the protective posture of an organization. The primary goal of the Blue Team is to gauge how protected are data, applications, systems, and networks. The Red Team, on the other hand, plays the offensive role. They simulate real-world attacks to identify deficiencies in the defenses of an organization's protective mechanisms. The Red Team's objective is to challenge the Blue Team's capabilities with the intent of improving an organization's overall protective posture.

The collaboration between the Blue and Red Team is referred to as a Purple Team. It involves war games and adversarial simulations such that knowledge is shared toward the pursuit of enhancement in an organization's protective capabilities. The iterative process of attacking, defending, testing, collaborating, and improving helps organizations strengthen defenses and try to stay ahead of evolving cyber threats.

Extending beyond the cyber and/or information security teams to the broader team, you need to ferret out if key roles, or pieces of the puzzle, are missing. In particular, these represent roles that don't necessarily exist in every organization:

- Chief Privacy Officer.
  - Is there a Privacy team supporting this individual?
- Chief Legal Officer.
  - Is there a Legal team supporting this individual?
- Chief Risk Officer.

An example here is, asking around to figure out who has the ability to accept, or reject, risk given some action (e.g., product acquisition, awarding a contract to a specific vendor, etc.). This element of information will yield important data points. Does anyone in this organization actually acknowledge risk or is it just handled in some loose informal fashion? Is there an Enterprise Risk Management (ERM) Committee in place? And if so, is it a mere formality with no power? If there isn't one, has the company tried implementing one in the past? If the company is public, then formal risk management may not be an option as a public company is typically required to have risk management practices in place.

INVENTORY YOUR ECOSYSTEM

The data generated from the ASM exercise will prove invaluable in your efforts. Many organizations aggressively pursue technology innovations and digital transformation efforts. Understanding what these efforts leave in place could greatly impact the success of your program. Moreover, these artifacts have the ability to positively or negatively impact your ability to protect the data, systems, applications, products, and revenue-generating processes.

It's critical to recognize that it will take time to do this in a granular fashion. And there is always the possibility that you won't see, or know about, everything. Organization size and complexity are serious factors regarding this. Expect challenges with your visibility efforts and accept the fact that there may be some ambiguity no matter how aggressively you attack this. The idea here is to figure out what you have so you can eventually spend protective resources appropriately. On top of this, you want to get a sense of what the asset inventory, and the ecosystem, mean to the potential success/failure of both the business and your program.

Note: All of this can be overwhelming. Part of being a CISO is about being relaxed, and comfortable, with all this uncertainty and disadvantage. There is nothing wrong with seeking mentoring or coaching from peers that are willing to help. We are in this together, and peer networks represent valuable troves of knowledge and support.

At the end of the first 60 days, it is recommended that you:

- Inventory resources.
- Inventory the ecosystem.

FIRST 90 DAYS

You are now at a good stage in terms of intelligence gathering and discovery. Time to be a leader. Time to be a business partner.

IDENTIFY QUICK WINS

If possible, identify areas where quick wins are realistically possible. There is the possibility of these not existing but some of these can go a long way in showing your business prowess, hunger for productivity, and effectiveness as a leader. The goal is to have something concrete to show business stakeholders and other leaders. Demonstrate your ability to lead a project that positively impacts the business. Your credibility will rise and it will be a display of your collaborative approach, willingness to do what is best for the business, thought process, and operational capability. If this can be done within the first 90 days it will send a clear message about you and, more importantly, what the organization can expect from you.

The quick target(s) should have made themselves known to you as you performed your conversations and established relationships. Pick something meaningful, discuss it with the relevant teams that can execute it, and figure out how to get some short-term wins. This not only delivers a message to the business and relevant stakeholders but it also establishes confidence with your team as well.

Regarding your team, they may already possess strong domain knowledge. If that is the case, they can add tremendous value when it comes to identifying some possible quick wins:

- Brainstorm threat scenarios and known areas of deficiency.
- Conduct quick tabletop exercises.

OUTREACH

If you achieve some short-term accomplishments, then you have to make them known to the relevant audience. If you get something done and it remains in the shadows, there will not be any benefit in terms of establishing yourself within an organization. Consider an internal series of outreach meetings to share the accomplishments and start sharing your plans and observations. Get feedback. Educate the business stakeholders, and any other relevant players, about your team, your observed ecosystem, and the program you are starting to envision. Make it known that you are here, a team player, and willing to be a business partner looking to align on business priorities and objectives.

As part of this outreach, make it known that business stakeholders and senior leaders have a safe place to innovate, collaborate, and negotiate with you. The negotiation part is very important because your business counterparts need to see you as someone they can work with to achieve safe and successful business outcomes. You cannot become the anti-progress entity of the organization. The notion is to be seen as an entity that enables the business through the pursuit of safe business.

COMMENCE WITH CHANGES

Towards the end of the first 90 days, there should be consensus and alignment about what needs to happen to build the new security program. As a CISO you should have already built enough credibility with your team so that you can move forth as one unified force. So long as you don't make this feel like a dictatorship, and your security team members feel as though they're part of this journey, the building of the new program has a good chance of success. This is where decision-making comes into play and you cannot come across as indecisive. Without decisions, changes are not possible. Make decisions, be ready to fail fast, be ready to reset, own your decisions, and be humble enough to acknowledge bad decisions and pivot accordingly.

At the end of the first 90 days, it is recommended that you:

- Identify quick wins.
- Create positive outreach.
- Commence with changes.

This first three-month period can be daunting, but it is essential in laying down some of the foundational pieces you will build upon. The goals are aggressive but reflective of real-world needs. In order to set your company and you up for security and business success in the short and long term, aim to accomplish as much as you can given the material just covered.

Given the collective 90-day period, let's take inventory of some of the high-level goals:

- Understanding of the business – A new security leader's job starts with a lot of learning, and possibly some doing. New CISOs should familiarize themselves with their organization, its business model, its culture, its security history, its security appetite, its tolerance for security improvements, its perception with outside entities, and how it interacts with the market.
- Understanding the processes – Dig into processes, especially those that have touchpoints with external entities (vendors, partners, etc.). You need to become as familiar as possible with these processes, how they work, and how they don't work (are unsuccessful).
- Understanding the team – Dig into the security team(s). Understand how they act, how they interact with other teams, the perception outsiders have of them, their skill sets, their strengths, and their weaknesses.
- Understand security posture – This encompasses many elements including familiarity with your attack surface, familiarity with your defensive capabilities, and familiarity with cyber resilience levels. One of the biggest gaps in most security ecosystems is made up of their use of Software as a Service (SaaS) solutions. Because these can potentially be purchased and utilized in a fashion that bypasses policies and controls, they represent tremendous risks you should be aware of. No matter what SaaS solution may be in use, please remember, it's still your data on those external systems.
- Relationship building – Critical to security success are the positive relationships that need to be built. This is your time to meet with other business stakeholders, the C-Suite, and possibly board members to understand their needs and make yourself accessible to them.
- Strategy building – It's never too early to start building a new security strategy that will drive the buildout of your security program. It must obviously meet the organization's business goals and objectives but your work in the early stages of the 90-day period should have given you enough foundational knowledge to be able to do this. One area that is often overlooked in the strategy is career pathing for the security team members. This strategy should also include how to continuously test the protective/defensive mechanisms that have been put in place. Finally, regarding your strategy, it's important to get critical feedback from business stakeholders in order to start building your program and implementing this new strategy.
- Introduce process changes – This is obviously optional and dependent on the organization's culture and how far you got in the first 90 days. If appropriate, and based on your findings, you may consider exploring new ways to inspire the security team to become more responsive, more flexible, and possibly agile enough to adapt and overcome arbitrary challenges. This may include finding the right project management tools.
- Gather metrics – Metrics will guide you toward areas of strength and deficiencies. Use them to ensure that whatever is in place is effective and

properly working. If metrics are not in use, then that needs to factor into your new plans. If they are in place, make sure there is a regular cadence of measurements and reporting. Continuous metrics will prove useful in addressing states and levels of effectiveness with your security team(s), the C-Suite, the executive committee (if one exists), and potentially board members.

- Regarding your understanding of the protective ecosystem at hand, if you are unsure of its effectiveness, or if you have received conflicting information, bring in external help as a matter of urgency. Have assessments done, have penetration tests performed, get as much of the truth as is possible without the possible tainting of data from internal sources (irrespective of their motivation or reasons)

Given the collective 90-day period, these are some of the questions you should be asking, and hopefully answering:

- Can I explain this organization's business model and mission to someone else?
- Can I explain the general culture of this organization?
- How well protected is the organization?
- What are the largest areas of risk for this organization?
  - Do I have a sense of what it will take to mitigate risk in these areas?
- What is the security maturity level of this organization?
  - Maybe correlate this against some industry standard framework.
- What data is mission-critical to the organization?
- Is this organization properly equipped to stand up to attacks?
- Is this organization properly equipped to respond to events and incidents?

At this point, it is time to start paving the path toward the longer-term security program you want to build and maintain over time.

EXPERT ADVICE

The path to a successful career as a cybersecurity executive at any level or any business is to treat the business as a customer. When you think of how companies are passionate about their customers, this is the same thinking you should take in your role. Being laser-focused on the business, putting the time in to understand your peers' needs, and going deep on business functions outside of cyber will make people your champion. When people feel valued and heard they are more open to accepting new ideas. And if you are the first CISO that the company has hired, you are most likely bringing in a lot of new ideas and changes.

Cybersecurity is about helping the business manage risk. They've hired you to be that expert voice. Showing you understand how the rest of the business functions will demonstrate your ability to see a problem and solution end-to-end. While we have to do a lot of change management in cybersecurity, that requires trust. And when you solve business problems outside of cybersecurity you build immediate trust. Once that is established everything else you do from that point forward will be far easier.

– Chris Castaldo, CISO, Crossbeam

REAL-WORLD PERSPECTIVE

When starting a new CISO role, it's important to come into the organization with a certain level of humbleness. It's true that you were hired into the position as a security expert, and it is your job to make changes in the organization. However, you need to keep in mind that organizational traditions and culture preceded your arrival and to get your goals accomplished, you will need finesse and strategy that considers people even more so than the technology you are tasked with securing.

Pay special attention to your conversational style and avoid too many references to your previous jobs and experiences. We've all had that new colleague, who started a new job and often said, "Well, we did it this way at Previous Corp and it worked great, let's do this here as well". I've been this colleague and can tell you firsthand that your new coworkers usually do not appreciate this type of approach. Instead, if you did something that worked great at a previous job and could work in the organization, try using a more subtle approach such as "Would it make sense to solve this problem in the following manner . . ."? This will be less likely to alienate your new colleagues and may still get you to the outcome you desire.

– Vlad Brodsky, CIO and CISO, OTC Markets Group

I regularly work with new CISOs who are struggling to get their footing in the new role. My first questions are always the same: how many executives and business unit leaders have you spoken with, and have you built your stakeholder map? Every leader has a risk they are most concerned about, a project that must succeed, and a stretch goal they aren't sure they can reach. Buy individuals a coffee to introduce yourself and instead of talking about yourself, ask them indirectly about these things. Then, write it down. You will see opportunities to mitigate some of their risks, to help them reach their project goals faster and you will gain champions for your own projects in this manner. And all it will cost you is a few cups of coffee.

– Dan Elliott, Principal, Cyber Security Risk Advisory,
Zurich Resilience Solutions (ZRS) Canada

Outreach – Over the last ten years the CISO has gone from an executive who sat a tier below the C-Suite to a true C-Suite leader. One of the goals a CISO must set for themselves in the first 90 days is to claim that seat at the table and for this to be possible the CISO has to put in the work to make themselves visible. Being visible does not necessarily mean the CISO has to be singing their own praises or shouting out about the projects that have been completed. It could mean that over the first 90 days, they invite participation from their peers and identify shared objectives that can be accomplished in those early days. When these early wins are realized, the CISO can celebrate their collaborative success thus lifting not only themselves but also their peers. There is no better way to build allies in the workplace than to be the shoulders on which your peers stand to be recognized, and a CISO can always use all the allies they can get.

– Arti Raman, CEO and Founder, Portal26

Politician or CEO? Working with CISOs over the years, I always admire the diversity of skills required to be a successful CISO. Sometimes, jokingly, I would say a successful CISO has to be a successful politician, or a CEO running their own enterprise. Here is the why.

Go-To-Market – Many CISOs underestimate the amount of sales and marketing work related to their job. To begin with, a CISO needs to identify their internal customers – Who are the stakeholders? Who receives the services that the cyber team provides? What are the business problems that the internal customers are facing? What are the metrics that the internal customers are being evaluated on? Is that top-line revenues, profitability, customer acquisition, or process efficiency?

Once you can capture and articulate all of this it provides a tremendous amount of clarity to help a CISO formulate their own business plan, objective and key results, and staffing plan. Once the business plan is formulated, the CISO can develop a marketing plan to educate internal customers and increase security awareness across end-user communities and executive stakeholders. Oftentimes, understanding the who and why is more important than executing the blocking and tackling security tasks.

Communication skills are crucial in managing how the enterprise "perceives" the cyber team. Is the cyber team a pure cost center asking for a budget increase every year? Or are they a business partner who understands how to support business priorities and deliver differentiated business values for both internal and external customers? A successful CISO communicates the latter.

> Engineering – No successful CISO can pass the sniff test without a foundational grasp of technologies. An experienced CISO should have good fundamental training on the core components of cyber defense and offense. They need to have played active execution roles in proactive exposure reduction, active monitoring, and reactive response and incident management.

Other than mastering the fundamentals, a seasoned CISO is also a technologist at heart. They must be apprised of the latest technological innovation in general domains. They might not be a data scientist or expert in large language models but they must be conversational in the space. Whether that is identifying the technology trends that affect their industry, the impact on the cyber defense strategy, or the required knowledge for their cyber team to stay ahead of the game.

> CFO and HR – Negotiating the budget with the CFO is part of the job description for a CISO. However, what is more important is to articulate the "why" through the lens of a CFO – a highly analytical mind that primarily focuses on profitability and bottom line. As we all know cyber is a cost center. To be successful, you must speak of your cyber investments and returns in financial terms. Outline the cost savings in risk reduction, compliance achievement for regulated businesses, cyber insurance premium savings, and intangible reputational value to prevent a breach. This is one-to-one language your CFO will comprehend.

With regard to HR, the talent shortage in this space is well documented. Smaller talent pipelines and higher demands make keeping a healthy, happy, and productive cyber workforce critical. This is not an easy undertaking for CISOs. CISOs need to be constantly scouting for talent, developing an internal leadership bench, coaching underperforming staff, and developing a staffing continuity plan.

Legal and Vendor Management

Modern CISOs recognize the value of building partnerships with core and innovative vendors. Core vendors help develop the building blocks of the foundational cyber program. Think about exposure management, SOC operations, threat hunting, incident responses, and GRC all working together. Innovative vendors bring the next frontier of technology innovation to disrupt the traditional way of problem-solving. A good balance of core and innovative vendors can help CISOs achieve performance, speed, and agility while maturing cyber programs. Consolidating non-core vendors and putting strategic bets on innovative vendors are a good risk-reward playbook in vendor management.

On the legal front, CISOs do not need a JD or LLM to be effective but understanding the basics of indemnification and limitation of liability clauses in contract negotiation will help CISOs to become more well-rounded business executives.

PR and Crisis Communication

When the news drops – "we got hacked" – the clock starts ticking to test out the incident response plan and crisis communication to multiple dimensions beyond the annual tabletop exercises. Stay calm, things will eventually get sorted out. An experienced CISO will quickly adapt their role into the Head of Crisis Communication and PR agent. They will first understand the magnitude of the impact, develop a damage control strategy on demand, and communicate with calming confidence with the board, customers, legal, and the press. Certainty and transparency provide the highest level of comfort in the time of crisis.

Politician or CEO? The question came back. As a CISO CEO, they are running their own enterprise to deliver a business outcome for the organization. There will be a time to deal with "Layer 9" challenges, aka politics. The larger the organization, the more complex relationships a CISO has to navigate through to be successful in her career and in building allies/securing sponsors. Find an informal mentor, who has been there and done that, or hire a professional coach. All top-performing athletes have coaches who keep them at the top of their game, the same rule applies to CISOs.

– Lisa Xu, CEO, NopSec

3 Be a Builder

The journey has reached the point where the first milestone, the 90th day, is in the past. Now it's time to focus on building, or improving, a security program. This must be pursued while continuously building and/or managing all the relationships essential to success in this role. Building the security program may constitute a scenario where the program does not exist and the CISO starts at ground zero, or this may be building upon an existing program and either making adjustments or expanding what is already in place. The approach presented here will tackle the challenge from the former perspective. If a CISO is facing an existing program the advice and recommendations presented here formulate a checklist of sorts to gauge the completeness of the existing program.

Building a cybersecurity program involves several essential steps and/or elements to ultimately manage risk and protect an organization's data, end-users, employees, and systems. This will rely heavily on the intimate knowledge a CISO should already be gaining about the business and its needs. Building the program will also require intimacy with the risk appetite and attack surface at hand. This knowledge will be coupled with security assessments, the identification of risk areas, and an understanding of technical debt and known vulnerabilities within the ecosystem. The gaps must be understood in order to eventually implement active protective mechanisms that can autonomously stand up to nefarious activity. Assuming a certain level of corporate maturity, this program should also have continuously running programs, such as a Vulnerability and Threat Management (VTM) program and security awareness programs.

Part of being a builder is being a destroyer after asking yourself, and facing, some difficult questions. The questions in this scenario are being posed to the CISO by the CISO. A CISO needs to honestly assess the need for solutions. This person may very well be inheriting solutions that add little to no value. If something is not truly needed, get rid of it. Accept the exit terms of a contract, work with procurement, finance, and legal but let these situations linger. Any system, even security systems, that do not actively add value needs to go. Security systems are not immune to attack and there is a historical pattern of neglecting these systems because they perform background functions silently, and as security products are assumed to be secure. This is one area of risk that is seldom addressed. These systems are probably on a depreciation cycle, and this must tactfully be addressed with finance. But, even if a system needs to be allowed to run out a contract or depreciation cycle, it doesn't have to live up to that agreement while introducing risk (in a running state while adding no value).

One example of being a destroyer is doing away with outdated Identity and Access Management (IAM) paradigms and upgrading to modern techniques, such as biometrics-based solutions with a failover/fallback to Multi-Factor Authentication (MFA). This also includes upgrading SaaS solution security configurations and pushing those vendors for support of these advanced solutions as well.

 DOI: 10.1201/9781003477556-3

Another example of being a destroyer, for good, is pursuing a passwordless model given a current model that relies on passwords for authentication. Passwords made sense in the past because there was nothing better to leverage for proof of identity during authentication. The industry is way past that stage, yet passwords are still readily used. Remember, a CISO has to face and tackle those elements that are difficult. Sensibly target those legacy systems and replace them with modern ones wherever possible. The new ones can improve the security posture of your organization and actually provide a better user experience.

GENERAL FRAMEWORK

Here's a general framework for building a security program:

- Take inventory of assets.
- Implement continuous attack surface management (ASM).
- Understand your data.
- Create a risk register.
- Develop policies.
- Implement controls.
- Create an incident management program/plan.
- Create a culture of awareness.
- Implement continuous monitoring.
- Implement change management.
- Create a Vulnerability and Threat Management (VTM) program.
- Ensure defenses are adequate.
- Implement continuous testing.
- Pursue continuous improvement.
- Establish external partnerships.
- Third Party Risk Management (TPRM).
- Create a Metrics program.
- Create Steering Committees.

ASSET INVENTORY

An asset inventory is a vital component of any cybersecurity program. Baselining your assets and maintaining that inventory over time sounds straightforward. But the challenges start early. Every organization needs to define what constitutes an asset to it. Here are some of the challenges you should be aware of when it comes to asset discovery:

- Broad scope – cybersecurity assets can come to encompass a wide range of elements. These can include the obvious hardware, software, data, intellectual property, networks, and human resources. But the scope starts to expand when considering things like software, most software packages come with many dependencies (more details in the upcoming SBOM section). Defining and categorizing these more complicated assets can be difficult due to the complexity and interconnections.

- Dynamic nature – some assets to be considered from a security perspective are not static; they expand, contract, evolve, and change over time. New assets are constantly being added, while existing assets may be modified, upgraded, or decommissioned. Keeping track of these changes can be a challenge, especially if there is a lack of automation.
- Cloud and ephemeral assets – with the increasing adoption of cloud technologies and elastic capabilities, assets can be ephemeral. Identifying and defining assets in these dynamic ecosystems can be complex; traditional boundaries just don't apply.
- Shadow IT – shadow IT makes an accurate inventory virtually impossible. The ecosystems where employees use unauthorized applications, services, or devices without the knowledge of IT departments, pose a serious challenge in asset inventorying. These untracked assets can obviously introduce serious security risks without proper visibility.
- Data classification – identifying and classifying data assets is particularly challenging. Organizations store vast amounts of data, ranging from sensitive customer information to intellectual property. Determining which data is critical, sensitive, or public requires a thorough understanding of the data's location, value, sensitivity, and potential impact if compromised. See section "Understand Your Data" for more details.
- Human element – people (employees, contractors, etc.), can be both assets and potential vulnerabilities in a cybersecurity context. Determining how to define and manage human assets, including their roles, privileges, and access rights, requires careful analysis.

The absence of standardized asset classification frameworks, and terminology across the cybersecurity industry, certainly makes asset definition challenging. Different organizations may use varying criteria, definitions, and approaches that lead to inconsistencies and difficulties in sharing asset-related information.

Now that you are aware of the challenges you still have to take on the inventorying challenge. Simply put, it is very difficult to build a security program if you don't have clear targets for protection. The inventory will provide much-needed visibility that should become a guide. As you conduct a thorough assessment to understand assets and potential related vulnerabilities, look closely for areas of technical debt that can be of potential impact to your organization. Many organizations have the natural, and understandable, disease of looking forward and ignoring what is behind – technical debt. But this represents a risk area a CSIO needs to address. This generally lowers your popularity rating within an organization because it is not sexy work that energizes folks.

Your asset inventory aims to become a comprehensive, and continuously updated, record of all entities defined as assets within your organization. Here are some reasons why an asset inventory is something you should aggressively pursue:

- Guidance – your asset inventory will organically guide you toward the entities that you need to protect. It represents an awareness of your ecosystem of responsibility.

- Risk assessment – your asset inventory forms the foundation for assessing and managing security-related risks. Your organization will have the ability to correlate potential vulnerabilities per asset once you understand them. With accurate asset information, you can prioritize resources effectively.
- Vulnerability management – your asset inventory is crucial for effective vulnerability management. It will allow your organization to track the software versions, dependencies, patch levels, and configurations. By correlating this asset information with vulnerability databases, threat intelligence, and security advisories your organization will be able to identify assets at risk and in turn, remediation efforts.
- Attack surface foundation – understanding your organization's assets and their dependencies will serve as a key foundational component of your attack surface management program. With an asset inventory, organizations can focus on securing critical assets and implementing appropriate controls.
- Incident management foundation – during an incident management exercise, it is essential to have a clear understanding of the impacted assets. An accurate asset inventory will enable your incident management team(s) to quickly identify compromised assets and their dependencies. This data should facilitate efficient containment of the incident impact and point restoration teams to the realm of impacted assets.
- Asset lifecycle support – your asset inventory will support lifecycle management activities. Areas like asset acquisition, maintenance, retirement, and disposal will benefit from this dataset. It will help your organization maintain an overview of assets' age, usage, maintenance requirements, and retirement plans, ensuring that security considerations are factored in throughout the asset lifecycle.
- Compliance support – many regulatory frameworks require organizations to maintain an accurate asset inventory. An asset inventory helps demonstrate compliance with those framework requirements.
- Vendor and supply chain support – organizations with an accurate asset inventory can better manage relationships with vendors and suppliers. It helps track assets provided by external entities and can help organizations assess the security practices and risks associated with certain third-party assets.

SBOM

An important part of your asset inventory is an SBOM per piece of software. This can be software created in-house or it can cover commercial software as well. Many pieces of commercial software use open-source libraries, such as OpenSSL. SBOMs are now a critical aspect of the cybersecurity industry. The main reason for this is that nefarious actors have stealthily leveraged unchecked software dependencies to facilitate attack activities. An SBOM aims to counter these efforts by enhancing transparency and enabling effective risk visibility. To be clear, an SBOM alone does not solve any security problem, but it does facilitate your ability to gauge risk levels due to the use of some specific piece of software.

An SBOM is a structured inventory list that provides detailed information about software components and dependencies. Each SBOM is subjective and specific to some application or piece of software. It essentially becomes the "parts list" for software, mimicking a bill of materials used in manufacturing. Here are some key aspects of an SBOM:

- Dependencies – an SBOM obviously includes a comprehensive list of all software components, libraries, modules, frameworks, and the versions used within an application or piece of software. But one of the key benefits it provides is the identification of interdependencies. It identifies both proprietary and open-source software elements and their dependencies, forming a hierarchical view of the entire respective software stack.
- Version information – as stated previously, SBOM provides version details for each software library, component, and dependencies. This is important because some pieces of software have dependencies in large amounts. Having a version inventory in an SBOM helps organizations track which specific versions of software components are used. This is important in identifying risks associated with those versions.
- Licensing information – SBOMs may include licensing information. This is very important when using open-source software because it is easy to innocently violate some of those licenses assuming all open-source software is usable in any form. A great example is the GNU General Public License v2.0 or later, and the GNU Lesser General Public License v3.0 or later. These are quite restrictive and can become problematic if not treated seriously. Depending on how the software in question is integrated with a GPL-licensed component, it may be required that the software written by your organization be released under the same GPL license, as FOSS.
- Vendor information – in some cases, software components are obtained from external sources – third-party vendors. The SBOM may include information about these vendors that can be helpful in managing relevant relationships.
- Security vulnerability management – SBOMs are particularly useful for tracking and managing relevant software vulnerabilities. Organizations can assess the potential security risks associated with software stacks by correlating the software components in an SBOM with known vulnerabilities or threat intelligence data.
- Incident management – SBOMs can become reference points that add value to incident handling teams. A list of relevant security vulnerabilities, especially one that covers embedded libraries, allows organizations to quickly determine which applications are affected in the face of an incident. This expedites incident response and reduces the time required to address the extent of an impactful event.

Related to SBOMs you should consider frameworks such as "Supply Chain Levels for Software Artifacts" (SLSA), and the "CIS Software Supply Chain Security Guide", which are covered later in this chapter ("Controls" section).

To appreciate the importance of SBOMs within the context of cybersecurity, one has to understand some aspects of software development. Developing software typically consists of code being written through a series of stages that make up the Software Development Lifecycle (SDLC). Each stage in the life cycle represents a different set of code interactions (source code, libraries, etc.). Each stage is also a potential entry point for vulnerabilities to be introduced, or for code-level attacks (injections, etc.) to occur. If a compromise is successful at any stage in the SDLC of software that gets released to users, come run time, those entities will be put at risk.

The attack pattern just described equates to what is known as "supply chain attacks". These types of attacks are increasing because of the wide range of code touchpoints (entry points, library callouts, etc.). Relevant cybersecurity teams (AppSec, DevOps, etc.) are facing serious challenges in preventing these attacks when security is treated as an afterthought. This means applications are packaged and then possibly scrutinized from a security perspective. Compounding the challenge is the broad adoption of open-source pieces of software, especially in the form of imported libraries. Attackers have recognized these deep-rooted dependencies are hard for security teams to manage. Moreover, the volume of potential victims is substantially large given the amount of software that is written in the modern-day world. Hence, attackers have begun to leverage them as a main pathway to mount hard-to-detect attacks.

Some typical supply chain attack techniques are:

- Supply chain compromise – in this pattern, attackers target the SDLC to strategically inject malicious code, or backdoors, into legitimate software packages. This can occur at any stage, including during development, build, distribution, or update stages.
- Malware injection – this pattern is basically made up of injecting malware into commonly used pieces of software, such as libraries. Attackers aim to inject malware into legitimate software packages that are later distributed to unsuspecting victims. This technique creates a situation where malware has the possibility of spreading across many organizations, especially those that rely on highly targeted elements such as open-source libraries. The malware can be designed to exfiltrate data, establish persistent backdoors, or perform lateral moves on the victim's network.
- Firmware tampering – some supply chain attacks involve the modification of firmware. These are very difficult to detect unless firmware providers provide mechanisms to verify the validity of a given package. Attackers aim to insert malicious code into compiled/packaged firmware that enables them to gain unauthorized access over the compromised devices.
- Rogue or fake updates – in this pattern attackers attempt to create and distribute fake software updates that appear legitimate. These updates may mimic the branding and distribution channels of trusted software vendors, tricking users into installing malware-infected software. A common modus operandi here is tricking developers into downloading malicious code via typosquatting.
  - Typosquatting is also known as Uniform Resource Locator (URL) hijacking. It represents a malicious technique in which attackers register domain names that are very similar to legitimate ones. They

typically contain subtle typographical errors or slight variations. The purpose of typosquatting is to deceive someone to use this fake URL to use altered software.

- Compromised development tools – in this pattern attackers target the software development tools used by software developers. By compromising these tools, the attacker can manipulate the generated code, insert vulnerabilities, or distribute altered pieces of software.
- Interception and modification – this attack pattern consists of attackers exploiting weak access controls to tamper with packaged software. Attackers intercept legitimate software shipments during transit and modify their binary form to include malicious instructions. This can occur at different build points in the supply chain.
- Insider threats – some supply chain attacks can involve insiders within a vendor that intentionally or unwittingly aids attackers. Insiders with privileged access or knowledge of the supply chain processes can easily assist in introducing vulnerabilities or malicious components. Sometimes these people fall victim to blackmail or social engineering tactics. Sometimes they simply get paid off.

ATTACK SURFACE MANAGEMENT

Attack surface management is a deceivingly complex endeavor. But getting the best possible grasp on this information can prove transformative in your CISO journey. To truly get a handle on your attack surface you must take a holistic approach and scrutinize many angles. The realm of External Attack Surface Management (EASM), while very important, is merely one angle to cover. EASM is often mistaken for some type of adequate attack surface understanding. These are some angles to consider so that you may possibly create, or expand, your program to cover your organization in a more thorough way.

External Perspective – EASM

The overt, and best-known, space regarding attack surface management is that of the external perspective. This basically covers what your organization looks like to the outside world, in particular to nefarious actors. This outside-in perspective generally focuses on public internet-facing resources, especially for businesses that actually sell, or host, web-based products. The angles here mostly focus on which hosts are public-facing, what ports are actively listening per host, and, in turn, what service is being hosted on each one of those ports. A good solution here actually probes the listening ports to verify the service being hosted. For the sake of accuracy and thoroughness please don't ever assume that everyone adheres to IANA's well-known port list. It is entirely possible, for instance, to host an SSH server on TCP port 80. That example, if not scrutinized deeply, would inaccurately imply that a web server is at play.

Shadow IT

A benefit of focusing on this outside-in angle is that it is a great way to expose shadow IT elements. That is, if they exist within your organization and are hosted in a public-facing capacity. It should be stated that for this angle coverage to be effective this must be a continuous process. When new public-facing hosts, ports, and/ or services are deployed, they should automatically be discovered in rapid fashion. There are many products that serve this space and provide relevant solutions. This is a typical blind spot and one that you would be wise to not ignore.

B2C/B2B

From the external perspective, the natural focus is on the Business-to-Consumer (B2C) angle. This is where the space is predominately based on end-users/customers and web applications. All of what makes up a web app stack comes into play there. But from a Business-to-Business (B2B) perspective there is the less familiar area of APIs, and other integration models (batch processes, nightly job runs, etc.). Most modern-day integrations are API based though. Whether you run a REST shop or a GraphQL shop there are unique challenges when protecting APIs. Some of those challenges revolve around authentication, authorization, and possible payload encryption in transit. For instance, is TLS enough to protect data in transit? Or do you consider an orthogonal level of protection via payload encryption, something like JSON Web Encryption (JWE) (if you use JSON Web Tokens (JWT)) for instance? It's certainly an angle that needs consideration.

Insiders

There are threats and there are employees. Sometimes an employee becomes a threat and the angle here is that they are already inside your network. This angle is typically one where there is high risk because certain employees possibly have authenticated access to sensitive systems and data. To complicate this, enter a hybrid or work-from-home setup. Now your attack surface has expanded to areas outside of your control. Home networks are clearly high-risk environments. Since our traditional network perimeters no longer exist, now those home networks are part of your attack surface. Imagine a home network with kids downloading all kinds of crazy stuff. Then imagine a user that has your hardened work laptop at home. Then imagine the day that person feels like accessing work content from their personal machine. Or better yet they figure out how to copy crypto certificates and VPN software to their personal machines. The angle here is an insecure machine with direct access to your corporate network, that, in turn, potentially has direct access to sensitive resources, such as your cloud environments.

Non-Generic Computing Devices

In reference to non-standard computing devices, there are risks based on this equipment being generally unknown to traditional IT teams. Imagine the Heating, Ventilation, and Air-Conditioning (HVAC) controllers or motors, or Programmable Logic Controllers (PLC), required to operate the building you work in. Or maybe you are responsible for security in a manufacturing context. Today, many of those devices are networked with IP addresses, they typically reside on your network and are part of your attack surface. Consider the administrators of said equipment and the fact that they may very well have remote access capabilities. Some VPN paths bring traffic in via your cloud environments with paths back to the building equipment.

That is one angle. Then there are direct remote access scenarios, which put human resources on to your network, and in turn, there is the possibility of access to your cloud environment. Misconfigurations like these happen all the time and are angles to be considered when analyzing your attack surface.

Alternate Ingress Pathways

A typical cloud provider setup only accepts sensitive network connectivity from specific networks (owned by your organization). This is by design so that sensitive communication paths, like SSH, are not routed via the public internet. Typically, these specific networks are our corporate networks, and those, in turn, get remotely accessed via VPNs. Or it could also be the case that your VPN traffic itself flows into, and/or through, your cloud environment. An angle to scrutinize is exactly where VPN connections get placed on your network and what is accessible to those connections. This may be leaving pathways open to your cloud infrastructure.

Another pathway of concern is direct, browser-based, access to your cloud infrastructure. A successful authenticated session could give a user a privileged console for them to get work done. If this account was ever compromised, then there is substantial risk. The real danger with this ability is that it facilitates users to log in and do their work from personal machines that may not have the same protective controls as a work computer.

Privileged Users

Site Reliability Engineers (SRE) and System Administrators (sysadmin) typically have elevated privileges and the ability to make impactful changes in cloud environments. The scripts and tools they use need to be considered part of your attack surface because I am sure your teams didn't write every piece of administrative software they use. These scripts, software tools, the SRE engineer machines, and so on all become possible alternate access paths to sensitive elements.

Database Administrators (DBA) are valued team members. They typically have the most dangerous levels of access from a data perspective. This is obvious given their role, but this also should raise your risk antennas. Imagine a DBA working from a home-based machine that, for instance, ends up with a keylogger installed on it. This is a machine that will also have data dumps at any given time, this is a normal course of DBA business. There are a few angles to scrutinize here, are those data dumps somehow protected? DBAs and software engineers do not always sanitize data dumps (for their stored local working copies), and this becomes another angle to look at.

Source Code Repositories

There are many known examples of sloppy software engineering practices around hard coded, and in turn, leaked elements of sensitive data (DB passwords, API keys, application secrets, etc.). One important angle to look at is the use of secrets managers. Analysis must take place to sniff out hard-coded credentials, API keys, passwords, encryption keys, and so on, and then ensure re-engineering takes place to remove those angles from your attack surface. The removal obviously being a migration to use something like a secrets manager as opposed to statically storing sensitive elements where they are easy to access.

SSH

SSH tunnels and backdoors are both interesting and challenging. Unquestionably they represent a set of angles you need to home in on. For instance, detecting if some SSH traffic is a reverse tunnel is not trivial, but is possible. From an attack surface perspective, you can be assured that tools like SSH represent a double-edged sword providing benefit to administrators but also introducing risk since that traffic cannot be inspected. Something like the use of reverse SSH tunnels can expand your attack surface in a dangerous and stealthy way.

Ephemeral Port Openings

Temporary port openings can be a real problem. Ephemeral entities within cloud deployments are challenging enough, legitimate ones can be public-facing. As an example, let's say you have containerized your web servers. And you are using elastic cloud technology and orchestration to successfully react to web traffic spikes. That is an ephemeral use case that is entirely acceptable and can add a lot of value. Typically, these entities are placed behind protective layers (Web App Firewall, etc.) and because of this you may consider this part of your ecosystem to be in the space of mitigated, or lessened, risk. But what happens when the human factor at play creates bypasses to those protective controls in order to facilitate ease of use? Here is an example of a bypass: a security team discovered a case where a specific host, on a specific port, was open to the public internet on specific days for a limited amount of time. That port opening was otherwise non-existent. Their investigation led to the finding that the SRE and DBA teams had an automated process to allow for the running of remote DB maintenance scripts hitting some DB servers directly. The SRE/DBA teams felt it was such a limited exposure that there was no risk. As a CISO, you need to decide if you agree or not. There is no formula here, but this is an interesting angle from an attack surface perspective.

Supply Chain

Supply chain angles are a big area of concern. For some time now the software industry has, unfortunately, shifted from methodical testing while building (i.e., slow, time-consuming, etc.) to agile and fast-moving (i.e., unthorough testing, continuous releases, etc.). There has been a price to pay for this, especially on the upstream software (libraries, packages, etc.) components used by other pieces of software. The price is that the need to cut time from lengthy development cycles has introduced substantial risk. The risk is due to a lack of scrutiny of those elements of upstream software. This makes your attack surface quite complex because just knowing that something is problematic (e.g., having it in your SBOM) doesn't mean you can do anything about it.

Be aware that nefarious actors will target these upstream pieces of software since you have little to no control over their security posture. Targeting upstream components is attractive to attackers because third-party vendors and software components represent a known black box element to any organization. From the perspective of understanding your attack surface, know that bad actors will target these upstream resources based on efficiency. The efficiency comes by way of multiple pathways to your ecosystem, especially through commonly shared, or used, libraries.

Free and Open-Source Software (FOSS)

Part of modern-day supply chains is open-source code, especially in the form of importable, or includable, libraries. The angles here vary but most custom applications, and cloud environments, are full of open-source code. Look no further than support for cryptographic functions. There is a strong likelihood that no software engineer writing code for your organization is writing these from scratch. So, there is the use of externally developed libraries that your organization has no control over. It is an angle that cannot be avoided in the modern world.

Software as a Service (SaaS)

SaaS solutions are part of your attack surface, period. They may be so by way of their direct usage, via integrations, or as part of your supply chain(s). Are they your responsibility from a security perspective? Maybe, maybe not. But your data goes into these external systems. While it is an organizationally subjective decision if your data in a SaaS solution is part of your attack surface, it is an angle to consider. You should at least scrutinize the security configuration of the SaaS components that get accessed by your employees. The goal is to make sure the tightest security configurations possible are in use. Too often consultants are brought in to set up SaaS environments and they may take the easiest path, meaning the least secure. It happens.

SaaS-to-SaaS integrations are even riskier. Now your data is being exchanged by N number of SaaS solutions outside of your control and again, it's your data being sent around. Were those integrations, typically API-based, configured to protect your data or purely to be functional? It is up to you whether you want to contextually be in the cynical category.

Data

Data is the real, and ultimate target, the heart of your challenges. This is also where multiple angles exist. Let's start with some simple questions. Each one should make you realize the angles at play:

- Regarding all the data you are responsible for, do you know where it all is?
- Do you know all the databases at play?
- Do you know every storage location where files are stored?
- Within those previous answers (files, DB columns, key/value stores, etc.), do you truly know where all your sensitive (Personally Identifiable Information (PII), Protected Health Information (PHI), etc.) data is?

If you answered "No" to any of those questions, then those are angles you need to cover with some urgency. Ultimately, those are the real targets for attackers.

Once you know where the data is . . . then for each location you need to at least map, and understand ingress pathways. What and/or who can touch some DB? Web apps, admin scripts, APIs, people? And what about egress pathways? Once someone touches a data store how can the data be exfiltrated? The angles within the ingress/ egress challenge can be vast, and some skilled analysis needs to take place in order to properly understand this part of your attack surface.

Data exists in three states:

- At rest.
- In motion/transit.
- In use.

At Rest

Data at rest is data that is in a state of persistent storage. This implies that the data is not currently being accessed or used. The protection of data in this state could be entirely dependent on the storage mechanism used. For example, some DB products provide native column-level encryption features. Column-level encryption is a type of encryption method that allows for specific columns in a table to be encrypted instead of encrypting an entire database file.

In Motion/Transit

Another data-related angle to consider is that of your data in transit. One angle is that the data flows to and from the outside world. By this point, chances are those have been addressed, at least at a transport layer. But is your transport security tight on the inside of your networks and/or cloud environment? More often than not, the following scenario is real. You have strongly protected TLS 1.2+ streams from the outside to a tier of load balancers and/or WAFs, possibly controlled by your cloud provider or some other external service. The load balancers, or WAFs, terminate the relevant sockets and, in turn, terminate the stream encryption at play. From that point to the back end all the streams are in the clear. A lot of people assume that is a trusted part of your network. A CISO is not in the business of trust. This is a dangerous angle, often assumed to be safe. Depending on your level of healthy paranoia, you may want to push for encrypted streams on the inside of your networks and cloud environments. Otherwise, that part of your attack surface is susceptible to prying eyes.

In Use

A challenging state by way of protecting data is when it is in use, it's currently being modified, processed, created, deleted, accessed, or read. Examples of data in use are when data is in volatile Random Access Memory (RAM), in cache memory, opened by a specific application, simultaneously being used by multiple users via cloud-based shared document technology, etc. An example of a respective threat is an attacker gaining access to the RAM of a running instance. That memory can be parsed to locate an encryption key that an application has in use at that time. Or this could be application credentials to a DB.

UNDERSTAND YOUR DATA

We already touched on the importance of data from the perspective of your attack surface. After all, it is the ultimate target for nefarious actors. It is imperative to focus on the data that is truly important to your organization. Some of this should have come to light while you were having probing conversations with key players. Beyond importance to your organization, one has to simply realize that data is the basis of the modern-day global economy. Putting aside the amateurs wanting to show off, or looking for bragging rights, digital attacks are generally after something of value. That is data. Your organization's data. Your data. Even something like a Denial of Service (DoS) attack can be traced back to the importance of data. A DoS attack makes a service or system unavailable. The availability of said service or system matters because it is what users must use to access their data.

A component to consider as part of your security program is an exercise in the classification of your organization's data. We have already established the need for a data classification policy. It is supposed to categorize your organization's information according to the risk it represents. Data classification generally includes three categories (or at least consider these as your starting point if you have nothing):

- Confidential – the organization's crown jewels. If this data were to be exposed, there could be harm to your organization. Confidentially classified information includes virtually anything that provides your business with a strategic advantage.
- Internal – this is data that represents moderate risk to the organization.
- Public – this is data that carries with it no consequence if exposed. It should already be meant for public consumption.

Limiting your policy to these few simple types may make it easier to classify larger volumes of data.

RISK REGISTER

A cybersecurity risk register is a key element in helping your organization proactively stay focused on cybersecurity risks. It is generally a structured document, or database, that houses a list, or lists, of identified risk areas. Categorization of these risks, and possibly related threats, is also managed in a risk register. The focus is one central, and accessible, source of risk data in reference to an organization's data and/or systems. This is an essential component of a comprehensive cybersecurity program and one that needs to be easily referenced in the face of an audit. The risk register should be clear in terms of identification, categorization, assessment, quantification, and management of identified risk:

- Risk identification – the register should seamlessly facilitate the identification of risk areas.
- Risk categorization – the register should have clear categorization of risks covering data points such as severity, likelihood, and potential impact.
- Risk assessment – the register should facilitate the assessment of each identified risk by providing a structured approach of evaluating the likelihood and potential impact to your organization.

- Risk quantification – the register should provide correlations to potential financial impact of a given risk if it is actualized. Cyber Risk Quantification (CRQ) is the practice of using statistical methods to generate estimated financial impact per area of risk.
- Risk management – once a central, and accessible, risk register exists, organizations can develop and pursue effective risk management, and mitigation, strategies. The register should provide a centralized view of risks, identifying necessary resources for mitigation efforts.

Beyond those base benefits, there are others:

- Compliance and/or audit – a risk register is a point of evidence that demonstrates an organization's commitment to cybersecurity and risk management. If certain compliance or regulations are part of your organization's remit this may assist in meeting some requirements. During audits, the register serves as proof of a systematic and structured approach to managing digital risk.
- Monitoring – the risk register helps organizations track and monitor the status of identified risks over time. Regular updates and assessment of risk treatment effectiveness can be obvious through an effective register. This is especially important when considering sharing access to the register with business stakeholders, the C-Suite, and potentially board members.
- Incident management – in the event of a cybersecurity incident, the risk register can be referenced to understand the potential impact at hand.

POLICIES

Cybersecurity policies are crucial for organizations as they provide roadmaps for acceptable and safe conduct within business operations. They introduce structure for an organization's employees to protect sensitive information and ensure compliance with regulations. They also promote consistency and education with the goal of contributing to a more secure and resilient organization.

These policies are formal documents that should clearly outline an organization's stance, approach, guidelines, and requirements for ensuring the confidentiality, integrity, and availability of its data and systems. Here are some reasons behind why companies should have cybersecurity policies:

- Establishing a framework – policies provide a documented foundation for creating a structured and organized approach to protecting an organization's assets. They define the rules, standards, and guardrails that employees must follow to protect the organization and mitigate cyber risks.
- Promoting consistency – policies aim to ensure consistent behavior across disparate departments and functions within an organization. They set clear behavioral expectations and guidelines for all employees, contractors, and third parties interacting with organizational assets.

- Protecting confidentiality and integrity – policies help by specifying appropriate controls. They address areas such as data classification, access controls, encryption, and secure handling and storage of data.
- Compliance with regulations – policies ensure that organizations meet legal and regulatory requirements as set forth by the target regulation. They align the organization's practices with industry standards and guidelines, such as NIST CSF and ISO 27001.
- Demonstrating maturity – well-documented policies demonstrate an organization's commitment to information security and a level of maturity. This can enhance the organization's public persona and build trust with customers and partners. This can also facilitate the ability to conduct business with customers requiring a mature security posture.
- Raising awareness – policies serve as educational tools, helping employees understand their responsibilities and obligations. They contribute to creating a security-aware culture within the organization.

In Chapter 2 (Inventory Your Resources – Policies) a list of common policies was provided.

CONTROLS

The controls that you will either put in place or verify are totally subjective to the ecosystem you are aiming to protect. The objective is to mitigate identified risks. The controls may include measures like WAFs, firewalls, IDS/IPS, secure configurations, secrets management, encryption and decryption mechanisms, multi-factor authentication, and regular software updates. One path to consider is adopting one of the many industries' best practices and frameworks. Some of these are based on a self-attestation model while others are actual formal certification processes to put your organization through. Here are some to consider or compare to what you already have (keeping in mind that new revisions are always possible):

- Center for Internet Security (CIS) Controls – www.cisecurity.org/controls/
  - The CIS Controls is a set of cybersecurity best practices designed to help organizations establish mature practices when protecting their systems and data. It currently consists of a prioritized list of 18 (the number varies over time) controls that provide actionable guidance for implementing and maintaining effective cybersecurity measures.
  - As a point of reference, here are the current CIS controls:
    - 1: Inventory and Control of Enterprise Assets.
    - 2: Inventory and Control of Software Assets.
    - 3: Data Protection.
    - 4: Secure Configuration of Enterprise Assets and Software.
    - 5: Account Management.
    - 6: Access Control Management.
    - 7: Continuous Vulnerability Management.
    - 8: Audit Log Management.

- 9: Email and Web Browser Protections.
- 10: Malware Defenses.
- 11: Data Recovery.
- 12: Network Infrastructure Management.
- 13: Network Monitoring and Defense.
- 14: Security Awareness and Skills Training.
- 15: Service Provider Management.
- 16: Application Software Security.
- 17: Incident Response Management.
- 18: Penetration Testing.
- NIST Cybersecurity Framework (NIST CSF) – www.nist.gov/cyberframework
  - The NIST CSF is a voluntary framework that provides a set of guidelines, best practices, and standards to help organizations manage and improve their cybersecurity posture. Verson1 focused on five core functions: Identify, Protect, Detect, Respond, and Recover. Version 2 adds a Govern function. Because of its comprehensive nature, compliance with NIST CSF can pave the way to compliance with other security frameworks.
- NIST SP 800-53 – https://nvlpubs.nist.gov/nistpubs/SpecialPublications/NIST.SP.800-53r5.pdf
  - The NIST 800-53 security rules categorize controls into low, moderate, and high. The controls are split into 18 security control families, allowing organizations to select only the most applicable to their requirements. The 18 areas include access control, incident response, business continuity, and disaster recovery. Compliance for NIST 800-53 is voluntary for organizations that are not USA-based federal agencies and are not affiliated with the US federal government. NIST SP 800-53 introduces the concept of baselines as a starting point for the control selection process. This enables organizations to establish a baseline that can be used to measure progress toward the development of a secure organizational infrastructure.
- NIST SP 800-171 – https://nvlpubs.nist.gov/nistpubs/SpecialPublications/NIST.SP.800-171r2.pdf
  - Organizations doing business with the US Department of Defense (DoD) must comply with NIST Special Publication 800-171, Protecting Controlled Unclassified Information (CUI) in Non-Federal Information Systems. This is focused on DoD contractors that process, store, or transmit CUI.
- NIST Secure Software Development Framework (SSDF) – SP 800-218 – https://nvlpubs.nist.gov/nistpubs/SpecialPublications/NIST.SP.800-218.pdf
  - NIST released the SSDF to be focused on helping government organizations address software supply chain threats. The SSDF outlines a set of practices that are meant to be implemented within an existing SDLC. The NIST SSDF organizes secure software development practices into four groups:
    - Prepare the Organization (PO).
    - Protect the Software (PS).

- Produce Well-Secured Software (PW).
- Respond to Vulnerabilities (RV).
- Supply chain Levels for Software Artifacts (SLSA) – https://slsa.dev
  - SLSA came about partially as an industry response to the government-focused SSDF. SLSA is a security framework intended to create software supply chain integrity. It started at Google and has evolved into an industry-level collaboration, maintained by the Open-Source Security Foundation (OpenSSF). The path for applying the framework is represented by levels of graduated maturity. Higher levels indicate a stronger posture regarding the application of software security practices. SLSA Levels are designed to introduce protections against tampering, or unauthorized modification, during the package build process of a respective software build lifecycle. There are four levels within SLSA, each representing a different level of security maturity. In the latest version, there are now the following tracks:
    - Build L0 – no guarantees, no requirements. This level represents a total lack of SLSA. It is intended for non-production environments, such as self-contained ones that run on a single machine and perform unit tests.
    - Build L1 – provenance exists. L1 calls for organizations having to build environments that are consistent and reproducible. This means that the build environment must be documented, and changes are tracked. At this level, there is also a requirement for organizations to track critical components, including dependencies. This should allow your organization to quickly identify changes within those critical components.
    - Build L2 – signed provenance exists. L2 compliance relies on an organization being able to prove the existence of a repeatable build process; including the verification of critical component integrity. At this level, there is an expectation of regular vulnerability scans covering critical components and ensuring that any vulnerabilities are quickly addressed.
    - Build L3 – hardened builds. Once L1 and L2 are covered organizations must implement automated tooling to enforce consistent builds and verify that only authorized individuals can modify a given build environment. This now places an organization at a level where the build process is automated and repeatable and has checks and balances to ensure that only trusted individuals can make changes to the process. To augment the existing progress there is the addition of organizations ensuring that cryptographic signatures are used to sign artifacts and that these signatures are verified throughout the entire build process. This includes verifying the signature of build artifacts as well as verifying signatures at each step of the build process.
- CIS Software Supply Chain Security Guide – www.cisecurity.org/insights/white-papers/cis-software-supply-chain-security-guide

- This guide focuses on enterprise development cycles and considers new industry standards like SBOM and other best practices intended to foster secure software development practices. It includes generic guidelines divided into five areas:
  - Source code – this area calls for code changes to be validated by at least two strongly authenticated users. Branch protection rules are checked to ensure verification of signed commits for new changes and to identify inactive or orphaned branches. Further, protective guides focus on Source Code Management (SCM) controls regarding authorization and authentication, user creation and deletion, users with administrative access, and inactive users. It also calls for the use of MFA, hardened email configurations (email authentication protocols such as Sender Policy Framework (SPF) and DomainKeys Identified Mail (DKIM), etc.), limiting repository access based on SSH certificate presentation and/or source IP addresses, and logging of anonymous activity. In the spirit of least privilege, the guide also requires that third-party source code is approved and limited to the least needed and that scanners are used to identify exposed credentials, sensitive data, and infrastructure as code misconfigurations.
  - Build pipelines – the guide makes a point of the fact that you should ensure build environments are immutable. This includes build pipeline infrastructure, configurations, and relevant access. Least privilege rules are to be enforced here as well with a call for build configurations to be single-purposed, isolated, and to have minimal network connectivity. The code in the pipelines should also be automatically scanned for vulnerabilities and guardrails should be enforced at runtime. Pipeline instructions defined as code is a recommendation and this should introduce the ability to track and review activity. The guide makes a point of the need for pipeline integrity, all release artifacts should be signed. Moreover, all external dependencies should be frozen at build time in order to produce a signed SBOM and ensure that the built pipeline has created a reproducible artifact.
  - Dependency integrity – to achieve dependency integrity, the guide states the need for validation of items in the SBOM, especially regarding third-party suppliers. This can be challenging, so set realistic goals. Optimally, trusted packages and repositories should be no older than sixty days. For dependencies, it is also recommended that you scrutinize packages for vulnerabilities, license implications, and ownership changes.
  - Artifacts – artifact verification is intended to ensure that artifacts are signed by the build pipeline itself, encrypted, and best security practices are followed for safe distribution. Access to artifacts should be tightly limited and, using MFA, best practices for access to the package registry (GitLab, GitHub, etc.), should be followed.

- Deployment integrity – the guide calls for a clear separation between deployment configuration files and source code files. This way deployment changes can cleanly be tracked, and scans are possible for sensitive data exposure. The guide also covers the fact that deployment environments should enforce limited access and be both automated and reproducible.
- ISO/IEC 27001 – www.iso.org/standard/54534.html
  - ISO/IEC 27001 is an internationally recognized standard that outlines the requirements for establishing, implementing, maintaining, and continually improving an Information Security Management System (ISMS). It provides a systematic, repeatable, approach to managing data, identifying risks, and implementing security controls to protect assets. The end result of an assessment is an actual certification that is valid for three years. To maintain compliance, your organization is required to undergo annual spot audits.
- ISO/IEC 27002 – www.iso.org/standard/75652.html
  - ISO/IEC 27002 is an internationally recognized standard that provides guidelines for implementing information security controls. It provides a comprehensive set of controls and measures that organizations can adopt to establish, implement, maintain, and improve their information security management. These controls cover various areas, including organizational security, asset management, physical and environmental security, access control, information systems acquisition, incident management, business continuity, and compliance. It should be noted that ISO/IEC 27002 is often used in conjunction with ISO/IEC 27001. While ISO/IEC 27001 provides the framework for implementing an ISMS, ISO/IEC 27002 offers detailed guidelines and controls that organizations can follow to address specific information security risks. ISO 27002 follows the renewal pattern of ISO 27001.
- System and Organization Controls 2 (SOC 2) – www.aicpa.org/interestareas/ frc/assuranceadvisoryservices/aicpasoc2report.html
  - SOC 2 is an auditing standard developed by the American Institute of Certified Public Accountants (AICPA). It focuses on the controls and processes related to security, availability, processing integrity, confidentiality, and privacy of customer data. This is an optional auditing, not certification, process that provides an externally generated report as the end result and is typically renewed annually.
- UK Cyber Essentials – www.cyberessentials.ncsc.gov.uk/
  - Cyber Essentials, and Cyber Essentials Plus, is a cybersecurity certification scheme developed by the UK Government. It provides a set of basic security controls and best practices that organizations can be measured against in order to gauge an organization's resilience to common cyber threats. This is a formal certification process and Cyber Essentials certificates are valid for 12 months. Hence, there is an annual renewal process.

- Payment Card Industry Data Security Standard (PCI DSS) – www.pcise-
curitystandards.org/
  - PCI DSS is a set of security standards developed to protect cardholder
  data. It applies to organizations that handle, process, or store payment
  card information. It provides requirements for network security, data
  protection, access controls, and ongoing monitoring. There are four
  levels of PCI compliance, and they are based on the number of transactions a merchant, or organization, handles. A transaction is defined as
  any of the following, regardless of geographical region:
    - Credit card-based transactions.
    - No card transaction.
    - E-commerce transaction.
    - PCI DSS Compliance Level 1 applies to merchants that process
    more than six million transactions annually. Level 1 requires that
    merchants use an external, third-party, auditor. External audits are
    performed by Qualified Security Assessors (QSA). The auditor will
    detail findings in a Report on Compliance (ROC). Level 1 mer-
    chants must also perform the following:
      - Quarterly network scan, basically a minor audit. It is normally
      performed by Approved Scanning Vendors (ASV). These may
      be performed remotely and are not as detailed as the full assess-
      ments performed by QSAs.
      - Attestation of Compliance (AOC) form. This is an opportunity
      to explain the organization's compliance efforts in writing. The
      AOC is written, and submitted, by internal staff.
  - PCI DSS Compliance Level 2 applies to organizations that pro-
  cess between one and six million transactions per year. PCI DSS
  Level 2 merchants must submit a Report of Compliance (ROC)
  but it is performed by internal evaluation, not an external audit.
  This internal evaluation is created by completing a Self Assessment
  Questionnaire (SAQ). Level 2 merchants must also perform a quar-
  terly network scan and submit an AOC.
  - PCI DSS Compliance Level 3 applies to merchants that process
  between 20,000 and one million transactions each year. PCI DSS
  Level 3 merchants do not need to perform an external audit. They
  do not need to submit a ROC either. They may submit a voluntary
  ROC to establish an improved security posture. Level 3 merchants
  must also perform a SAQ, quarterly network scan, and submit an
  AOC.
  - PCI DSS Compliance Level 4 applies to any merchant processing
  fewer than 20,000 transactions per year. PCI DSS Level 4 merchants do not require audits, do not submit ROCs, and may not
  need AOC forms. Level 4 merchants must also perform a SAQ and
  a quarterly network scan.
    - There are varying SAQ levels (number of questions may change
    over time):

- SAQ A is for e-commerce/mail/telephone-order merchants that have fully outsourced cardholder data functions. No electronic storage, transmission, or processing of any cardholder data takes place on this merchant's systems or premises. This is the shortest of the SAQs with 24 questions.
- SAQ A-EP is for e-commerce-only merchants that use a third-party service provider to handle customer card information. These merchants typically have a web presence but do not handle card data. No electronic storage, transmission, or processing of any cardholder data takes place on this merchant's systems or premises. This SAQ has 192 questions.
- SAQ B is for merchants that use physical card reading machines and/or standalone, dial-out terminals. These merchants have no electronic cardholder data transmissions, processing, or storage; these merchants do not support e-commerce environments. This SAQ has 41 questions.
- SAQ B-IP is for merchants that use only standalone, PIN Transaction Security (PTS) approved payment terminals. PIN is an acronym for Personal Identification Number. These terminals do have remote connections to payment processors. But, they have no electronic cardholder data storage; this merchant does not support e-commerce environments. This SAQ has 87 questions.
- SAQ C-VT is for merchants that use a virtual terminal on one computer dedicated solely to credit card processing. They have no electronic cardholder data storage; this merchant does not support e-commerce environments. This SAQ has 161 questions.
- SAQ C is for any merchant with a payment application connected to the Internet. They have no electronic cardholder data storage. This SAQ has 84 questions.
- SAQ P2PE is for merchants using approved point-to-point encryption (P2PE) devices, with no electronic card data storage. This SAQ has 34 questions.
- SAQ D is for merchants that do not outsource their credit card processing or use a P2PE solution. This merchant may store credit card data electronically. This SAQ has 328 questions.
- SAQ D for Service Providers is for service providers deemed eligible to complete an SAQ. This is the longest of the SAQs with 370 questions.
- National Cybersecurity Center of Excellence (NCCoE) Cybersecurity Framework (CSF) – www.nccoe.nist.gov/projects/use-cases/cybersecurity-framework
  - The NCCoE CSF is a practical implementation of the NIST CSF. It provides detailed guidance and reference architectures to help organizations implement the framework's main principles.

- SANS Critical Security Controls – www.sans.org/critical-security-controls/
  - The SANS Critical Security Controls is a set of prioritized actions to improve an organization's overall cybersecurity posture. It focuses on fundamental security measures that organizations should implement to mitigate common threats.
- International Electrotechnical Commission (IEC) 62443 – www.iec.ch/iec62443/
  - IEC 62443 is a series of internationally accepted standards for Operational Technology (OT) and/or Industrial Control Systems (ICS) security. It provides a comprehensive framework for validating the implementation of cybersecurity measures in industrial environments, addressing aspects such as network security, system hardening, secure development practices, and incident handling. This is an actual certification process but there is no hard requirement for certificate renewal. Once obtained your certification is considered current for a three-year period.
- Cloud Security Alliance (CSA) Security Guidance – https://cloudsecurity alliance.org/guidance/
  - The CSA Security Guidance is a cloud computing-focused framework for securing environments. It offers best practices, controls, and recommendations to help organizations assess their risks associated with cloud-hosted services.
- Cloud Security Alliance (CSA) Security, Trust, Assurance, and Risk (STAR) – https://cloudsecurityalliance.org/star/
  - The CSA STAR program is an assurance framework for cloud service providers. It provides organizations with cloud-specific information for their security programs. STAR is a voluntary self-assessment, and set of attestations, aligned with the standards outlined in the Cloud Controls Matrix (CCM) that validate an organization's security posture. The STAR Registry is a publicly accessible registry. Publishing to the registry allows organizations to show current and potential customers their security and compliance maturity and posture, potentially reducing the need to fill out multiple customer questionnaires.
- Information Security Forum (ISF) Standard of Good Practice (SoGP) – www.securityforum.org/
  - The ISF SoGP is a guide that provides organizations with a comprehensive set of controls and measures to address cyber and information security risks. It covers various domains such as governance, risk management, incident response, physical security, and employee awareness. This is not a formal certification program or process; it is a guide.
- Open Web Application Security Project (OWASP) Application Security Verification Standard (ASVS) – https://owasp.org/www-project-application-security-verification-standard/
  - The OWASP ASVS is a framework that provides guidelines for secure application development and testing. It helps organizations ensure that

their applications are designed and implemented with proper security controls, aiming to protect against attacks.
* OWASP Software Assurance Maturity Model (SAMM) – https://owasp-samm.org/
    * Experts at OWASP observed that some frameworks targeting software security were not designed to factor in specifics of a given development process. To address this OWASP came up with, and maintains, the community-driven OWASP SAMM. Its intent is to improve secure software practices in any organization. OWASP aims for its SAMM to be a flexible and open framework to help organizations implement a software security strategy that can be subjectively designed for it. The framework is mapped to the NIST SSDF.

There are other frameworks. And there are some that are generic but can be applied to the cybersecurity space. One worth mentioning is the Capability Maturity Model Integration (CMMI – www.cmmiinstitute.com). Choose what makes sense to your organization given that, at this stage, you should have some solid intimacy with what a good fit will be.

INCIDENT MANAGEMENT

Depending on the size of your organization this may be a full-blown program, consisting of multiple plans, or simply a singular plan. This is hands down one of the most important areas for a CISO to focus on. There is a reality to security events and incidents; that reality is that if your organization operates with a dependence on technology, impactful things will happen. Regulatory requirements aside, you must make sure there is a well-defined set of responses for when these negative events take place.

By having a well-defined incident management, or incident handling, process in place your organization will be given the ability to efficiently respond to security incidents. The detection of an incident is pre this stage. And the remediation is post this stage. This proactive approach of having processes ready aims to minimize the impact of incidents. Containing the sprawl, controlling the damage, ensuring business continuity is possible, and ensuring touchpoints with external entities (law enforcement, peer groups, etc.) take place are also part of the strategic goals of the incident management program.

Your incident management program will either have a plan or multiple plans. Each plan should be detailed to empower your team(s) to respond effectively to cybersecurity incidents. Each plan should include steps for investigation, containment, and moving toward recovery from the incident. Each step may have explicit playbooks with step-by-step instructions. Each plan should leave as little as possible to guessing or a process of "figure it out". Each plan should document assigned roles and responsibilities, contact information, and establish communication channels. All of the plans that make up an incident management program need to be continuously tested and improved as needed. More details are covered in Chapter 6.

AWARENESS

Security awareness programs are an essential requirement for any security program at this point. Due to an increase in strong technical controls and improved protection mechanisms, the easier targets became the humans, our users, our family members. Attackers have shifted gears based on this awareness. This has led to sophisticated campaigns targeting users who are typically less security savvy or simply too trusting. Security awareness campaigns are designed to raise user's levels of scrutiny when faced with potential digital attacks.

It is the CISOs responsibility to properly invest in cybersecurity awareness and training programs for all users, typically employees of the organization. The goal is to help those users understand their role in maintaining a positive security posture. Typically, the awareness programs a CISO and team will design teach users about common threats like phishing and social engineering. They also provide guidelines on safe practices for data handling, password management, and device usage.

Tabletop exercises (TTX) are a good set of exercises that can be designed to target the unique needs of specific groups (executives, privileged users, etc.). TTXs are an informal, discussion-based session that simulates scenarios in a low-risk environment. Teams discuss their roles and responses during a set of synthetic scenarios usually controlled by someone skilled in this practice. The atmosphere is relaxed and exploratory and is not meant to be judgmental but to put participants in the mindset they'd have when handling a disaster.

CONTINUOUS MONITORING

The need for continuous monitoring, of many things, is just a reality in the cybersecurity industry. The bad actors don't take days off, hardly play within boundaries, and don't honor holidays in your country. So, it is up to you to ensure that your program, and its people, are equipped to keep an eye on things even when the rest of the business is off going about their lives and not thinking about work.

Continuous monitoring does require proper tooling. But it also requires relevant processes to benefit from that tooling. The goal is to continuously monitor your systems for potential threats, especially activity that may seem benign but is actually part of a campaign against your organization. Some examples of tool types that are used for this type of functionality are:

- Vulnerability scanners – these tools scan networks, systems, and applications for areas that require remediation. They typically have scheduled and/or automated features that facilitate continuous activity.
- Endpoint Detection and Response (EDR) – EDR solutions monitor endpoints such as workstations, servers, and mobile devices for signs of malicious activity or suspicious behavior. They continuously collect and analyze endpoint data in real-time and typically report upstream into some centralized mechanism (data lake, dashboard, SIEM, etc.).
- File Integrity Monitoring (FIM) – FIM solutions monitor and track changes to critical files and detect unauthorized modifications or tampering. They typically operate in a continuous runtime model adding to the goal at hand.

- SIEM – these solutions collect and analyze log data from various sources within an organization's network. They continuously correlate and analyze events, detect anomalies, and generate alerts for potential security incidents.
- SOAR – these platforms sometimes work in conjunction with SIEM systems. They facilitate the integration of various tools and continuously automate specified actions.
- IDS/IPS – these solutions continuously monitor network traffic, looking for patterns and signature matches that indicate malicious activities or known attacks. IDS passively monitors, while IPS actively blocks traffic.

CHANGE MANAGEMENT

From a cybersecurity perspective, change management is a critical element of risk management and overall governance. It is necessary for balancing the need for change with the need to protect resources. Change management involves a structured approach to ensuring that modifications to an organization's resources (IT elements, applications, data stores, etc.) are tracked and do not introduce new risks. Here are some key aspects of change management in cybersecurity:

- Risk assessment – before any changes are made, a thorough risk assessment should be conducted to identify potential security implications. This includes evaluating the impact on existing security controls so as to not introduce regressions.
- Proper planning – planning for change involves documenting and reviewing (from multiple perspectives) the steps required to implement said change safely. This should include responsibilities, security implications and requirements, timelines, and clear and verified rollback procedures in case of a negative impact.
- Approval process – changes affecting business systems and operations should be approved by a Change Advisory Board (CAB) that covers all relevant business functions. This way no business operation or function is caught by surprise, they had a voice in the process. This board typically includes representatives from finance, legal, internal audit, IT, cybersecurity, compliance, and other business units.
- Thorough testing – before a change is rolled out, it should be thoroughly tested and validated in a controlled (non-production) environment. This testing phase should validate that the change does not negatively impact anything.
- Continuous monitoring – once a change is implemented, continuous monitoring is crucial to detect any operational or security issues that arise because of the change. The security monitoring tools that are part of the security program should suffice.
- Audit trails – maintaining detailed, query-able records of changes, including who approved them and when, who implemented them and when, is crucial for accountability and future reference. This documentation is also vital for audits and compliance reviews.

- Post-change review – when possible, a post-change review should be conducted to assess the effectiveness of the change management process as well as the security impact of the change. Lessons learned should be documented and used to improve future change management processes.

Implementing, or pushing for, change management can be challenging. This is especially so in a world where agile and speed to market get pushed really hard. Change management can actually be perceived as being somewhat anti-agile. Employees may resist this based on the time necessary and the formality of it. They may just view it as inconvenient or anti-progress given that they must keep up with the fast pace of technological change. Other challenges can come from the rapid evolution of threats and how those impact changes that are being pursued.

Effective change management will require a keen business-driven balance between innovation and security. Ensuring that changes are implemented in a safe manner needs to be presented in a way where it enables safe business practices, operational, and revenue protection.

VULNERABILITY AND THREAT MANAGEMENT

By implementing a comprehensive VTM program, organizations can proactively reduce their exposure to cyber risks. The main objective of this program is to ferret out issues before nefarious actors do with the goal of minimizing the potential impact of a successful attack. The results of a VTM program are data points to identify, assess, and prioritize threat areas. The real goal is to pursue mitigation of threats once they have been discovered. Here are some of the key components in a VTM program:

- Threat identification – this phase involves actively hunting for and analyzing threats. There is a subjective nature to this based on the environment at hand. To be effective threat hunters must stay updated on the latest attack techniques and also have familiarity with the target environment.
- Vulnerability assessment – regular vulnerability assessments are part of the VTM program remit. These are performed to identify weaknesses and vulnerabilities in the target environment. This process often involves the use of automated vulnerability scanning tools coupled with manual techniques.
- Risk prioritization – once threats and vulnerabilities are identified, they must be analyzed for their potential impact on the target environment. This analysis will yield some prioritization levels. This is important because it is virtually impossible to uniformly address all discoveries. Risk-scoring methodologies are typically used to establish a level of criticalness and giving organizations the ability to allocate resources in a relevant fashion.
- Vulnerability remediation – the program should include playbooks and processes for working with relevant teams in pursuit of remediating findings. This may involve applying security patches, code-level changes, configuration changes, system updates, improved awareness training, or

implementing compensating controls toward mitigating the risks associated with findings.

- Continuous monitoring – an effective VTM program implements continuous monitoring of their target environments. This can be achieved through various security monitoring techniques such as the use of an IDS on live network flows, a SIEM that is receiving relevant logs, and analytics tools that can operate on large datasets.
- Reporting and metrics – regularly generated metrics provide insights into the effectiveness of the VTM program. Metrics may include the number of vulnerabilities discovered, the number that gets remediated, the number of remediated vulnerabilities that resurge, and the average time to remediation. Metrics are covered more in Chapter 10.

Threat Hunting

While the overall VTM program covers the points listed previously and becomes continuous with effective metrics generated, a key component is solid threat hunting. Threat hunting is what will actually unearth areas of concern. It is an active, and iterative, process of proactively searching for potential threats within your target environments. It encompasses identification of those threats along with indicators of compromise that could expose activity related to some threat area. The overt goal of threat hunting is to detect threats before they become something a nefarious actor can take advantage of. Covertly, the goal is to also have these threats addressed and mitigated. Here are some key aspects of threat hunting:

- Proactive – threat hunting needs to be based on a proactive approach rather than relying solely on reactive security measures. It involves actively searching for areas that are vulnerable to attack and searching for signs of anomalous activity.
- Hypothesis driven – threat hunting is often guided by an expert's hypothesis or gut feel. While this may seem un-scientific, there is a reality to the experience one gains over time. Threat hunters can formulate hypotheses based on signals, log data, threat intelligence, and knowledge of the target environment.
- Contextual understanding – threat hunters rely on their intimate understanding of the target environments. This can lead to advanced insights such as knowing the difference between typical user behavior and related anomalies. This contextual knowledge is important in identifying anomalous behaviors that may otherwise go unnoticed.
- Tools and techniques – threat hunting leverages many tools and technologies. In order for those to yield useful output they need quality data. This normally comes from SIEMs, EDR solutions, and threat intelligence feeds.
- Collaboration and expertise – threat hunting often involves collaboration between disparate teams. Security analysts, business analysts, incident response teams, IT personnel, and threat intelligence experts typically work together when analyzing complex potential threats.

A VTM program, with solid threat-hunting capabilities, will actively expose threats that may have eluded traditional security controls. It enables organizations to proactively address and hopefully defend against things like Advanced Persistent Threats (APT), zero-day exploits, and AppSec issues. From a proactive perspective, the obvious goal is to pursue successful mitigation before a negatively impacting act takes place. But, a successful VTM program can also add value by reducing the dwell time (the amount of time a malicious actor has access to a compromised environment before it is detected) of threats, minimizing their impact.

Ensure Defenses are Adequate

There isn't much worse than a false sense of security in this industry. In the spirit of trusting nothing, you should always have your team(s) spend time and/or resources on ensuring the effectiveness of the protective mechanisms that have been put in place. Assume nothing.

A part of this is to stay current with the latest security developments, technologies, and threat intelligence. Another part is to pursue regular patching. A lot of noise has been made over the years about this, but the space of patching is not as straightforward as some make it seem. There are challenges given that patches cannot be blindly applied. Your team(s) must understand the repercussions of applying patches. This assumes there is some regression test suite that can be run to ensure that some patching does not adversely impact an existing solution. Maybe this ends up being manual testing in your organization. Either way, make sure the impact of a patch is understood and then you can pursue software patches to address known vulnerabilities. Consider partnering with cybersecurity vendors or experts to leverage their expertise and stay ahead of emerging threats. A trusted partner full of experts is invaluable in this industry.

Given that cybersecurity is a journey, an ongoing effort, you need to regularly reassess and adapt your protective mechanisms to address both evolving threats and changes in your organization's environment. It is a good practice to conduct regular assessments and audits of your defensive capabilities. External expertise may be something to consider because the necessary depth of expertise is typically not something within existing team members. It's important to note that pen testing and assessments should be conducted by skilled professionals targeting a controlled environment, one that mirrors production.

Penetration testing (pen testing), vulnerability assessments, and security audits are all endeavors that need to be pursued to identify any weaknesses or gaps in your defenses. They offer several benefits to organizations in terms of identifying vulnerabilities and ensuring effectiveness of your defenses. Here are some key benefits:

- Assess security controls – pen tests and assessments evaluate the effectiveness of existing security controls and measures (WAF, firewall, IPS, etc.). By using a varied set of techniques, experts attempt to bypass the security measures in place. This will give you clear answers in terms of whether your defenses are adequately protecting your assets.

- Identify vulnerabilities – pen testing and assessments help identify existing vulnerabilities. By simulating real-world attack scenarios, experts will exploit existing weaknesses and uncover potential problems at your core elements (web applications, APIs, etc.). Identifying these potential vulnerabilities will enable your organization to proactively address them before malicious actors can exploit them.
- Test incident handling – if you simply don't forewarn your incident management team(s) these exercises can test their incident response capabilities. By simulating security incidents and assessing the response process, you may be able to identify strengths and weaknesses in the incident response plans, procedures, and coordination.
- Regulatory requirements – simply put, some regulatory frameworks require that your organization undergo regular pen tests and security assessments. By conducting these assessments, your organization will meet those requirements. This can help enhance trust with external entities (clients, partners, etc.) and you may even want to consider the transparent option of sharing the resulting reports.
- Enhance security awareness – these exercises can contribute to building a security-first culture consisting of awareness within the organization. When employees are made aware of simulated attacks or vulnerabilities being exploited, it sends a message that the organization takes security seriously. This increased awareness can lead to a more security-conscious workforce, actively contributing to the organization's security posture.
- Continuous Improvement – pen testing and assessments are not one-time activities but part of an ongoing cybersecurity strategy. They allow organizations to continuously improve defenses and adapt to changing threat landscapes.

Pen testing typically targets the B2C space by way of targeting web applications (what users interact with via a Browser). But pen testing can also be conducted targeting APIs to cover the B2B space. There are some key differences in these focal areas:

- Web application – when pen testing a web application, the primary focus is on assessing the security of the application's reaction to input, weaknesses in the user interface, and weaknesses in functionality. The pen tester typically explores the web application's behaviors based on ingress and egress, and various components, such as authentication, session handling, forms, input fields, and backend logic. The objective is to identify vulnerabilities that can be exploited through the web-based transport mechanisms (Browser, direct HTTP requests, etc.), such as cross-site scripting (XSS) and SQL injection (SQLi).
- API – in API pen testing, the primary focus shifts to assessing interactions on machine-to-machine level, typically the interaction between a code-based client and a server. The pen tester examines the APIs' endpoints, request and response structures, and authentication/authorization

mechanisms. The objective is to identify vulnerabilities and weaknesses in the actual API implementation. Unique issues come up, for instance, the fact that there is no Browser to enforce X.509 data elements (Common Name matches, etc.). Other elements a pen tester will look for are insufficient input validation, lack of proper authentication and access controls, or potential data exposure through API responses.

In order to test the adequacy of your defenses both of these areas need to be covered. It is important to consider both areas when planning and conducting penetration tests. Typically, APIs are ignored because they are not understood, or in some cases not even known about.

Chaos engineering is another technique to consider when testing your defenses. While a chaos engineering exercise aims at testing the overall fragility of an ecosystem or solution, it does add value here. Chaos engineering is a practice that intentionally introduces controlled failures and disruptions into a system. This aims to assess a solution's resilience and uncover relevant weaknesses. If part of your defensive strategy is proactive high availability, then an exercise of this sort will certainly test that capability. The objective of chaos engineering is not to cause damage but to proactively unearth a lack of resilience before a real situation does. Chaos engineering is covered in more detail in Chapter 6.

Continuous Testing

A portion of continuous testing is covered under the umbrella of continuous monitoring. For example, a continuously running vulnerability scanner is constantly testing components within your target environment. But there is another important area where testing touchpoints should be introduced. The space of Continuous Integration/Continuous Deployment (CI/CD) is the one where some focus needs to be applied. It represents an area that meets an important business need by way of agile, quick, and automated build (software, applications, etc.) deployments. Benefits aside, a CISO needs to recognize that if these build pipelines are not implemented and managed properly, they can easily lower the security posture of an ecosystem and can introduce risks to an organization's security posture. Here are some potential risks associated with CI/CD and automated builds:

- Insider threats – CI/CD pipelines and automated build processes often involve multiple individuals with varying levels of permissions. If proper access controls are not in place, insiders with malicious intent can misuse their privileges to introduce vulnerabilities or compromise the integrity of the built software. Sometimes this is not intentional, and people are victims of social engineering campaigns but the risk an insider poses is of serious concern. This is especially so when builds are automated. This type of automation is simply a reality these days, imagine an organization that performs hundreds of automated builds per day. Any human involved in that flow will become a hindrance to business progress. Hence, the risk from the inside of your organization needs to be scrutinized carefully.

- Expanded attack surface – CI/CD and automated build systems typically involve customer-facing solutions. This implies that an automated deployment will create, or expand the number of, world (public Internet) facing open ports. A build typically touches multiple interconnected components, such as code repositories, build servers, artifact repositories, and deployment environments. Each additional component introduces potential entry points for attackers to exploit. If these components are not properly secured, monitored, or updated they can become targets for attackers seeking to disrupt the build process, inject malicious code, or compromise the integrity of the deployed software.

- Dependency vulnerabilities – everything concerning supply chain risk applies here. Automated build processes often actualize all that exists in an SBOM and rely on various third-party dependencies. These dependencies may have their own security issues, potentially exposing the end result of your build process.

- Insecure configurations – CI/CD pipelines and automated build systems require configuration. Some of the software utilized within a set of pipeline callouts require their own configuration. If any of these are not properly secured, they can become a target for attackers. The configuration of the CI/CD software itself can fall prey to weak access controls, excessive permissions, or inadequate authentication mechanisms. It is crucial to ensure that the CI/CD infrastructure is properly configured to prevent unauthorized access and tampering. An example of software that a pipeline can callout to, is a vulnerability scanner. If this is misconfigured, it could generate false negatives or false positives, leading to potential security gaps or unnecessary delays as results are reviewed for accuracy. Proper configuration and regular testing are crucial to ensure CI/CD effectiveness and reliability.

CONTINUOUS IMPROVEMENT

Cybersecurity is a journey. There really is no concrete destination. When acknowledging this, one realizes the journey is an ongoing process under the surface. This calls for continuous improvement because the cybercrime space is always in flux. By embracing continuous improvement, your organization can steadily improve its cybersecurity posture. Moreover, this facilitates the organization's ability to adapt to emerging threats and meet regulatory requirements given that some do change over time. Continuously pursuing improvement can also organically start pushing your stance into a proactive one. The weaknesses of manual processes will just expose themselves. Some of the relevant concepts to embrace are:

- Technology innovation – technology advancements have become a matter of agility and rapid changes. Modern-day business demands this to be competitive. From the CISO perspective, these developments bring about new opportunities but also introduce new risks. History has shown us that as organizations adopt new technologies, cybercriminals will exploit them. A continuous improvement approach allows organizations to keep pace with evolving technologies and associated risks. But this requires that you very closely align with business leaders and/or developments. If you are made aware of new deployments after the fact, it is already too late. Security as an afterthought is known to be sub-optimal.

- Evolving threat sophistication – cyber threats are constantly evolving and becoming more sophisticated. New techniques are always showing up and lowering the bar of technical knowledge needed to launch successful attack campaigns. To stay ahead (as much as possible) of these threats, a CISO and team must continuously assess and enhance their cybersecurity measures. The minute they think something is enough the mistakes begin. Regular updates to security controls, monitoring systems, and response capabilities are essential to address evolving risks effectively.
- Regulatory requirements – regulatory frameworks, and industry standards related to cybersecurity, are continually evolving. They must evolve to stay relevant. This industry is the opposite of static. Regulatory requirements impose requirements and/or standards on organizations to improve security posture. By embracing continuous improvement, you can ensure your organization's adherence to evolving regulations and demonstrate commitment to security.
- Organizational changes – organizations undergo changes over time. These changes can come by way of mergers, acquisitions, structural changes, or changes in business models. These changes often impact the organization's cybersecurity posture due to the introduction of new risks, or lack of existing controls, in the case of an acquisition.

PARTNERSHIPS

Most CISOs who walk the path of this journey understand that taking on all these fights alone is just not a sensible approach. Most CISOs are more than willing to extend a helping hand and you should be open to seeking out these partnerships. It is in your best interest to actively seek out, and develop relationships with, industry-specific groups and cybersecurity communities. Make it a bi-directional engagement and give as much as you take, the benefit will become obvious very quickly. You should aim to openly participate in information-sharing programs and collaborate with peers to stay informed about the latest threats and share knowledge. Be warned though, if you work for a public company there are most likely policies, and rules of engagement, that you must adhere to. If your organization is not public, they may still have these guardrails in place. Seek those out and understand them before you engage with peers, journalists, or any entity outside your organization.

For a CISO, one key area of partnership is that of establishing partnerships with law enforcement agencies. This can be extremely beneficial in enhancing your organization's security posture and managing cybercrime-related activity. Here are some general steps you can take to establish a partnership with law enforcement:

- Identify relevant agencies – please be realistic. The likelihood of cold-calling the Federal Bureau of Investigation (FBI) and getting their help

instantly is pretty low. It's not like dialing 911 and getting someone's attention. Research and identify the law enforcement agencies that are relevant
to your organization and/or sector of business. Not all law enforcement
agencies specialize in cybercrime investigation and prevention. The goal
here is to build a relationship with relevant ones. Here is a general list of
agencies (some are technically not law enforcement but are nevertheless
relevant) to consider:

- Federal Bureau of Investigation (FBI) – United States – www.fbi.gov/
- United States Secret Service (USSS) – United States – www.secretser
  vice.gov/
- Department of Homeland Security (DHS), Cybersecurity and
  Infrastructure Security Agency (CISA) – United States – www.cisa.gov/
- National Security Agency (NSA) – United States – www.nsa.gov/
- United States Postal Inspection Service (USPIS) – United States –
  www.uspis.gov/
- United States Department of Justice (DOJ), Computer Crime and
  Intellectual Property Section (CCIPS) – United States – www.justice.gov/
  criminal-ccips
- United States Department of the Treasury, Financial Crimes Enforce-
  ment Network (FinCEN) – United States – www.fincen.gov/
- United States Department of Defense (DoD), Defense Cyber Crime
  Center (DC3) – United States – www.dc3.mil/
- United States Department of Energy, Office of Cybersecurity, Energy
  Security, and Emergency Response (CESER) – United States – www.
  energy.gov/ceser
- National Crime Agency (NCA) – United Kingdom – www.national
  crimeagency.gov.uk/
- National Cyber Security Centre (NCSC) – United Kingdom – www.
  ncsc.gov.uk/
- Canadian Centre for Cyber Security (CCCS) – Canada – https://cyber.
  gc.ca/
- Cybercrime Investigation Unit (CCIU) – Canada – www.rcmp-grc.gc.ca/
- Bundeskriminalamt (BKA) – Germany – www.bka.de/
- Australian Cyber Security Centre (ACSC) – Australia – www.cyber.
  gov.au/
- Federal Police (AFP) – Australia – www.afp.gov.au/
- Central Bureau of Investigation (CBI) – India – https://cbi.gov.in/
- Dutch National Police – Netherlands – www.politie.nl/
- National High Tech Crime Unit (NHTCU) – Netherlands – www.poli-
  tie.nl/onderwerpen/cybercrime.html
- Cyber Security Agency of Singapore (CSA) – Singapore – www.csa.
  gov.sg/
- Cyber Crime Unit (CCU) – New Zealand – www.police.govt.nz/advice-
  services/information-and-data/cybercrime
- National Cyber Security Centre of Lithuania (NCSC-LT) – Lithuania –
  www.cybersecurity.lt/

- Cyber Defense Institute (CDI) – Japan – www.cdi.go.jp/
- Swiss Cybercrime Coordination Unit (CYCO) – Switzerland – www.melani.admin.ch/
- Europol – European Union – www.europol.europa.eu/
- INTERPOL – Global – www.interpol.int/
- Attend industry conferences and events – in the spirit of building the relevant relationships you must participate in industry conferences, workshops, and seminars where law enforcement representatives are likely to be present. These events provide opportunities for human networking and will give you a platform to begin establishing connections with these professionals.
- Engage with public-private partnerships – many areas have support for public/private partnerships aimed at combating cybercrime. Look for such initiatives in your area and actively participate in them. Here are some:
  - Infragard – www.infragard.org/
  - National Cyber-Forensics & Training Alliance (NCFTA) – www.ncfta.net/
  - Cyber Threat Alliance (CTA) – www.cyberthreatalliance.org/
  - Cybersecurity Tech Accord – https://cybertechaccord.org/
  - National Cybersecurity Center of Excellence (NCCoE) – www.nccoe.nist.gov/
  - CISA, Stakeholder Engagement and Cyber Infrastructure Resilience (SECIR) Division – www.cisa.gov/cybersecurity-public-private-partnerships
  - National Cyber Security Partnership (NCP) – www.cyberpartnership.org/
  - Financial Services Information Sharing and Analysis Center (FS-ISAC) – www.fsisac.com/
  - Multi-State Information Sharing and Analysis Center (MS-ISAC) – www.cisecurity.org/ms-isac/
  - Industrial Control Systems Cyber Emergency Response Team (ICS-CERT) – www.us-cert.gov/ics
- Develop relationships – initiate outreach efforts to law enforcement agencies by contacting their cybercrime divisions or dedicated units. Introduce yourself as a CISO and express your interest in establishing a partnership. Share information about your organization's cybersecurity initiatives and your willingness to collaborate.
- Make this bi-directional – offer your team's expertise and highlight the resources available within your organization that may be valuable to law enforcement agencies. This can include sharing threat intelligence, providing technical assistance during investigations, or participating in joint wargame simulations.
- Try to establish a partnership agreement – once initial contact has been made, see if agency representatives are open to formalizing the partnership through a written agreement. This agreement should outline the objectives, scope, and responsibilities of each party as well as the protocols for sharing information and coordinating activities. Be aware that not all agencies

will be receptive to this, but the effort shows you are serious about the engagement.

- Share information on cyber threats – regularly communicate with law enforcement agencies to share information. Timely sharing of information can help law enforcement agencies in their investigations, and it is a great way to show value-add on your part.

Establishing partnerships, especially with law enforcement, is an ongoing process that requires patience, tenacity, continuous engagement, and mutual cooperation. Building trust, maintaining open lines of communication, and demonstrating bi-directional value-add are essential for successful partnerships.

TPRM

Most modern-day businesses cannot operate and/or succeed on their own. The reliance on external entities, or third parties, is simply a reality. From the perspective of protecting your organization, these external entities need to be carefully scrutinized before commencing a business relationship. This relationship may come in the form of partnerships or a vendor/customer relationship. In either case, a CISO has to tread carefully in terms of how much blind trust they place on these external entities. Is it enough to accept a SOC-2 report, or an ISO-27001 certificate, as proof of security maturity? There is no formula here, and you will have to determine personal and organizational thresholds. Is it ok to conduct business with an organization that has placed no external scrutiny on its own security posture? Again, a business call but from a security perspective antennas should be active if this is a scenario you encounter.

TPRM (Third Party Risk Management) is a program, or set of processes, for identifying and assessing risks associated with the use of third-party vendors, suppliers, partners, or service providers by an organization. It is not realistic to include "mitigate" in that initial statement because more often than not mitigation is totally out of your control. You should be trying to push for it but there may be limiting factors on the third-party side. Your TPRM program should at least evaluate potential risks associated with third parties as they may negatively impact operations, systems, data, or your reputation. Typical risks to look out for include:

- Financial – financial instability on the third-party side can negatively impact your organization's operations, financial standing, contractual obligations, or revenue streams. Part of your scrutinization process must include some review of a third party's financial health.
- Security – as part of a business arrangement, third parties may be granted access to data that is under your stewardship. This access could also expand to systems or networks and could open up attack surface elements under the guise of legitimate business. Clearly, this requires a "trust nothing" mindset when analyzing the technical touchpoints of this business relationship.
- Operational – third-party disruptions or failures can impact your organization's operations, especially if they are tightly coupled with your supply

chain model. Scrutiny here may require you to tap into some of the relationships you should have already built. For example, if a third-party mishap can negatively impact some manufacturing processes within your business, an OT leader would be best suited to point out the details and potential impact.

- Legal – third parties may fail to comply with compliance, legal or regulatory requirements. If this results in legal liabilities or regulatory penalties, there could be an obvious negative impact to your business. The safety of your business is part of your remit as a CISO, and so you should make sure to rope in your legal experts so that this is analyzed properly.

- Reputational – the actions or behaviors of third parties can reflect positively or negatively upon your organization's reputation. For instance, if a third party engages in publicly exposed unethical practices, this can indirectly impact your organization's image. Another example could be that your organization is publicly known to be conservative. A third party your organization is partnered with has a more liberal stance and their employees are all over social media posting about their views. This could put a strain on your organization's reputation or your organization's relationships with other third-party vendors that are also relied on.

One of the more frustrating aspects of dealing with third-party vendors is that if any of these areas becomes an actualized risk, your organization could be impacted, and yet none of this by your doing. This is simply part of your reality as a CISO. To effectively manage third-party risks, typical TPRM programs follow an approach that involves the following steps:

- Risk identification – identify the third parties that have, or are going to have, access to data and/or critical systems. Each relationship needs to be assessed individually. This assessment includes understanding the nature of the relationship, services, or goods to be provided, sensitivity levels of data being accessed or exchanged, and the state of security maturity (do they have external proof, etc.) of the respective third party.

- Risk assessment – evaluate the identified risks in terms of their likelihood of occurrence and, if actualized, what is the potential impact on your organization. This is very much a prioritization exercise and should establish risk levels that could dictate management strategies.

- Due diligence – this step calls for thorough due diligence. When selecting third-party vendors or partners, it is optimal that you do not cut corners. This generally means probing into their security posture, security practices, financial stability, regulatory stance, and overall reputation. Depending on the depth of the relationship, this may involve traveling on-site to see things yourself, reviewing certifications, and requesting objective and independent audits of the third party.

- Contractual agreements – a CISO will most likely not be establishing contractual agreements with third parties. Legal entities typically handle that. But it is your responsibility that written contracts outline the consequences

of violations, non-compliance, or breach of terms as well as address other factors such as:
- Rules of engagement.
- Risk management responsibilities.
- Security requirements.
- Data protection requirements.
- Compliance obligations.
- Boundaries of responsibilities.

- Continuous Monitoring – this is where some TPRM programs fall short making the mistake of a strong initial assessment and no further follow-ups. Typically, this is due to a lack of resources. But, a good program covers the continuous monitoring of the third-party state of affairs, performance, compliance, and security practices. Changes at the third-party level, years into a relationship, could push it out of compliance with your original contractual agreement. Or structural changes could introduce a degradation of security and/or risk practices. Push hard for a cadence of periodic reviews, assessments, and/or audits.
- Incident response – you must ensure that your organization's incident management plans address the touch points with third-party vendors. This is bi-directional. An incident or breach on your end that involves third parties needs to be addressed. You should also have a playbook that covers how to handle an incident on the third-party side that touches your organization. These playbooks should cover communication channels and escalation procedures to minimize the impact of any negative events.
- Termination and transition – while this type of an agreement is again outside the scope of a CISO's role the business will most likely define these terms and steps somewhere. Your job is to ensure that an exit strategy properly covers the handling of systems access, the secure transfer and/or disposal of data, and potentially the secure transitioning of services to alternate providers.

Metrics

The subject of cybersecurity metrics is a highly subjective one. The same set of metrics may not resonate with every audience or organization. Your target audience matters as well, for instance, you may present one set of metrics to the members that make up your cybersecurity steering committee, but then only use a subset of those metrics with the members of your board. In either case, effective metrics are essential for showcasing the effectiveness of an organization's cybersecurity program, identifying areas of improvement, and demonstrating the value of investments in cybersecurity. The real key is that metrics help you cover these areas over time. Please don't expect an upward linear trend all the time. Realistically, there are business situations such as an acquisition of an organization with a weak security posture that may move things backwards and that is ok. Metrics are covered at a deeper level in Chapter 10.

CREATE STEERING COMMITTEES

Steering committees will allow you to democratize some decision making but the real value is in the name, the committee should legitimately help you steer your initiatives in the right direction. To reinforce a CISO's stance as a collaborator, the members will feel included because they have a say in matters that aim to enhance the organization as a whole. By establishing a cybersecurity steering committee, and subcommittees as needed, you are demonstrating your commitment to making cybersecurity a strategic business priority. These committees if run properly, provide a forum for collaboration, decision-making, and collective risk management ensuring that cybersecurity efforts are aligned with organizational objectives.

You should use a subset of the committee to create a voting arm. The voting members should represent all important facets of the business. All others should be there to gain information and collaborate when appropriate. Typically, you include stakeholders and senior representatives from legal, privacy, IT, HR, the C-Suite, and operational leaders.

A documented charter is a sound step in this journey. It will solidify the direction of the committee, its goals, and its members. And then decide the committee meeting cadence that makes the most sense for your organization. One other technique to consider is always sending reading material, including the deck that will be used, ahead of the meetings. This way conversations are meaningful because committee members should have already digested the information.

The following points represent the value that steering committees will bring to your program:

- Collective decision-making – committee meetings bring together key stakeholders from different departments. By having this diverse representation, the committee can make informed and strategic decisions regarding cybersecurity initiatives. The goal is an integrated approach, aligned with the organization's overall goals and objectives.
- Resource allocation – cybersecurity initiatives require adequate resources, including budget, personnel, and technology. The steering committee should help in allocating resources because all members should instantly realize legitimate needs. The committee should become a voice of advocacy for necessary resources to strengthen the organization's cybersecurity posture. The aim of this centralized decision-making body is to ensure that resource allocation is optimized based on priorities and organizational objectives.
- Communication – committee meetings act as a central hub for disseminating information, best practices, and updates regarding cybersecurity. The committee can promote employee education and training initiatives, ensuring that cybersecurity awareness is embedded in the organization's culture.
- Risk management – committee sessions play a vital role in assessing and managing cybersecurity risks. The risk register should be covered at meetings so that there is enterprise-level risk awareness. If your committee is

really dynamic, you may find your scribe adding and modifying register data based on live interactions. Committee meetings will facilitate a prioritization of risks and guide the implementation of appropriate mitigation strategies.

- External engagement – cybersecurity steering committee members can facilitate external engagement with stakeholders such as industry peers, government agencies, and regulators. The collective group should represent broad coverage across multiple industries. Engaging with external entities can help your organization stay updated on regulatory changes and industry trends.

There is a technological reality to the landscape a CISO will oversee and protect. This requires intimacy with an organization's business operations, risk areas, attack surface, and technical debt. A security program needs to push into the proactive space and move the needle away from a purely reactive mode of operation. A CISO needs to emphasize this as a business goal while building, or expanding, a security program. Ultimately, building a security program is an essential strategic initiative on a business level. It will improve the resilience of an organization's operations, data, and reputation. While it requires commitment, resources, and much focus, the benefits far outweigh the costs, especially in a modern time where cyber risks are increasingly sophisticated and pervasive.

REAL WORLD PERSPECTIVE

When becoming or improving one's role as a builder, it's important to assess where the security organization is in its maturity. What I've seen to be most successful is looking at building or improving the security program by looking at things from a risk-based approach. For this, you will need to leverage insights from your teams, vendors, and the business units you support to identify and quantify the current risk posture and thresholds associated with the identified risks. It's important to build upon processes to de-risk your environment as well as provide your team and business units you support with the best training possible so they can adhere to these processes. Furthermore, it's important to push your vendors to share any industry-specific data and/or insights related to your organization that they possess. This is often something that leaders miss but can be a free way to get valuable data to build and improve upon your program based on the budget you're already spending. Building and/or improving your program can seem daunting, but once you start breaking up and delegating tasks to your team and vendors, it progresses rapidly.

– Brian Arellanes, Independent Director, Board of Directors, Lynx and North Bay Steel and Recycling

Over the past decade, I've been fortunate to have helped contribute to one of the fastest-performing companies in cyber security, offering services and tools to some of the largest companies in the world. This has afforded me face time with hundreds of CISOs, spanning verticals such as healthcare, fin-tech, media, manufacturing, and energy (to name a few).

These engagements with cyber leaders usually involve a large conference room (sometimes uncomfortably small ones, but who's judging), and dialogue that outlines an organization's tech stack (the tools they use to manage their cyber program). We dive into an in-depth explanation of how said tools are designed, are managed, and are, hopefully, integrated with each other. It's during these discussions where terms like MTTR (mean time to remediation) and BVA (business value add) are mentioned superfluously, dissecting time invested in different response approaches. We discuss the strategy of how a cyber program can mature, often leading the conversation to a capability gap that my team can help address in some fashion. But out of all those conversations I've had over the years, there's always one common denominating "issue" that stands out: human capital.

Most CISOs that I've met have a "go-to-guy/gal" that becomes the core component to the success of that cyber program. This person has an understanding of the complexities of, not only the tools themselves but the landmine-riddled political landscape that their CISO leaders need to navigate in order to make the program successful. It's a skillset only matured with experience, an ability to be convincing, and an affinity for not hating people (or at least not telling them). Eye rolls and sighs aside, the discussion usually questions the need to expand that "go-to" role to a potential successor. Call it human-high-availability, where protecting the company involves preparing for events such as that "go-to" person being hired by a competitor or technology vendor; or worse, them getting hit by a . . . winning lottery ticket. My suggestion? Create a human-maturity program that builds redundancy, establishes trust, and enforces stability in an industry where the availability of cyber professionals is at a deficit.

– Cristian Rodriguez, Americas Field CTO, CrowdStrike

Leading With Purpose – Building a community or a team is an art. It takes time when time is limited and is one of the most important aspects of our lives as we try to balance family, pleasure, and work. A strong leader has the ability to see gaps and close these voids by incentivizing and leveraging each team member's strengths and weaknesses. As a leader, walking with purpose towards a higher calling helps ensure the team/community you are building to remain cohesive, stay focused, and do so with a strong sense of mission to whatever the team's objectives are. Having an ethos or mission statement can provide something worth striving for.

– Robert D. Rodriguez, Chairman SINET &
Partner at SYN Ventures

4 Be a Risk Manager

While the CISO function has many responsibilities and must cover many angles, it ultimately comes down to managing risk for an organization. Protective mechanisms are important but protecting 100% of even important assets is simply improbable. And so, the role boils down to managing risk. In some organizations, even the notions of "minimizing" or "mitigating" risk are difficult to pursue, if possible, at all.

Risk management can become a borderline academic endeavor. Some leaders formalize risk management to the point where it becomes scientific and ineffective. But risk management can be handled in a pragmatic way, especially if founded in identified and assessed risks and then linked to business risk. More importantly, you must aim to quantify risk, in this case cyber risk, into business terms, a language that business executives can relate to. Executives are generally interested in risk as it pertains to the potential negative impact to the future of the organization. Being a risk manager, your objective is to make clear any areas that have the potential to negatively impact the organization and, in particular, its ability to create revenue or pursue its mission.

Stripping away the emotion surrounding risk management allows one to focus on the real-world areas of concern. For most organizations, cyber risk is primarily attached to potential reputational damage and financial loss. Some of the actual risks are:

- Loss of existing customers.
- Diminished ability to gain new customers.
- Loss of productivity due to outages and/or downtime.
- Cleanup costs and/or damage control.
- Theft of intellectual property.
- Regulatory fines.
- Personal liability for some executives.

RISK MANAGEMENT

There is a strong correlation between industry and the requirement to have risk management practices. Regulations play a big role here as well. Some industries may have industry-specific regulations that require risk management practices. Some examples of industries that may be required to have risk management practices:

- Healthcare – they are generally required to have risk management practices in place to protect patient safety. They handle sensitive patient data, so a requirement makes sense.
- Energy – these companies are required to have risk management practices in place to protect their assets and to help prevent physical impact (loss of life, environmental damage, etc.).

DOI: 10.1201/9781003477556-4

- Financial – these institutions are required to have risk management practices in place by law. This is because financial institutions are responsible for managing large amounts of money and assets.

Other organizations may not have an actual requirement for risk management practices but simply treat it as a sign of maturity. This means that even if an organization is not required to have risk management practices by law, it is still considered good practice. Risk management aims to help organizations identify risks with an eventual goal of mitigation. Some of the benefits of having risk management practices:

- Reduced risk – a solid risk management program can help organizations make sound decisions and identify risk areas, reducing risk if properly addressed.
- Increased compliance – a solid risk management program can help organizations comply with relevant regulations, in particular, when aligned with a proper framework.
- Improved maturity – a solid risk management program can help organizations prove their security maturity and demonstrate that they are serious about protecting customer assets.

Here are some areas that make risk management important for organizations of all types (public, private, government, non-profit):

- Stakeholder protection – organizations of all types have stakeholders. Public companies, for instance, have shareholders. The organization has a duty to protect the interests of these key players. Effective risk management helps mitigate potential threats that could negatively impact the organization. As the last layer of protection of your organization, your risk management function directly impacts the organization's key-player protective duty. By implementing a solid risk management program, you will demonstrate your organization's commitment to being protective of stakeholders.
- Cyber resilience – most modern-day organizations operate in complex, fast-paced, and ever-changing business environments. Proper risk management helps identify and assess, risks to business continuity. By proactively managing these risks, organizations can enhance their resilience and ensure continuity of operations.
- Financial reporting – most organizations are required to provide accurate financial reporting. Effective risk management plays an important role in ensuring the integrity of financial information. This insurance comes by way of identifying and mitigating risks that could impact revenue, financial data accuracy, or a lack of controls.
- Compliance – some organizations, especially public companies, are subject to various compliance, legal and/or regulatory requirements. Regulatory bodies and/or business partners often mandate that organizations have risk management programs in place that adhere to industry-known frameworks.

- Corporate governance – bodies of organization directors and/or stakeholders will have a fiduciary duty to oversee the risk management activities. In some cases, this body is a board of directors. Risk management practices provide this oversight body with critical information, and derived insights, to make informed decisions. Generally speaking, a solid risk management program will enable this body to meet its obligations to organizational stakeholders.

While a large component of a risk management practice starts with the identification of risk, the measurement of this risk is of great importance. Not all risk will impact an organization equally. And short of some unicorn cases, the CISO will not be able to uniformly address all identified risks. This makes effective measurement a major factor in the prioritization of risk.

Risk Measurement

Risk can be measured in different ways. Ultimately you need to home in on a model that makes sense to you and fits in well with your organization. Risk measurement in cybersecurity comes down to a way of assessing the potential harm/impact that could result given the likelihood of some negative event taking place. Here are some of the common methods used to measure cybersecurity risk:

- Qualitative assessment – a qualitative risk assessment is a subjective method that involves analyzing potential impact and likelihood based on domain and/or environmental expertise. This type of method is useful when you do not have a lot of data to work with.
- Quantitative assessment – a quantitative risk assessment is a more objective method that uses data and statistical analysis to measure likelihood and impact. This method uses quantitative factors such as the value of the asset being protected, the likelihood of some attack, and potential financial impact.
- Risk scoring – risk scoring is a method of measuring cybersecurity risk that involves assigning numerical scores to cybersecurity threats based on different criteria. The scores are then normally used to prioritize risks and determine which areas should be addressed accordingly. Some common formulas of measuring risk include:
  - Risk = Likelihood * Impact
    - Likelihood – sometimes referred to as probability. This represents the chance of some risk event occurring. It's often expressed as a percentage even though there are examples of it used with a numerical score. The higher the likelihood percentage, the more probable it is that the risk event can occur.
    - Impact – sometimes referred to as consequence. This refers to the potential harm if some risk event occurs. It could involve financial loss, operational disruptions, or other negative outcomes. Impact is often quantified as a numerical value.

- By multiplying likelihood by impact, you get a risk score that helps prioritize risks and can be used in comparative exercises if you stay consistent (e.g., always use percentage for likelihood and decimal value for impact).
- Here are a few examples:
  - Example 1 – IT system vulnerability.
  - Likelihood – the likelihood of a specific vulnerability being exploited in an IT system is assessed based on multiple factors (security controls, patching, etc.). Let's assume the likelihood rating for this vulnerability is determined to be 0.2 on a scale of zero to one. In this scale, one represents the highest likelihood.
  - Impact – the potential impact (data leakage, system downtime, financial loss) of a successful exploitation of this vulnerability are evaluated. Let's assume the impact rating for this vulnerability is determined to be 0.6 (on a scale of zero to one). In this scale, one represents the highest impact.
  - Risk score – in this example the risk score = 0.2 * 0.6, or 0.12 (out of a maximum of one, where one is the absolute worst).
  - Example 2 – breach of an unpatched system.
  - Likelihood – in this example the likelihood of a breach is 70%
  - Impact – the impact of this breach will be a severe nine (on a scale of ten).
  - Risk score – in this example the risk score = 0.7 * 9, or 6.3 (on a scale of zero to ten where ten is the absolute worst).
  - Example 3 – third-party risk assessment.
  - Likelihood – the likelihood in this example will be based on factors such as the financial stability, history of incidents, and documented security standards. The likelihood will be set at 0.6 (on a scale of zero to one), where one represents the highest likelihood.
  - Impact – the potential impact of the risk materializing will be set at 0.8 (on a scale of zero to one), where one represents the highest impact.
  - Risk score – in this example the risk score = 0.6 * 0.8, or 0.48 (out of a maximum of one, where one is the absolute worst).
- Risk = Hazard + Outrage
  - Hazard – this represents actual, technical risk or potential harm. It's usually quantifiable and the values are set by experts.
  - Outrage – this represents an emotional reaction to some risk. The factors behind a level of outrage are often human-centric, such as control, fairness, and trust.
  - This is a concept developed by Peter Sandman and was developed mainly as a risk communication technique. The adaptation here is to use the formula to develop a risk score that can be used for prioritization and comparison. Conceptually, the "Likelihood * Impact" formula can be seen as what could end up as a value of a hazard in this

formula. It is a very dry mathematical approach. But a lot of people act emotionally (e.g., express outrage) in the face of risk, and this is the reason this formula is interesting and should at least be considered. This formula needs to be considered with a solid understanding of an organization's culture. If the culture is human-centric, this formula accentuates the important role that emotion plays in managing cyber risks. Where this formula is a good fit, it allows those in cybersecurity to communicate risks effectively, factoring in both the technical aspects (hazard) and the emotional responses (outrage) to provide a comprehensive understanding of some risk.

- Here are a few examples:
  - Example 1 – unauthorized data exfiltration risk assessment
  - Hazard – the technical risk of a data breach and exfiltration event is based on many factors, such as the existence/effectiveness of security controls, the presence of known vulnerabilities, and the value of the data (should have been set during a crown jewels analysis). Let's assume the hazard rating for this example is a seven on a scale of one to ten.
  - Outrage – the potential emotional and/or reputational damage caused by this event is evaluated by considering factors such as the nature of the data at hand (e.g., customer information, trade secrets). Let's assume customer PII is involved and the outrage rating for this risk is determined to be nine on a scale of one to ten.
  - Risk score – in this example the risk score = 7 + 9, or 16 (out of a maximum 20, where 20 is the absolute worst).
  - Example 2 – phishing.
  - Hazard – the hazard here is the potential for damage if a person falls for a phishing attack. You should be able to get some good statistics for this from your phishing simulations. For the sake of example, let's assume your organization is well trained, and only 13% of employees fall for phish simulations. This will put the hazard value at 1.3 on a scale of one to ten.
  - Outrage – the outrage, however, can be fueled by the feeling of being personally violated. This means that the perceived low hazard can be offset by the outrage. For this example, the outrage rating will be set to eight on a scale of one to ten.
  - Risk score – in this example the risk score = 1.3 + 8, or 9.3 (out of a maximum 20, where 20 is the absolute worst).
  - Comparing the two examples we have a risk score of 16 for the data exfiltration assessment and a risk score of 9.3 for phishing. This makes sense considering the impact radius of a data exfiltration will impact many people. In comparison, phishing generally impacts specific individuals, sometimes just one.

As a further point of depth consider the following scenario: your company is considering outsourcing its IT department.

When using "Risk = Likelihood * Impact":

- Likelihood – the company estimates that there is a 30% chance outsourcing will be successful and a 70% chance that it will fail.
- Impact – if outsourcing is successful, the company estimates a 60% savings per annum. We will simply use a one to ten scale, so 60% = 6.
- Risk score – in this example the risk score = 0.7 * 6, or 4.2 (out of a maximum ten, where ten is the highest risk).
- This makes the outsourcing effort one of relatively low-risk with a risk score under the midpoint of the scale. Acceptance of this risk is obviously subjective to the organization's leaders.

When using "Risk = Hazard + Outrage":

- Hazard – for the sake of simplicity we will use the risk score from the previous formula as our hazard value. In this case, the value is 4.2, and the maximum is ten.
- Outrage – the outrage in this example can be fueled by the fact that many known people will lose their jobs based on this move. We will use a nine (out of a maximum of ten) for the outrage value.
- Risk score – in this example the risk score = 4.2 + 9, or 13.3 (out of a maximum 20, where 20 is the absolute worst).
- This makes the outsourcing effort one of relatively higher risk with a risk score over the midpoint of the scale. Acceptance of this risk is obviously subjective to the organization's leaders.

As you can see, company culture plays a big part in what risk measurement model you choose to employ. Choose wisely once you have a good understanding of your organization's culture. Overall, a risk score model is useful for organizations so long as the chosen model is a good cultural fit.

RISK MITIGATION PLANS

A risk mitigation plan is a document that outlines the steps that an organization will take to reduce the potential impact of some identified risk. Each plan represents a proactive approach that outlines specific actions to reduce the likelihood and/or impact of some identified risk. Risk mitigation plans are an important part of the overall risk management process as they help organizations in addressing and preparing for risk areas such as operational disruptions and negative financial impact. You will want to create one for each important area of risk your team has identified.

A risk mitigation plan generally includes the following elements:

- Identification of the specific risk – identify the risk that the organization is facing.
- Assessment of the risk – the risk needs to be assessed. This involves determining the likelihood and potential impact of the risk. This is a good spot to

include the risk score that should have already been calculated. This could also include some relevant data that establish where this risk sits on some subjective priority scale.

- Risk mitigation strategies – the next step is to outline risk mitigation strategies. This involves identifying the implementation steps to put the strategies into action and, eventually, monitoring their effectiveness.
- Monitoring the risk mitigation plan – the risk mitigation plan needs to be monitored on a regular basis to ensure its effectiveness. Ecosystem changes, M&A deals, and many factors can render one strategy ineffective and expose the need for change.

Here are some additional tips for creating a risk mitigation plan:

- Be specific – each risk mitigation plan should be specific and detailed.
- Be realistic – each risk mitigation plan should be realistic and achievable.
- Be flexible – each risk mitigation plan should be adaptable based on real-world events.
- Be vocal – each risk mitigation plan should be communicated to all relevant stakeholders.

Here are some example plans:

- Example 1:
  - Risk – the risk of an unauthorized data exfiltration event against X (X = a specific data store housing customer information).
  - Assessment – the likelihood of this risk is high because there are multiple ingress pathways, some that are not secured but needed by X (X = specific business units). The impact of this data being exfiltrated could be severe. A data breach of this sort could lead to the exposure of sensitive customer data. This could take the form of a leak on social media, or the data being sold on some dark web site. The damage could range from a negative impact on the organization's reputation to financial losses due to customers losing faith in the organization and taking their business elsewhere.
  - Mitigation strategies:
    - Implement a strong security policy.
    - Implement strong protective controls, such as data column encryption (where there is sensitive data), password protection for access to relevant data stores, and tight access control pursuing a zero-trust model where only entities that need access are granted it.
    - Implement continuous security audits to identify vulnerabilities and ensure the effectiveness of implemented controls.
    - Train employees on best practices when handling customer data.
    - Ensure that a resilience plan exists and is effective (should cover business continuity and disaster recovery).
  - Monitoring – the risk mitigation plan should be monitored and reviewed on a regular basis. This could be a continuous model, either way, you

need to ensure it is still effective as things evolve within the organization. This review needs to cover the relevant ecosystem, the risk mitigation strategies, and the effectiveness of those strategies. This also needs to cover the effectiveness of controls, the detection of data exfiltration activity, and evidence of nefarious activity that has possibly gone undetected (relevant data exposed and/or sold on the dark web, etc.).

- Example 2:
  - Risk – the risk of a software supply chain disruption.
  - Assessment – the likelihood of this risk is mid-level. Given the focus on this type of attack, there is concern, certainly not allowing this to be a low risk. Also making this not a high risk, for this example, we acknowledge that a number of software libraries in our SBOM are known to have tight security practices. Even so, the impact of this risk could be substantial with future releases of our own software being possibly impacted. If actualized this risk can lead to increased costs and customer dissatisfaction. It could also derail multiple projects within our organization if a release deadline is missed due to a disruption in the supply chain.
  - Mitigation strategies:
    - Diversification of suppliers:
      - Where possible, identify alternative software libraries for critical components.
      - Develop relationships with multiple suppliers of similar libraries in order to mitigate our reliance on a single source.
      - Regularly evaluate and assess the capabilities and reliability of key library suppliers.
    - Contingency Plans:
      - Develop contingency plans to address disruptions, such as ensuring new code works properly with older, known good, versions of a given library.
      - Establish communication channels with library suppliers to quickly address and resolve any issues.
  - Monitoring – implement SBOM management software that will provide continuous awareness of dependency status. Make sure this software provides insights based on integrations with threat intelligence sources. Also, ensure this software is integrated into any automated build (CI/CD) systems such that a dependency problem blocks a build from completing along with the standard model of sending out notifications.
- Example 3:
  - Risk – the risk of losing key personnel due to attrition.
  - Assessment – the likelihood of this risk is high because talented human resources generally tend to attract new opportunities. These opportunities may bring with them benefits that are more appealing than what your organization can afford. And so attrition is a real challenge when dealing with key personnel that have market appeal. The loss of such personnel can lead to disruptions in project timelines, decreased

productivity, the loss of domain expertise, and possible instability with the personnel that do stick around.

- Mitigation strategies:
  - Implement a succession planning strategy:
    - Identify and document critical roles and key personnel, especially where there exists a single point of failure situation.
    - Develop a succession plan to ensure minimal disruption in the face of personnel loss.
    - Identify, document, and train people with replacement potential.
  - Employee retention:
    - Implement measures to continuously keep employees engaged with measurable satisfaction levels. Surveys, bi-directional employee performance reviews, and interviews are good ways to measure satisfaction levels.
    - Offer competitive compensation packages, to include career development opportunities and pathways.
  - Cross-Training and redundancy:
    - Encourage knowledge sharing and collaboration (e.g., knowledge management systems) among team members. Make sure that no single point of failure is in possession of critical domain knowledge.
    - Identify critical skills and ensure multiple team members possess those skills.
    - Conduct cross-training sessions to equip team members with knowledge of each other's roles and responsibilities.
    - Establish backup resources or contingency plans to address temporary personnel gaps.
    - Conduct regular training sessions to disseminate knowledge and cross-train employees.
  - Recruitment and onboarding:
    - Maintain a pipeline of potential candidates as replacements for key positions.
    - Ensure that candidate pools are sourced from valuable and reputable sources.
    - Implement a comprehensive onboarding process to ensure new hires are quickly integrated into the team.
  - External Partnerships:
    - Develop relationships with external consultants, or agencies, that can provide the appropriate skill set coverage in case of personnel shortages.
    - Maintain a network of trusted contractors, or freelancers, who can assist during attrition cycles, peak workloads, or special projects.
- Monitoring:
  - Regularly monitor team health. This should factor in a deep understanding of individuals where possible (will most likely come from

direct leadership of the staff member in question). Seek out performance issues and identify any signs of discontent and/or burnout.
- Actively provide feedback and support to address concerns from either the staff member or their direct leadership.
- Recognize and reward outstanding performance to boost morale and motivation.

ENTERPRISE RISK MANAGEMENT (ERM)

ERM is really a process. The process becomes possible through the creation and management of an ERM program. Building an effective ERM program requires a comprehensive, enterprise-wide, approach to identify, assess, and manage risks across the entire organization. The real goal of an ERM program is to gain support for addressing risk. The program, if effective, can help organizations achieve their business goals by reducing the likelihood and/or impact of risks.

In some organizations, the CISO will be seen as part of the ERM committee. In others, the CISO will be an advisor. And in others, the CISO will be one of the entities that actually report risk to the ERM committee. Understand your organization's approach to risk management so that you know where you fit in. An example is that some organizations treat enterprise risk in a way where cybersecurity risk is merely one source of data to an ERM committee. The committee may have been constructed by the organization's internal audit function. In that model, chances are the CISO will be one of the sources of risk data that gets put in front of the committee for them to decide on how best to address.

The CISO may, however, also be called upon as an advisor when designing or improving an ERM program. Here are some elements to consider in reference to building, or maintaining an effective ERM program:

- Implement a risk management framework – The first step is to pick, and implement, an ERM framework. This framework should define the objectives, scope, and governance structure of your ERM program. The framework should outline roles, responsibilities, and reporting lines for risk management activities. Be ready to pursue executive leadership's support, without it an ERM program will be a useless formality that will lead to nothing but frustration.
- Stakeholder engagement – The members of the committee(s) that make up your ERM program will ultimately be the ones who accept/reject risk and upon acceptance, find you the resources necessary for mitigation. As such, you should engage stakeholders throughout the process and not just during scheduled ERM meetings. Create open communication channels to enable the exchange of risk-related information and concerns. The goal is to encourage a proactive approach to collectively managing risk.
- Identify risks – next, seek to identify risks. Conduct a thorough risk identification process to identify the subjective risks that the organization faces. This will involve engaging stakeholders, analyzing internal and external elements, and leveraging historical pattern data. The end result of these processes will live in your risk register.

- Assess risks – for those risks that have been identified, evaluate them on their likelihood of occurrence and potential impact on the organization. Use risk assessment techniques such as scoring to prioritize risks and determine their level of significance to your organization. Consider both inherent risks (the amount of risk that exists when some threat goes unaddressed) and risks after applying existing controls.
- Develop mitigation plans – once risks are assessed, develop appropriate risk mitigation plans per risk. Plan development was covered earlier in this chapter. Beyond specific plans, consider that risk avoidance and risk transfer may be options under certain unmanageable circumstances. Collaborate with relevant stakeholders to ensure support for the decided-upon mitigation strategies/plans.
- Integrate risk management into business processes – work toward embedding risk management into the organization's day-to-day operations and decision-making processes. Aim to ensure that risk management is considered in strategic planning, project management, budgeting, and other key business activities. A major factor here is how well you manage to create a risk-aware culture where risk is accepted as part of the business and employees understand their roles in managing risks.
- Communicate and review – a key step is to communicate and review the ERM process. This involves communicating the ERM framework and risk responses to key stakeholders and reviewing the ERM program on a regular basis to ensure that it is effective. Aim to establish a robust system for ongoing monitoring based on Key Risk Indicators (KRI). These should give you the ability to track the status and trends of risks. Assuming stakeholders are informed, then you should conduct periodic assessments and provide those results to the respective stakeholders.
- Leverage technology – leverage technology solutions to support the ERM program. Risk assessment tools, incident tracking systems, and metrics-based dashboards can all add value to the members of the ERM committee. Select and implement technology solutions that align with your organization's specific needs and appetite for risk data.
- Continuous improvement – regular review of the ERM program is necessary in order to mature it, and adapt to changing organizational needs and external conditions (regulatory requirements, emerging risks, etc.). Continuously assess the effectiveness of the risk measures that have been put in place and make necessary adjustments.

Here are some additional tips for building or maintaining an effective ERM program:

- Executive support – ERM is an enterprise-wide process, so it is important to get executive and board support.
- Involve stakeholders – an ERM program cannot be managed in isolation. ERM should actively involve all levels of the organization. This will help to ensure that the ERM program is legitimately aligned with the organization's goals.

- Be proactive – ERM is not just about responding to risks. It is also about being proactive and addressing risks before they occur.
- Continuously improve – ERM is an ongoing process. It is important to continuously improve the ERM program by reviewing it on a regular basis and making changes as needed.

Building an effective ERM program is an ongoing process. Irrespective of the organizational CISO role regarding the ERM program, make sure you are involved to your fullest capacity. This will require commitment, collaboration, and continuous improvement. As a CISO, you have a vested interest in the outcome (funding, support, etc.) of the ERM committee decisions and this is one area where your sphere of influence will be necessary.

ERM Frameworks

There are many ERM frameworks available that organizations can utilize to establish and enhance their risk management programs. When selecting an ERM framework, consider factors such as your organization's maturity, organizational culture, regulatory requirements, and the level of detail and guidance provided by the framework of interest. Ultimately, the chosen framework should align cleanly with your organization's business objectives while promoting a proactive and integrated approach to managing risk.

Here's a comparison of some commonly used ERM frameworks:

- ISO 31000:
  - Overview – ISO 31000 is an international standard that provides principles and guidelines for effective risk management. It takes a holistic approach, while making progress in increments, emphasizing the identification, assessment, handling, and communication of risks across an organization.
  - Strengths – ISO 31000 offers a flexible framework that can adapt accordingly to organizations of all sizes. It promotes risk management as a business function, an integral part of decision-making processes. In practice, it also supports continuous improvement.
  - Weaknesses – ISO 31000 while holistic in its approach, lacks detailed implementation guidance. This leaves room for interpretation and may require customization. Some organizations may be looking for a playbook style and they will find ISO 31000 less prescriptive than other frameworks.
  - Practicality – ISO 31000 is practical for mature organizations seeking a flexible, customizable, and scalable ERM framework that can be tailored to their specific needs.
- ISO 27005:
  - Overview – ISO 27005 is an international standard that specifically focuses on information security risk management. It provides a systematic approach to identify, assess, and treat information security risks within an organization.

- Strengths – ISO 27005 offers a comprehensive framework for managing information security risks, considering both technical and non-technical aspects. It provides detailed guidance on risk assessment methodologies and risk treatment options.
- Weaknesses – ISO 27005 is focused specifically on information security risks and may require the use of, and integration with, broader ERM frameworks to address other organizational risks comprehensively.
- Practicality – ISO 27005 is practical for organizations that prioritize information security risk management and aim to comply with international standards.
- COSO (Committee of Sponsoring Organizations of the Treadway Commission) ERM:
  - Overview – COSO ERM is a comprehensive framework that provides guidelines for integrating risk management with an organization's strategy and operations. It consists of five components: internal environment, objective setting, event identification, risk assessment, and risk response.
  - Strengths – COSO ERM is widely recognized in the industry and offers a robust framework for managing risks at an enterprise level. It emphasizes the importance of risk integration and aligning risk management with business objectives.
  - Weaknesses – implementation can be complex, especially for smaller organizations. It may require substantial effort and resources to fully adopt and embed within an organization.
  - Practicality – COSO ERM is highly practical for larger, more mature, organizations seeking a comprehensive framework to integrate risk management throughout their operations and decision-making processes.
- PRojects IN Controlled Environments (Prince2):
  - Overview – Prince2 is actually a project management methodology. It includes risk management as one of its core components. It focuses on managing risks within the context of individual projects.
  - Strengths – Prince2 provides a structured approach to project risk management, ensuring that risks are identified, assessed, and controlled throughout the project lifecycle. It offers well-defined processes and techniques.
  - Weaknesses – the risk management capability that Prince2 brings forth is primarily project-centric and may not fully address risks at an enterprise level. It may require additional integration with a broader organizational-level ERM framework.
  - Practicality – Prince2 is practical for organizations that adopt the Prince2 methodology for project management and want to manage risks effectively within their projects.
- Control Objectives for Information Technologies (COBIT):
  - Overview – COBIT is an IT governance framework that includes a risk management component. It focuses on managing risks related to information and technology.

- Strengths – COBIT provides a structured approach to IT risk management, ensuring alignment with business objectives and effective control over information and technology. It offers clear control objectives and processes.
- Weaknesses – COBIT's risk management primarily revolves around IT and may require additional integration with broader ERM frameworks to address enterprise-wide risks.
- Practicality – COBIT is practical for organizations that prioritize IT risk management and seek to align their IT governance practices with industry standards.
- NIST CyberSecurity Framework (CSF):
  - Overview – NIST CSF is a voluntary framework developed by NIST to help organizations manage and mitigate cybersecurity risks. It provides a common language and set of practices for managing cybersecurity risks effectively.
  - Strengths – NIST CSF is widely recognized, providing a structured approach to managing cybersecurity risks. It promotes a risk-based approach and supports continuous monitoring and improvement.
  - Weaknesses – NIST CSF primarily focuses on cybersecurity risks and may require additional integration with broader ERM frameworks to address other types of risks.
  - Practicality – NIST CSF is practical for organizations seeking to enhance their cybersecurity risk management practices and align with recognized industry standards.
- Project Management Institute Risk Management Professional (PMI-RMP):
  - Overview – PMI-RMP is a certification and framework offered by the Project Management Institute (PMI). It focuses on risk management within the context of project management.
  - Strengths – PMI-RMP provides a specialized framework for managing risks within projects, offering guidance on risk identification, analysis, response planning, and monitoring. It is aligned with PMI's project management methodologies.
  - Weaknesses – PMI-RMP is primarily project-focused and may require integration with broader ERM frameworks for managing risks beyond the scope of individual projects.
  - Practicality – PMI-RMP is practical for organizations that adopt PMI's project management methodologies and want to enhance their project risk management capabilities.

Here are some additional factors to consider when choosing an ERM framework:

- Organizational culture – the organization's culture must be considered when choosing an ERM framework. A framework that is too complex may not be effective in an organization that values agility and innovation. A framework that is too rigid may not be effective in an organization that values flexibility. A framework that is too flexible may not be effective in an organization that values strict structure.

- Organizational complexity – larger and more complex organizations may need a more comprehensive ERM framework. Smaller organizations may benefit more from frameworks that are customizable.
- Organizational sector – some sectors or industries are more regulated than others and this may affect the type of ERM framework that is needed.

While all these frameworks have their unique focus areas, they share the common goals of helping organizations manage risks effectively and assisting organizations in establishing a structured approach to ERM. The choice of framework depends on factors such as the organization's industry, specific needs, regulatory requirements, and the scope of risk management (enterprise-wide, project-specific, IT-focused, etc.). Organizations often adapt and integrate elements from multiple frameworks to create a customized approach that suits their specific risk management maturity. Organizations can always customize and integrate elements from multiple frameworks to suit their specific needs, regulatory requirements, and industry context. The selection of an ERM framework ultimately needs to consider the organization's risk culture, objectives, and risk appetite.

Third-Party Risk Management (TPRM) Program

TPRM covers the identification and addressing of any type of risk (e.g., cyber, financial, etc.) that comes along with third-party relationships. Most business operations these days have a digital or operational footprint that relies on third parties and beyond to N. An Nth party refers to the series of dependencies that exist beyond third-party, the relationships between a third-party vendor and its vendors. Any of these entities is an entity that provides a product or service directly to your organization for it to operate. They can include product vendors, partners, consultants, or suppliers.

Regarding TPRM, an organization may have the security team scrutinize third parties from an overall risk perspective or exclusively from a cyber risk perspective. In the latter case another entity, such as procurement or legal, would cover the non-cyber areas of risk. Vendor and supply chain risk management can also be brought into this arena. The focus here will be a generic stance on TPRM.

TPRM is a critical area of an organization's overall risk management strategy, with many examples of breaches impacting organizations due to indirect third-party relationships. Building a successful TPRM program involves several components, each crucial for ensuring that third-party relationships do not create unmanaged risk. Those components are generally:

- Identify and classify third parties – start by identifying all third parties your organization works with. Maintaining this to become an up-to-date inventory of all third-party relationships is essential. Then classify them based on the criticality of their services, the type of data or assets they access, whether they store any of your data in their environments, and the potential risks they pose.

- Develop a risk assessment framework – establish or use an existing framework to assess the inherent risks associated with each third party. Conduct thorough risk assessments of these vendors to identify, analyze, and evaluate the risks they pose. If your ecosystem is large enough it is challenging to do this thoroughly for all vendors. If this is the case, use your classification of third parties. When you can pursue a thorough risk assessment, assess their security practices, compliance with relevant regulations, and potential impact on the organization's operations. From the operational perspective do not overlook factors such as the nature of their services, their geographical location, and their financial stability.

- Conduct due diligence – before entering into business agreements, perform thorough due diligence on these entities, particularly those classified as high-risk. This may involve reviewing their policies, processes, certifications, financial statements, and security controls. On-site audits or assessments may be in order for mission-critical third parties. Ensure that the relevant contracts include clauses that address compliance, data protection (when they are used in your environment and when they are stored in theirs), and audit rights. Service Level Agreements (SLA) should clearly define expectations, responsibilities, and performance metrics.

- Implement risk mitigation strategies – in some cases, third-party risks will be identified but not be addressed by the third party. Most likely the business folks who pursued this relationship will want it to continue. The CISO needs to pursue whatever risk mitigations are possible to protect their organization. These may include contractual clauses, requirements for additional security controls over some time period, regular monitoring and audits, or termination of the relationship based on some number of incidents on the third-party side. Optimally, identified risk means that the business relationship does not happen, but the real world consistently shows us that is not the case.

- Continuous monitoring and review – resources allowing, pursue establishing a process for ongoing monitoring and periodic reviews of the third-party entities. This may involve periodic reviews and audits to ensure that third parties adhere to agreed-upon standards and practices and continuous monitoring of relevant risk indicators, such as security breaches, financial instability, or regulatory changes.

- Develop policies and procedures – seek to establish clear policies and procedures for TPRM, including guidelines for due diligence, risk assessment, risk mitigation, ongoing monitoring, incident management, and contingency planning. Explicitly develop and implement processes for managing incidents involving third parties. This involves having contingency plans in place for critical third-party failures that cause disruptions to business operations. Ensure these policies are communicated and understood across the organization.

- Implement governance and oversight – seek to establish a governance structure that defines roles, responsibilities, and the overall framework for managing third-party risks and relationships. This may involve a dedicated TPRM team, cross-functional collaboration, executive-level oversight, and standards for engaging with third parties. It may also involve training employees on the risks associated with third-party relationships and the importance of adhering to TPRM policies and procedures.

Regarding what to look for during a risk assessment of a third party; the specific components may vary depending on the nature of the third party's service offering, the industry they operate in, and also the risk appetite of the organization you (the CISO) work for. However, some common elements that are typically checked during a TPRM review include:

- Cybersecurity:
    - Evaluation of their cybersecurity practices, including SecOps, AppSec, IR, and VTM.
    - Review of their certifications and/or compliance with industry standards (ISO-27001, SOC-2, UK Cyber Essentials, etc.).
    - Assessment of their security controls, policies, and procedures.
    - Assessment of their ability to protect sensitive data and maintain both privacy and confidentiality.
- BCP/DR:
    - Evaluation of the third party's BCP and DR plans.
    - Assessment of their ability to maintain critical operations and services in the event of disruptions or incidents.
    - Review of their IR plan(s) and crisis management processes.
- Legal and Compliance:
    - Assessment of the third party's compliance with applicable regulations and laws.
    - Review of their policies and procedures related to government mandates, data privacy, anti-corruption, and other relevant regulations.
    - Evaluation of their ability to meet contractual obligations and SLAs, look for history of relevant legal action taken against the third party.
- Financial and Operational Stability:
    - Review of the third party's financial statements and credit ratings.
    - Assessment of their operational resilience, including their ability to scale and adapt to changing business demands.
    - Evaluation of their supply chain and dependency on sub-contractors, fourth parties, and beyond.
- Risk Management:
    - Assessment of the third party's governance structure, and overall risk appetite.
    - Review of their risk-related policies and procedures.
- Physical Security:
    - Where applicable, assessment of the third party's physical security measures, such as access controls and surveillance.

- Review of their processes for managing and monitoring access to facilities and systems, look out for weak deprovisioning scenarios that leave stale user accounts dangling.
- Personnel:
  - Evaluation of the third party's employee screening and onboarding processes.
  - Assessment of their security training and awareness programs.
  - Review of their processes for managing and monitoring employee access and privileges.

These elements are typically pursued through a combination of interviews, questionnaires, site audits, documentation reviews, and utilizing external investigators and auditors. For example, a forensic accountant is the best resource to analyze a third party's financial statements. That may seem like overkill, but it is a level of interest when considering mission-critical third-party relationships.

It is important to note that TPRM reviews should not be a one-time exercise but should be an ongoing process. At the very least there should be an annual review of the more critical third-party entities. These regular reviews will help ensure that third-party risks haven't arisen after a clean initial review. Turmoil or instability at the third party can come about at any time and to protect your organization vigilance is in order.

None of this can happen in a vacuum. For this type of program to be successful, the following are necessary:

- Executive support – strong support from senior leadership ensures that the TPRM program receives the necessary support, resources, and importance.
- Collaboration – cross-functional support, including finance, legal, IT, and procurement ensures a holistic approach to TPRM.
- Clear communication – clear bi-directional communication with third parties needs to exist, covering expectations, requirements, and change management.

Typical challenges to creating and/or maintaining a successful TPRM program are:

- Resource constraints – more than anything resource constraints is the enemy of a TPRM program. Resources are simply needed, and adequate staffing and funding TPRM programs can be challenging. This is especially so for smaller organizations.
- Evolving regulatory requirements – keeping up with changes in government mandates, regulations, and laws across different countries, regions, and jurisdictions is a constant challenge.
- Cybersecurity landscape – the ever-evolving and sophistication of cyber threats makes managing third-party cyber risks challenging.
- Complexity – modern-day N-party relationships and supply chains can be deeply complex, making it difficult to manage all third-party risks.

RISK PRESENTATION

The presentation of risk-related information to C-Suite and stakeholders involves communicating complex information in a clear and concise manner. But it also requires an understanding of the audience and that they may not care about risk itself, however, they likely care about the impact of that risk to the organization. This is important because executives need to understand the potential impact of cybersecurity risks as opposed to the risk itself. Linking risk to potential financial impact, disruptions to the organization's operations, and possibly reputation represents a sound approach. Here are some recommendations for presenting cyber risks to stakeholders outside of the security team:

- Speak the right language – executives are not always familiar with technical terms used in cybersecurity. But they speak the language of business. Therefore, it is important to use language that resonates with them while using data points to link risk to business impact.
- Focus on the risks that matter – know your organization and you will know what matters to executives and stakeholders. Cybersecurity risks can vary greatly, so it is essential to focus on those that matter to your organization.
- Provide financial impact – to help executives understand the potential impact of cybersecurity risks, it is essential to provide financial context and potential impact. This includes providing information on things like the potential loss due to operational disruptions, and costs of a data exfiltration event. CRQ is covered in Chapter 10.
- Use metrics – executives generally appreciate data-driven points. Presentations that use metrics and financial data to convey the potential impact of cyber risks should be the goal. It is important to use metrics that executives and stakeholders can understand. These are covered further in Chapter 10.
- Offer solutions – presenting risks without solutions is ineffective. It is essential to provide solutions and recommendations for managing risks. Presentations should outline the security controls that are in place and recommend additional ones to reduce the risk of a cyber attack.
- Focus on action – risk presentations should focus on action, not just sharing data points of how bad things are. Executives and stakeholders will generally act when they are empowered to make informed decisions. The insights you share should be specific and relevant to the organization's business objectives, providing a clear path forward for managing cybersecurity risks.

Presenting cybersecurity risks to the C-Suite, board members, stakeholders, and executives requires a balance between technical information and clear business language. Often the technical information is only offered when questions arise and warrant such information. Risk presentations should prioritize the risks that matter, provide financial context, use strategic metrics, offer solutions, and focus on actionable insights. In this way, a CISO empowers business partners (executives, stakeholders, etc.) to make data-driven decisions about managing cybersecurity risks.

More than anything, a CISO is a custodian and manager of risk. As such, it is essential for CISOs above all else to prioritize risk management for multiple reasons:

- Alignment with business objectives – by identifying and prioritizing risks based on their potential impact to the business, a CISO can direct security measures that are effectively supporting organizational operations, goals, and priorities.
- Instilling trust and confidence – by demonstrating a disciplined and proactive approach to risk management, a CISO can build trust and confidence amongst business partners. This can pave the path to a security-first culture throughout an organization.
- Protection of organizational assets – a CISOs primary responsibility is the protection of organizational assets. By focusing on risk management, a CISO can expose areas that need security attention, assess potential impact, and pursue controls to manage risks to an acceptable level. Risk management factors include areas such as resilience, BCP, DR, and IR. Managing risk has a direct positive impact on an organization's ability to develop resilient business operations that can continue in the event of a security incident or disruption.
- Efficient resource allocation – security teams generally have limited resources. By focusing on risk management, a CISO can effectively direct protective resources, targeting the areas with the highest risk exposure that can have the greatest impact on an organization.
- Regulatory and compliance requirements – some industries have specific regulatory and compliance requirements they must adhere to. Effective risk management helps a CISO identify and address these requirements, ensuring that the organization becomes and remains compliant, avoiding potential fines or legal consequences.
- Continuous improvement – risk management as an ongoing process is a part of the overall journey that is security leadership. By focusing on risk management, a CISO can ensure that security measures are constantly positively evolving to address emerging threats, new technologies, and changing business landscapes.

While other responsibilities, such as implementing protective security controls, SecOps, AppSec, and promoting security awareness are major aspects of being a CISO, the primary focus should be on effective risk management. By prioritizing risk management, a CISO can ensure that an organization's security efforts are aligned with the relevant business objectives, efficiently evolving to address ever-changing threat landscapes.

EXPERT ADVICE

One of the most important epiphanies a CISO can have is that they are not a technology manager, they are a risk manager. Your primary mission should be to provide your expertise, support, and advice to all stakeholders to help them manage technology and information security risks. All businesses make data-driven decisions on taking or avoiding business risks. The approach to technology and information security risks should be no different. Not every technology and information security risk can be reduced or eliminated. The CISO must provide the business with the data, advice, and rationale so the business can decide which technology and information security risks to accept, mitigate, transfer, or avoid.

– Rod Aday, CISO, Bank of China USA

To transition into an effective risk manager, a CISO must quantify cyber risks in financial terms, focus on significant threats that could impact the organization's revenue or mission, and integrate risk management into business processes for strategic alignment. Proactive stakeholder engagement is crucial to ensure that cybersecurity initiatives are in harmony with the company's broader goals, fostering a security-conscious culture throughout the business. This approach enables the CISO to communicate the importance of cybersecurity in business language, ensuring that it is a core component of the organization's resilience strategy.

– Terence D. Jackson, Chief Security Advisor, Microsoft

REAL WORLD PERSPECTIVE

CISOs and Risk Managers (Chief Risk Officers or equivalent) really should be best of friends. However, I find far too often they aren't speaking the same language. The Risk Manager, as the steward of the risk register, often has direct access to the Executive Committee and the Board, who are very concerned about what top three to five risks could send the company to ruin. Every effective CISO I have met makes sure they can communicate clearly with their Risk Manager as to why technology risk is near the top of that register. What makes a specific asset susceptible to damage? And what event could take advantage of that vulnerability? Explain it plainly and talk about potential outcomes in terms of business interruption (days or dollars). Working together increases the visibility of technology risk, and, in my experience, the funds assigned to risk mitigation.

– Dan Elliott, Principal, Cyber Security Risk Advisory, Zurich Resilience Solutions (ZRS) Canada

5 Be an Operator

Part of a CISO's remit is to manage security operations. While this does not necessarily mean having hands on a keyboard, a CISO is ultimately held responsible for the managing and maintaining of security within an organization's information systems, infrastructure, networks, and data. Given that, gaining as much operational knowledge as possible can be very empowering. This is especially so when situations get to a point where decisions need to be made. Being an educated consumer can go a long way in making coherent decisions.

Security Operations, often referred to as SecOps, is the practice of managing and maintaining the security of an organization's information systems, infrastructure, networks, and data. It involves the continuous monitoring, detection, response, and prevention of security incidents and threats to safeguard the organization's assets and mitigate risks.

SECOPS

At a very high level, a successful cybersecurity operations program requires a strong foundation built on multiple crucial components, specifically people, processes, technology, governance, and metrics.

PEOPLE

Irrespective of how much automation one can introduce into an environment, people are what make up a successful security operations program. People also happen to be the ones who currently create automation. If you decide to outsource an entire SecOps program to an MSSP, for instance, there will still be people behind the scenes at the MSSP taking care of things. If you do keep this function in-house, whether entirely or partially, consider the following people-related elements:

- Skilled workforce – having a team of skilled, knowledgeable, and experienced cybersecurity professionals with diverse perspectives is vital for effective threat detection, analysis, and response.
- Strong leadership – dedicated and strategic leaders are needed who can set direction, enable collaboration, and ensure realistic workloads as well as efficient resource allocation. This is needed at multiple levels, not just at the CISO or Deputy CISO level. This concept really applies to anyone placed at the leadership (people or team) level.
- Continuous learning – encourage a continuously up-to-date skillset. This may require ongoing training and development to keep up with evolving threats and technologies.

DOI: 10.1201/9781003477556-5

- Cross-functional collaboration – push hard for active collaboration between the relevant teams (SecOps, IT operations, business departments, privacy, legal, and compliance) to ensure information and cyber security considerations are integrated into the very culture of the organization while also being factored into processes such as software engineering.

PROCESSES

While people are clearly important, they need to be provided with operational guidelines and/or playbooks. Basically, processes are needed so that operational functions are covered in a consistent fashion by all people involved. When staff changes, or gets rotated, there should be consistency in operational functions. In order to achieve that consistency, consider the following necessary elements:

- Mature Incident Response (IR) – defined, repeatable (as much as possible), well-practiced, and tested IR processes ensure quick and effective containment, mitigation, and recovery from cyberattacks.
- Vulnerability management – continuously identifying, prioritizing, and pursuing the remediation of vulnerabilities minimizes attack surfaces and strengthens defenses.
- Security awareness and training – empowering employees with essential cybersecurity knowledge and best practices empowers them to be part of the overall protective posture of the organization.
- Threat intelligence – gathering, analyzing, and making actionable threat intelligence helps anticipate and proactively defend against emerging threats.
- Risk management – a robust risk management process needs to identify, assess, and prioritize cyber and information security risks based on potential impact and likelihood.
- Security architecture and design – pursue the implementation of a process for secure architecture. This process needs to cover security concerns from the onset of any new systems or initiatives, addressing security matters throughout the lifecycle of projects.

TECHNOLOGY

Technology is simply a reality in this space. After all is said and done, the elements (data, crown jewels, systems, etc.) a CISO is responsible for protecting are mostly, if not all, based in technology.

- Security tools and solutions – having the right solutions, tools, and technologies for data security, application security, network monitoring, threat detection, vulnerability scanning, and endpoint protection is crucial. The most important point here is that tools and solutions need to be a good fit for a given environment.

- Cost is a real-world factor here. For example, if a SIEM is in place does that environment truly warrant all logs getting piped into it? Storage costs can grow dramatically if that is the approach.
- Integrations and automated processes – streamlining processes with automation and integrated tools generally improves efficiency and reduces human error. Utilizing integrated solutions around SIEM, pen testing, vulnerability scanning, endpoint protection, and IAM can provide comprehensive protection and monitoring.
  - While there is great benefit in pursuing automation, be warned that this space comes with numerous challenges. If done incorrectly, this can become an enormous problem very quickly. For example, a SIEM is taught to query its compiled data sets for anomalies against patterns of usage. Then a new set of data gets piped into the SIEMs dataset while forgetting to update that query. People will assume that the original automated query process will still yield accurate results but that is not the case. The dangers of thinking automation will always be up to date is real, and humans tend to not want to touch legacy elements of technology that "just work".
- Data security and privacy – implementing robust data controls, protective mechanisms, and privacy controls protects sensitive information and complies with regulations, where applicable.
  - Native data security is essential. Many known breaches have shown that when all other controls fail, data needs to be secure in standalone form. This means native protective capabilities, such as column-level encryption within a relational DB table where sensitive data is housed. This way a data exfiltration exercise, such as a successful SQLi attack, would be less impactful.
  - Data Loss Prevention (DLP) solutions aim to prevent unauthorized data exfiltration and ensure information confidentiality. This type of solution is generally more focused on user actions and endpoints.
  - Encryption for sensitive data both at rest and in transit aims to protect data confidentiality and integrity.
    - Encrypting data in transit is tricky because the use of stream protection, such as SSL and TLS, is typically confused with this notion. SSL and TLS encrypt transport streams, not the data itself. If the true goal is encrypting data in transit, then the payloads put on transport streams would need to get encrypted and in turn, decrypted on the receiving end.
    - Encrypting data at rest is also tricky. Volume or disk encryption is typically confused with the encryption of actual files. They are very different things. Encrypting files is an action that impacts each file individually while volume-level encryption only covers use cases of physical volumes being targeted.
- Continuous monitoring and logging – continuously monitor systems and networks for suspicious activity and maintain detailed logs for forensic analysis and incident response. Also, create centralized storage for logs such that authorized SIEMs and analytical tools can leverage those elements of data.

GOVERNANCE AND METRICS

People, processes, and technologies have been established as necessities to design, create, and run a SecOps program. But, the program also needs to be owned and managed or governed. Moreover, the program also needs to track progress, show maturity, and show growth toward stronger maturity and/or prove its results. For that purpose, one needs to pursue sensible metrics.

- Governance and oversight – establish some type of governance body with representatives from various departments to provide oversight and guidance for the overall SecOps program. In many organizations this takes the form of a steering committee, in others, they form working groups. The point is that the oversight and direction for the program do not exist in a bubble and leverage diverse sets of input from multiple departments and/ or teams.
- Policies and procedures – establishing clear operating guidelines and expectations to ensure everyone understands their roles and responsibilities. Document these so that there is no ambiguity.
- Effective communication and collaboration – regular communication across cross-functional departments and stakeholders goes a long way in creating a collaborative environment while also sharing intelligence and information. It is the job of a CISO to demonstrate the impact of a SecOps program. Resources outside of security need to be made aware of this impact on risk reduction and business resilience and continuity.
- Pursue sensible metrics and reporting – focus on sensible metrics, meaning that they must be relevant to your organization and its stakeholders. Tracking relevant and key metrics helps share and measure program effectiveness, identify areas for improvement, and demonstrate value to leadership and peers.

Focusing on these four general areas will provide a solid foundation for a SecOps program. They will also support you in fostering a culture of continuous improvement. Remember that this is only one part of the continuous cybersecurity journey, it is not a destination. By investing in these foundational components, and adapting to the ever-changing threat landscape, you can build a resilient and effective SecOps program that safeguards your organization.

Beyond those foundational higher-level components, there are some more concrete elements that should be considered when designing a SecOps program.

SECURITY OPERATIONS CENTER (SOC)

If a SOC does not exist, the first question is: will your organization benefit from having one? For example, some small and mid-size businesses don't see the need for a SOC. They may feel their risk exposure does not warrant the expense of a SOC, and that is a fair point. The rest of this section assumes that a SOC must be built or improved. If one will not be built internally it can be implemented via an external entity such as a Managed Security Service Provider (MSSP).

A SOC is basically a dedicated facility, a virtual entity, or a team responsible for managing cyber and information security operations. The SOC serves as a centralized resource where security analysts, incident responders, and other security professionals collaborate to monitor, analyze, track, and respond to security incidents and events. Given the cost of physical facilities, Virtual Security Operations Centers (VSOC) have sprung up. These are basically a package of software tools that virtually provide the same capabilities as the traditional SOC described earlier.

Whether in a physical facility, virtually, or just a bunch of humans (i.e., a team), SOCs typically encompass the following key components:

- Monitoring – these components continuously monitor the organization's systems, networks, applications, and APIs to detect potentially nefarious events, anomalies, or potential threats. These components can take the form of various tools and technologies such as IDS, SIEMs, and other pieces of software that perform log analysis.
- Threat Intelligence (TI) – this component consists of collecting and analyzing relevant information about existing and emerging threats, including vulnerabilities, malware, and Tactics, Techniques, and Procedures (TTP). Often threat intelligence comes in from external sources focused exclusively on the function of gathering and disseminating these valuable data points. TI helps in understanding the threat landscape from both a micro (your environment) and macro (impacting multiple organizations) level. When used properly it gives you the proactive ability to prevent or mitigate potential attacks. TI sources may include security vendors, industry reports, security research communities, and government agencies.
- Vulnerability and Threat Management (VTM) – this component, or program, consists of identifying and addressing vulnerabilities in the organization's systems, applications, and APIs. The function consists of conducting regular penetration tests and vulnerability assessments. Based on the resulting findings, then there is typically a prioritization effort followed by the pursuit of remediations or the implementation of mitigating controls. These can come in the form of patch management (OS and application level) and the pursuit of secure coding practices. Ultimately, VTM programs aim to minimize the attack surface of an organization while reducing the likelihood of successful exploitation.
  - Threat Hunting is often managed under a VTM program. Threat hunting consists of proactively searching for potential security gaps, deficiencies, threats, or indicators of compromise within an organization's network, applications, APIs, or systems. The process can be highly manual and often involves using advanced analytics, TI, and security expertise to identify and mitigate threats that may have evaded traditional security controls.
- Incident Response (IR) – this component consists of promptly identifying and assessing security events and incidents. An event doesn't always turn

into an incident. Generally speaking, an incident is a breach, violation, or unauthorized event that negatively impacts the confidentiality, integrity, or availability of an organization's assets. IR involves a concerted response effort that first aims at containing the damage, then moves into investigating activities, analyzing data, and determining the severity and impact of the incident. IR teams play a crucial role in mitigating incidents and minimizing their impact on the organization. This generally involves following well-documented processes via playbooks that define roles and responsibilities, establish communication channels, incident classification, containment, eradication, and recovery measures.

- Continuous Improvement – it is imperative to continuously assess the effectiveness of security controls, processes, and technologies to identify areas for improvement. A SOC can become very complex and creating feedback loops for constructive feedback can prove very valuable. This can include conducting post-incident reviews, analyzing trends and patterns (response times and patterns, for instance), and updating documented procedures accordingly.

The overall goal of a SOC is to maintain the confidentiality, integrity, and availability of an organization's information assets and protect them from unauthorized access, misuse, or disruption. It represents an ongoing effort that requires a combination of technology, skilled personnel, focused metrics, robust processes, and a proactive mindset to stay ahead of evolving security threats.

Security Incident and Event Monitoring (SIEM)

A CISO oversees all aspects of cybersecurity and data protection within an organization. A critical part of that role is the timely detection and response to threats. Very often the centerpiece of this operational capacity is a SIEM solution. An effective SIEM can become the central nervous system of a SOC. The SIEM is meant to aggregate and analyze data from disparate sources across an organization. The intent is to identify anomalies and potentially negative events that may indicate cyberattacks or policy violations. To be effective, a SIEM needs visibility into as many data sources as possible, including application logs, network traffic, endpoint activity, access logs, malware alerts, etc. It is possible to go overboard here and ingest many log sources that add little value. This can become costly due to storage but also slows down computing processes where needed. Expertise is needed to find the right balance between effective sources of log data and valuable insights as output from the SIEM.

Strong correlation rules, Machine Learning (ML), AI, and advanced analytics options help the SIEM detect genuine threats amongst what can become a very noisy landscape of data points. It is imperative to fine-tune these engines and rules based on the subjective risk profile of an organization while possibly also leveraging TI. ML capabilities in a SIEM can be effective at establishing clusters of data, such as normal baselines for user and system behavior. These clusters can then be used for the identification of anomalies, or outliers. Be warned that SIEMs are sort of like cars and need regular tuning and maintenance to maximize derived value.

Cybersecurity demands and landscapes are constantly evolving. Complexity grows and sometimes traditional SIEMs no longer suffice. SIEMs, like so many elements in this space, evolve, adapt, and overcome. One example of this is a Next Generation SIEM (NG SIEM).

Next Generation (NG) SIEM

NG SIEMs focus on new security challenges that have emerged with larger volumes of data, data lakes, and the explosion of cloud computing. These elements have forced SIEM evolution to be more efficient at analyzing and correlating very large amounts of security data. NG SIEMs also bring with them a newer generation of ML algorithms that have also evolved over time.

A subset of NG SIEMs is Cloud-native NG SIEMs. They aim to deliver important benefits, including streamlined systems management, seamless software updates, and feature upgrades that are deployed more efficiently. Moreover, NG SIEMs are stressing the value of security data science, particularly security data fusion. Data fusion is a process of combining data from multiple disparate sources and databases so that the performance of the overall analytical system can be improved, while the accuracy of the results also increases.

SECURITY ORCHESTRATION, AUTOMATION, AND RESPONSE (SOAR)

SOAR solutions are not standalone in nature. These types of solutions are actually a set of tools that integrate into other solutions, like SIEMs. As the acronym directly implies, they aim to give organizations automated and orchestrated capabilities that replace traditional human involvement. By effectively using SOAR technologies an organization can gather security data and respond to security events and incidents automatically, or at least with minimum human involvement. Many in the cybersecurity field regard SOAR technologies as complementary to SIEM, augmenting its abilities.

This complementary nature of SOAR is seen in many commercial solutions that come out of the box with integrated SIEM and SOAR. While SIEM typically handles the collection and analysis of security-related data, SOAR orchestrates operations against triggers from these SIEM-consumed data sets, boosting security management efficiency. This orchestration intends to automate the human out of the loop in order to introduce efficiencies. Various tasks, including incident response, host isolation, event ticketing, and threat isolation can be handled by SOAR automation. These capabilities are not present in traditional SIEMs, which means that response is time-consuming and prone to errors. Moreover, humans need to be involved. While SOAR solutions will most likely not replace humans, they don't take sick days, go through family emergencies, etc.

It should also be noted that SOAR solutions are designed to integrate with technologies beyond SIEMs. They can also supplement Endpoint Detection and Response (EDR) and Threat Intelligence Platform (TIP) solutions. AI developments are also pushing into this space and creating great opportunities of value. As an example, consider that building SOAR processes are not a trivial endeavor. That specialized skill set can get costly. To improve this space, Generative Pre-trained

Transformer (GPT) based applications have popped up that allow for natural language descriptions of what is needed by way of a SOAR process. The GPT engine in turn translates the need into that SOAR process without a human having to code or design any of it.

As an example of a SOAR process let's consider a trigger of a piece of malware getting detected on a user's laptop. The process, which for example could be in the form of a Python script, could perform the following steps without human involvement:

- Isolate the infected host.
- Gather details (IOCs, etc.) about the detected malware.
- Kick off scans across the environment where the host sits.
- Quarantine malicious files.
- Perform notifications and create an incident ticket.

This simple example showcases SOAR's capability to take intelligent, coordinated actions across networks, systems, and teams to rapidly isolate, establish root cause, document, and recover from malware events.

ENDPOINT DETECTION AND RESPONSE (EDR) AND NETWORK DETECTION AND RESPONSE (NDR)

EDR and NDR are popular security solutions thrown around whenever SIEM alternatives come up. EDR is powerful in that it addresses last-mile concerns at an endpoint level, where the end user is typically operational. EDR, when effective, has the ability to effectively detect and address memory-based (fileless) malware, hardware-related matters (use of USB ports, etc.), ransomware, DLP, and other endpoint-targeting threats, including zero-day malware.

NDR focuses on real-time network traffic monitoring and analysis. This focal area is interesting in that it represents a significant gap for traditional SIEMs. NDR is focused on traffic analysis in as close as possible to real-time, SIEMs are generally always after the fact. In the era of fast-moving cloud computing, elastic solutions, ephemeral entities, and the Internet of Things (IoT), the value that SIEMs offer has slightly diminished due to the time required to gather data and analyze it.

From the perspective of analytical depth, SIEMs are at the mercy of the data they are provided. As such, they lack the inherent ability to autonomously dig deep into endpoint and network threats. In a world where speed (detection, response time, etc.) matters, solutions like EDR and NDR are becoming interesting SIEM alternatives. These detection and response solutions have deeper, more advanced, and accurate detection in their respective focal areas. They simply cover a more proactive space where, for instance, an NDR solution could detect a network-focused attack way earlier in the attack chain. Imagine command-and-control connectivity and lateral movement attacks being caught as they commence, a good NDR solution can do that. However, neither EDR nor NDR may be a full replacement for a SIEM solution as it can correlate data points from many solutions and for instance, piece together things forensically with great accuracy when speed is not the driving force.

THREAT INTELLIGENCE PLATFORMS (TIP)

As the acronym suggests, TIPs collect and analyze threat intelligence data from various sources. There are many entities focused exclusively on generating these valuable elements of intelligence, such as government agencies, private security firms, and open-source initiatives, or Open Source Intelligence (OSINT).

TIPs are not limited to the gathering of threat intelligence from these disparate sources. Some can perform advanced analytics and contextualize threat data based on subjective data (what matters to a given organization). The downside to TIPs, as well as many other security solutions, is the overlap of data from multiple sources. The normalization of this data becomes critical in order to minimize noise. TIPs can handle this and generate strategic and actionable insights for cybersecurity analysts. This cutting out of noise can help ensure that the most crucial and applicable threats are prioritized instead of getting buried in a sea of irrelevant and benign data points.

TIP solutions can be integrated with SIEMs to improve the cleanliness of the threat data a SIEM is leveraging. This makes for a more efficient incident detection and response cycle. The goal is to leverage a TIP to enhance the performance of SIEM operations and add contextual awareness.

USER AND ENTITY BEHAVIOR ANALYTICS (UEBA)

UEBA is another rising technology that is challenging the value a SIEM can provide. However, in the real world, it is used to augment SIEM solutions. UEBA solutions help address the weaknesses of traditional SIEMs. They also aim to augment NG SIEMs to achieve better threat detection and response.

UEBA solutions focus on detecting threats without relying on volumes of log data, threat intelligence, or rules-based analytics. These solutions can spot threats, including zero-day attacks, even if such threats are still unknown. This is possible because of UEBA's baselining of behavioral patterns. These solutions learn what becomes considered normal for each user in an ecosystem. They scan an organization's entire IT ecosystem to determine what constitutes normal or safe behavior. Based on the learned baselines, UEBA solutions aim to flag outliers, or actions, that do not appear to be in line with what has been learned and deemed as normal.

UEBA solutions detect anomalous behavior using a combination of ML, modeling techniques, and advanced analytics. These solutions leverage AI to identify zero-day attacks, including insider attacks. This area is a gap for SIEMs where they can overlook insider threats because the origin of activity is not from the outside of the environment. UEBA solutions do cover these types of gaps as they generally do not presume anything based on the source of activity, or the access/authority of the person performing some actions.

Managed Security Service Provider (MSSP)

There are multiple values to engaging with an MSSP, one of the major ones is that they provide 24/7 operational capacity, monitoring, alerting, and incident response capabilities. They generally have human and technical resources that would be very expensive and difficult to build internally. The technical resources are of great value in that they can expand an internal capacity with the leverage of a global network of SOCs and experts. As a CISO, you must understand that not all MSSPs are created equal, and they have different service offerings. Closely review these offerings, or service catalogs, to select what is relevant and will add value to your environment. The MSSP should be seen as an extension of your own operations team if you have one. If you don't have one, then the MSSP is your team.

Ensure that strict Service Level Agreements (SLA) exist with your MSSP of choice. These should cover acceptable response times once something is happening, alerting, reporting, and investigation timeframes. A point of reality is that things change and needs evolve. This means that you need to be ready to re-evaluate a given MSSP service to ensure it still aligns with your business priorities. If it doesn't, time to change providers. Another point of importance is constant open collaboration. The MSSP may think its people are doing a stellar job while your team may disagree. Silence is sub-optimal here as it can create a contentious situation where no one really wins.

Any organization that conducts digital business will generate a substantial volume of data that needs to be processed. Given this volume and the legitimate need for analysis of all that data, proper SIEM, MSSP, and related tool management are in order. A business-focused approach is essential to maximize the value of these security operations platforms and the outcomes they derive. Choose your SecOps tooling and strategy based on your organization's unique needs and risks, not on best practices or analyst advice. What works well for one organization may not be a good fit for your organization.

SECOPS MANAGEMENT

As a CISO a SecOps program is a tool that can either add great value or become an expensive endeavor. To make it a value-add, a CISO needs to be able to make coherent, informed, and data-driven decisions. A CISO also needs to gain enough understanding of SecOps to have intelligent discussions with the human resources managing these operational arms on their behalf. To effectively manage a SecOps program consider the following:

- Goals and objectives.
- Metrics and Key Performance Indicators (KPI).
- Data Analysis.
- Communication.

Goals and Objectives

Defining goals and objectives for a SecOps program is very important. Sometimes these types of programs get to a mode of Steady State Maintenance (SSM) and improvements and direction could suffer. Tracking and reporting on sensible metrics and KPIs can be of much help here. It is ultimately the CISOs responsibility to put together a clear vision of where a SecOps program needs to go. It's ok if this direction changes so long as there is a direction that the team can execute on. When crafting these goals and objectives, consider the following questions:

- What are the business stakeholders looking for as a set of results?
- What data points or metrics make sense to stakeholders at your organization?
- What are the organization's security-centric strategic goals and priorities?
- What are the organization's operational challenges and risks?
- What are the organization's compliance and regulatory requirements?
- Are your security operations aligned with the organization's business goals and values?

By defining goals and objectives for the SecOps program, you can identify the most relevant and meaningful metrics and KPIs that support them. To set meaningful goals, knowledge is crucial, knowledge of SecOps and knowledge of the business you are protecting. This knowledge will make you aware of what makes sense to measure. If you don't have intimate knowledge of what you are measuring, building meaningful KPIs is very difficult.

Keep in mind that every element that is measured is contextual. It is important to stay focused on this, and present information that speaks to the audience. Always develop metrics and KPIs considering who will see and use them.

METRICS AND KPIS

Not all metrics and KPIs are meaningful to every member of an audience. Some are more useful and actionable than others. Some are more accurate and reliable than others. Some are more relevant and timelier than others. But all that value (actionable, accurate, relevant, etc.) is relevant to the audience at hand. As such, a CISO needs to choose the right metrics and KPIs that reflect the quality and impact of a SecOps program for a given unique organization. For example, you can build a metrics program and develop KPIs that measure the efficiency, effectiveness, and maturity of your SOC. These measures can include incident response time, detection rate, false positive rate, remediation rate, root cause analysis, and SOC maturity level. And then your target audience can react with something like, "What does all of that really mean for this organization"? Or "How much money will all of that save us"? Clearly, those seemingly great metrics missed the mark, given an audience that looks at the world through a different lens.

Beyond knowing your audience, consider a tactical separation of operational and improvement metrics. A good improvement is a great win, but it does not mean that any relevant risk is reduced. Again, some audiences may not care about the improvement if it doesn't yield risk reduction. Operational improvements probably only matter to you as the individual leading the SecOps program.

DATA ANALYSIS

Once a solid set of metrics and KPIs have been identified, data is needed to make them meaningful, the data needs to support the business value of the program.

You need to ensure that the data is accurate, complete, consistent, and timely. You also need to use the appropriate tools and methods to collect, store, process, visualize, and interpret the data. For example, SIEM platforms represent a central repository of large data sets. But, the SIEMs' analytical capability may not meet business needs, only technical ones. In this case, treat the SIEMs' dataset as what is important for business analysis. Dashboards can be built outside of the SIEM platform that can leverage the data sets housed by the SIEM, or by an independent data lake also used by the SIEM. This way the analysis looks at the same data as the SIEM but crafts outputs that are relevant to business stakeholders.

COMMUNICATION

To complement the quantity and quality of SecOps metrics and KPIs, communicate and act on the insights derived from them. These results and findings need to be shared with the relevant stakeholders to communicate value. Beyond stakeholders, the value needs to be shared with your SecOps team(s). This can be motivational where they understand the value they are adding to the organization. But it can also lead to process optimizations, capability brainstorming, and identification of gaps within the team. By regularly communicating and acting on these types of insights, a CISO can demonstrate the value and positive impact of a SecOps program as well as its related metrics and KPIs.

EXPERT ADVICE

How do you know the strength of your SecOps strategy? Now this introduces the concept of measuring your SecOps Maturity Level. This is a critical component because without this you have no real comparison to how good your program is performing, and it doesn't allow you to plan ahead to adapt to the constantly changing threat landscape.

The first step in assessing your organization's maturity level is to determine where your power actually lies. Do you want this to cover the entire SecOps program or do you want to break this out into specific functions like "Incident response, threat hunting, or even specific tools that one might have"?

Break down the SecOps function into key domains that the maturity model will evaluate. Typical domains might include:

- Governance and Policies – Management of security policies, compliance, and oversight.
- Process and Standard Operating Procedures (SOPs) – Efficiency and effectiveness of processes.
- People and Skills – Training, team structure, and skills development.

- Technology and Integration – Use of technology, automation, and integration of security tools.
- Incident Management and Response – Capabilities in detecting, responding to, and recovering from security incidents.
- Threat Intelligence and Analytics – Utilization of threat intelligence and analytical capabilities.
- Continuous Improvement – Mechanisms for feedback, learning, and process optimization.

Once the scope has been determined, the next step will be to set the maturity indicators. This is the only way to find exactly what Level your program is on. For example, let's consider the maturity level indicators for a Threat Intelligence Domain.

- Level 1 – Ad hoc threat data collection.
- Level 2 – Regular threat data collection with manual processes.
- Level 3 – Automated threat data collection and initial analysis.
- Level 4 – Advanced analysis with proactive threat-hunting capabilities.
- Level 5 – Integration of machine learning and AI for predictive threat analysis.

You can also outline several maturity levels that apply to each domain. A common approach uses five levels:

- Initial (Ad hoc) – Processes are unorganized and inconsistently applied.
- Managed (Reactive) – Processes are repeatable but may not be well-documented; reactive rather than proactive.
- Defined (Structured) – Processes are standardized, documented, and followed throughout the organization.
- Quantitatively Managed (Measured) – Processes are measured and controlled.
- Optimizing (Continuous Improvement) – Focus on continuous process improvement and state-of-the-art practices.

If you're not well equipped to perform this self-assessment, you could bring on third parties to help or even do both. Once this is complete, you must go ahead and perform a Gap Analysis between your current capabilities and your desired maturity levels to highlight areas of improvement as well as opportunities for immediate results/wins.

"Now you can build a roadmap that outlines the steps to get to that desired state. Note: This roadmap should contain specific projects, necessary resources, timelines, and milestones".

– Felix Kyei Asare, Deputy CISO, Putnam Investments

The impact of Artificial Intelligence (AI) on Security Operations is yet to be fully realized as a benefit as many organizations still struggle with proper implementation of over-arching security technologies. While the benefits of AI appear to be aimed at reducing mean time to detection (MTTD) and mean time to response (MTTR), the outcomes hardly translate to meaningful results due to the lack of large language models (LLM) to train AI in the appropriate detection and response procedures. In our adoption of AI, we could learn from the challenges that come with properly implementing and managing Security Orchestration, Automation, and Response (SOAR) technologies. The objective of SOAR is to automate security response workflow, typically called a playbook that is part of a security operations procedures for incident investigation and handling. In the implementation of SOAR, many organizations that did not have defined playbooks ended up adopting the standard workflows programmed into the SOAR, whether they were suitable to their organization or not. AI in security operations has promise. There is definitely a future security operations environment that can fully benefit from the adoption of AI in the use of security technologies and execution of operating procedures. Starting with well-defined use cases offers the best path to success. Training AI on meaningful data and evaluating the results for meaningful impact is essential to the adoption of AI in detection and response, especially since the cybersecurity landscape is built upon standards, regulation, compensating controls, and contingencies. Knowing when a risk is acceptable can be complex without all of the data associated with information that may not appear in detection logic or threat intelligence.

– Patrick Hayes, Chief Strategy Officer, Third Wave

6 Be a First Responder

Security events and incidents will take place. Regarding this realistic point, two things really matter most. One is the level of cyber resilience within an organization. The other is the level of maturity when it comes to responding to those events and incidents. Both areas are the direct responsibility of a CISO. As such, Incident Response (IR), Disaster Recovery (DR), and Business Continuity Planning (BCP) are key focal areas that must be mature and proven. They are also areas that make up a cyber-resilient environment.

RESILIENCE

Cyber resilience is an area that refers to the ability of an organization to rapidly adapt and recover from attacks, accidents, failures, or other negatively impacting cyber events. Pursuing resilience is of importance because this type of proactivity can mean the difference between an outage that is not even noticed, a temporary outage, or a business halting event. Within the mindset of a first responder cyber resilience should be viewed as an area where early investments take place. This is so as to minimize the number of future responsive and reactive endeavors. The aim is maturity. Maturity will prepare an organization's defenses and response readiness for real-world threats, rather than assuming anything and possibly stagnating in untested environments. Some key elements that make up a cyber resilience environment include:

- Anticipation – Anticipating adversarial moves is not easy. But covering as many angles as possible is doable. A CISO and the security team need to think like attackers so that anticipation can become a reality. Continuous monitoring for exposures and vulnerabilities holistically (both externally and internally) is in order. This way the security team has a chance to be ready for the evolving risk to an organization. Conducting what-if analytical processes is a healthy exercise. Many breaches have taught us that the angles we don't think of are sometimes exactly what crafty attackers use. Some folks in security have gone through unfortunate incidents that came about in ways those professionals thought no one would ever attack them. Train yourself and your team to think like attackers and then you may be able to anticipate.
- Absorption – A resilient environment can absorb failures or attacks and continue to function. Designing and building in high availability and redundancy of critical systems and cyber defenses will provide an organization with the ability to withstand inevitable failures, and/or attacks, without immediate operational or stability loss.

- Agility – Maintaining agility to handle unpredictable threats or operational failures is essential. By having multiple redundancies and controls an organization can gain the ability to have dynamic response capabilities while overcoming whatever comes its way.
- Recovery – Ensuring rapid restoration of essential services and operations requires proper design but also proper stress testing to ensure recovery in the face of a negative event. Backups, failovers, automated cloud deployments, and restorations need to be put through practicing runs to ensure they work as expected and positive recovery is realistic.
- Improvement – All areas already mentioned will need to be iteratively improved over time. These things are not always optimally achieved on the first try. Continuous improvement is part of the equation here. The CISO and team need to analyze all cyber incidents, outages, and failures with brutal honesty. The insights gained need to be fed back into a continuous loop of enhancing organizational preparedness, policies, and system architectures.

Cyber resilience is realized through relationships with relevant entities (IT, Operations, Engineering, the C-Suite, etc.) that are necessary for supporting it. But it also requires the pursuit of the aforementioned elements so that readiness is enriched over time.

INCIDENT RESPONSE (IR)

On the seemingly opposite end of proactive security controls is the need for an IR program as things will happen. While IR programs are reactive when they are put into play, they are actually proactive investments in building a resilient environment. Their importance cannot be overstated given today's increasingly complex and ever-changing cybersecurity landscape.

Security events and incidents are a reality, and even with strong security controls some attacks will inevitably bypass defenses and become incidents. An IR program provides a structured and documented approach to identifying, containing, mitigating, and recovering from nefarious incidents quickly and effectively, minimizing the blast radius, damage, and operational impact.

The Need for an IR program is relatively straightforward, it could be due to a security incident, or the need could be part of a maturing cybersecurity strategy. Irrespective as to why, building an enterprise-level IR program involves several steps. The specific components may vary depending on the organization's size, and structure, but here are some fundamental elements and steps:

- Align with risk management – this could mean digesting risk-related documentation or performing risk assessments themselves. A CISO and team need to understand the relevant threats and vulnerabilities to their organization. This understanding will help in identifying what kind of incidents they will need preparation for and respond to.
- Incident categorization and prioritization – once an incident is identified and/or reported, it needs to be categorized and prioritized based on

severity and possible impact and/or damage. Categorization and prioritization will guide the allocation of appropriate resources, determine the level of response, and ensure appropriate action.

- IR plan – an IR plan needs to be developed. This plan will be the central component of the IR program. It is a detailed document outlining how your organization will respond to a security incident. The plan needs to explicitly cover all stages of the incident response lifecycle, from detection to recovery. Think of it like this, if someone who has never performed IR needed to do so in an emergency, this is the document they will open and follow. There are exceptions to the point of explicit detail. For example, if the organization you work for is a holding company, then the IR plan the CISO organization puts together may want to be high-level and somewhat ambiguous by design. This way there is flexibility the child business unit can leverage for their unique needs.
- Incident response team – the incident response team consists of individuals responsible for managing the people and actions that make up the response to security incidents. This includes the incident commander, incident handlers, analysts, investigators, representatives from corporate communications and legal, and any other relevant personnel.
- Training – it would be wise to avoid single points of failure regarding IR. Within the scope of capabilities and value-add, as many people as possible within the organization should be aware of the IR plan. Moreover, they need to understand their specific roles in the plan. This includes not just IT personnel, but also other employees who might have to act of any sort given a security incident.
- Testing, testing, testing – regular testing of the plan is essential to ensure it works as intended. This could involve live fault injections, chaos engineering, tabletop exercises, and simulations. Assuming a plan works because it seems well-designed is an enormous mistake. Push hard for regular testing to make sure there is a high level of confidence amongst the relevant team members who need to spring into action in the face of a security incident.
- Modify the plan – IR plans are not static documents. They should be updated regularly to reflect realistic changes in the threat landscape, organizational structure, technology, etc. The plan should not be treated as an artifact that is forced or compliance related, this document needs to be treated as a real-world tool that humans can use in moments of high stress and chaos.
- Incident investigation – the focus here is on analyzing and investigating incidents to understand their root cause, extent, and impact. This is a forensic process and should involve collecting and preserving evidence; an understanding of chain of custody, identifying attack vectors and indicators of compromise, and determining the attacker's techniques. Sometimes the motive makes itself obvious and is important to document. There should also be a feedback loop from this step because great learning can come from those performing the investigative steps.
  - Chain of custody refers to the process of documenting and tracking the handling, transfer, and integrity of digital evidence. This process must

be honored from the onset of an investigation, from the initial collection of evidence to its presentation in a legal context. It is imperative to maintain detailed records of all actions and individuals involved in the handling and preservation of digital evidence. This way, if the matter ends up in a legal setting the authenticity, admissibility, and integrity of the evidence never comes into question. A digital chain of custody generally includes the following elements:

- Collection – document the location, date, time, and method of evidence collection. This may involve making a forensic copy, or digital twin, of the original data while leaving the original artifact intact.
- Identification and labeling – each piece of digital evidence should be clearly identified, labeled, and assigned a unique identifier. This will help in the tracking and referencing of evidence throughout its journey.
- Documentation – every action and touchpoint related to digital evidence should be meticulously documented. This includes capturing information (names, roles, contact details, etc.) about all individuals involved as well as date, time, and purpose of each transfer or access.
- Access control – digital evidence must be stored securely, relying on preventative mechanisms against unauthorized access or tampering. Access to the evidence must be restricted to authorized personnel, and appropriate measures, such as encryption at rest, and digitally signed access logs should be implemented to maintain integrity and confidentiality.
- Hashing – to establish the integrity of digital evidence, cryptographic techniques such as hashing should be employed. Hash values generated using algorithms, like SHA-256 or SHA-512 can be used to establish, and eventually verify, the integrity of evidence. This can also be used at different stages of the chain of custody. Blockchain techniques can come into play here as they are well suited for hash-based values that are linked in a chain.
  - Blockchain technology is based on a decentralized digital ledger. The ledger records individual transactions in a secure and tamper-proof manner. Blockchains can create an immutable and transparent chain of custody for evidence by recording every transfer of custody. Each transfer can be verified and recorded into the network of nodes. The fact that there are multiple nodes means that it is almost impossible to alter records once they are written into the network. This tamper-proof nature of blockchain ensures that the original source of the evidence can be referenced with complete transparency.
  - Blockchain's cryptographic mechanisms provide an extra layer of protection against data tampering. The mechanism provides a complex algorithm to encrypt data and also authenticate

transactions. Individual transactions are verified by a network of nodes. Once there is a record of a transaction, it is an immutable element in the blockchain network. Any attempt to tamper with transaction data is detected and instantly rejected by the network, ensuring the integrity of the evidence.

- Factoring in a chain of custody that will be used within some legal proceedings, blockchain technology can provide real-time access to the information it has stored. This means that authorized parties can access the chain of custody records at any time, making the evidence valuable throughout a legal process. This transparency and accessibility can save time and resources while ensuring the integrity of the evidence in court.
- Audit trail – a comprehensive audit trail of all actions, transfers, and accesses related to digital evidence must be maintained. This trail serves as a detailed record of the chain of custody and can be used for reporting purposes or to demonstrate the integrity of the evidence in legal proceedings.
- Incident containment – this involves containing the situation and mitigating its impact on the organization. It includes isolating affected systems, blocking detected malicious activity, system cleanup, possibly restoring backups, and implementing whatever measures are necessary to prevent further damage.
- Communicate the plan – transparency from security goes a long way in building trust and relationships. Communication is a key component of that transparency. Ensure that everyone in the organization, including senior leadership and stakeholders understands the plan. This will help ensure support and coordinated responses when the time comes.
- Document incidents – keep records of all incidents, including how they were handled and what was learned from them. This will form the basis of a knowledge base and can help improve future responses. There is great value in team members being able to query some data stores regarding historical events and how they are related to current events.
- Post-Mortem – once things settle there needs to be a focus on conducting a thorough analysis of the incident response process and outcomes. This involves a brutally honest review of the team and process effectiveness. Along the way, you should identify areas for improvement, update incident response plans, and make adjustments accordingly.

IR PLAN TEMPLATE

These are some baseline components for an IR plan:

- Introduction – a brief description of the purpose for this plan, and its scope. Clearly define the criteria that must be met to constitute an information security incident for your organization. It is good practice to include a version number and date of the plan.

- Roles, responsibilities, and contact information – identify the members of the incident response team and their respective roles and responsibilities. Clearly define the role, name, and contact information of the Incident Commander who will lead the response effort. Include role, name, and contact information for all other relevant team members and ensure this is kept up-to-date.
- Notification, detection, and analysis – describe the mechanisms and processes (email, ticketing system, online chat, etc.) used to be notified when an incident has been detected. Also, cover the scenarios when the detection of a potential security incident comes from security tooling. Cover these and any other ingress mechanisms regarding security incidents. Specify how identified incidents will be analyzed to determine their potential impact, root cause, scope, and severity. Outline in detail the procedures for evidence collection and preservation for forensic analysis in case matters reach law enforcement or legal arenas.
- Containment and eradication – define the strategies for containing the impact of an incident and preventing subsequent damage (isolating compromised host, disabling user accounts, etc.). Specify the steps to be followed for eradicating the threat and removing the root cause of the incident (DB cleanup, patching vulnerabilities, malware removal, etc.).
- Communication plan – document the communication channels and protocols used when in incident response mode. This needs to cover communicating with internal stakeholders, external stakeholders (impacted users, senior leaders, law enforcement), and the public at large, if applicable. This part of the plan needs to define communication strategies for different scenarios and impact/severity levels. It also needs to address subjective elements such as regulatory reporting requirements for publicly traded companies. It would also make sense to include a communication matrix with templated messages and relevant contact lists.
- Recovery and post-incident – document the procedures for restoring affected systems back to normal operational status. This may very well be pointers to other documents as complex systems will most likely have detailed restoration processes. These references may be to BCP and/or DR plans. Here you can also define the processes for conducting a thorough post-incident review. The goal of this review is to identify lessons learned and improve the plan for future events.

If you are looking for more material in this space a great resource is the NIST publications site at "www.nist.gov/publications". There is a search capability there and you could start with the string "incident response plan".

Ultimately, an IR program is an evolutionary and continuously adjusting process. It requires regular attention and updating to keep up with both business needs and the evolving threat landscape.

DISASTER RECOVERY (DR)

Disaster Recovery (DR) refers to a program that generally consists of policies, procedures, and technology solutions put into place with the objective of business operation restoration with the minimum amount of impact. An organization needs to resume business operations and restore critical technology components (endpoints, data stores, infrastructure, systems, etc.) as quickly as possible after a natural or man-made outage. The general elements that make up an effective DR program include:

- Crown Jewel Analysis (CJA) – this step is sometimes referred to by different names: High Value Asset (HVA) analysis, Strategic Asset Analysis (SAA), Critical Asset identification and prioritization (CAIP). Irrespective of the name used for the effort, the goal is the same. That being to identify and prioritize an organization's most critical information assets. These assets are considered mission-critical and invaluable due to their sensitive nature to the business at hand. This places these entities high up in reference to the potential impact on the organization's operations and reputation if compromised. Identifying these entities will direct protective resources toward them, maximizing return on security investment. The key steps in a CJA:
  - Asset identification and classification – this is the categorization of all assets (data, applications, hosts, etc.) based on their importance and sensitivity.
  - Threat identification and prioritization – an analysis of the potential threats and vulnerabilities specific to each categorized asset.
  - Impact assessment – an evaluation of the potential impact of a successful attack on each asset, including quantification (potential financial losses) and operational disruptions.
  - Risk calculation – the combination of the identified/prioritized threat and impact assessment for each asset, generating a risk score.
- Business Impact Analysis (BIA) – this analysis identifies critical business functions and establishes recovery time objectives. Its objective is to predict the potential consequences of disruptions to your organization's business processes and operations.
- DR plans – most organizations end up with many DR plans, one per area that warrants a plan. These plans document the detailed procedures for responding to operational disruptions. They also need to address crisis management, establishing clear structure for IR teams and decision-makers needing to appropriately steer recovery efforts.
- Awareness – creating awareness across the appropriate segments of the workforce will go a long way in minimizing downtime. Realistically, not everyone needs to be aware of DR plans, but they might get value out of knowing about the DR program itself.
- Testing, testing, testing – regular testing of a plan against its respective target is a must. It is the best way to identify gaps in a DR plan. The other way is during a postmortem at which point this becomes a painful learning exercise.
- Continuous improvement – analyzing gaps through testing or actual response experience will keep the DR plans current as landscapes evolve.

DR Plan Template

These are some baseline components for a DR plan:

- Introduction – a brief description of the purpose for this plan, and its scope. Clearly define the criteria that must be met to constitute an information security disaster for your organization. It is good practice to include a version number and date of the plan.
- Roles, responsibilities, and contact information – identify the members of this specific disaster response team and their respective roles and responsibilities (remember that an organization will most likely end up with one plan per critical system). Clearly define the role, name, and contact information of the team lead who will drive the recovery effort. Include role, name, and contact information for all other relevant team members and ensure this is kept up-to-date.
- Recovery procedures – these will be subjective and system-specific. Generally speaking, the following sections will be needed:
  - Activation criteria – these are conditions that trigger the activation of the recovery processes.
  - Actions – steps to take to contain the damage and stabilize the situation.
  - Recovery – steps to restore critical systems and applications to an operational state.
    a. Data recovery – procedures for restoring impacted data from backups or alternative sources.
  - Continuity – post-disaster actions to ensure essential business functions are, once again, operational.
  - Post-disaster activities – procedures for investigating the incident, documenting lessons learned, and updating the plan.
- Resources and assets – document all critical resources needed to put things back in an operational state based on this disaster recovery process, including:
  - Hardware and software.
  - Backup locations and DB details.
  - Contact information for entities on retainer, contractors, third-party vendors, and service providers.
  - Recovery scripts, processes, tools, and documentation.
- Communication plan – document the communication channels and protocols used when in disaster recovery mode. This needs to cover communicating with internal stakeholders, external stakeholders (impacted users, senior leaders, law enforcement), and the public at large, if applicable. This part of the plan needs to be strategic in terms of notification timing. For example, the part of the organization that is directly impacted probably needs to be notified before the rest of the organization at large. Noting this, define communication strategies for different departments, scenarios, and impact/severity levels. It also needs to address subjective elements such as regulatory reporting requirements for publicly traded companies. It would also make sense to include a communication matrix with templated messages and relevant contact lists.
- Testing and maintenance – document the schedule for regular testing of the DR plan through simulations and exercises. Make sure to include some baseline

measurements where appropriate. This way improvements can be measured. For example, a situation calls for the full restoration of a DB from backups. This is a process that can be time-consuming based on where the backups are and the volume of the data. When in full DR mode these estimated timings are necessary as senior leaders will want estimates in terms of how long before everything is back up and operational. As part of maintenance and the pursuit of continuous improvement, it makes sense to also describe the process for making improvements based on test results and lessons learned.

- Appendices – these are optional but can be useful in some cases. For example, an appendix could include supporting documents such as:
  - Decision-making matrix for different disaster scenarios.
  - Vendor contracts and service agreements.
  - Specific communication templates and escalation procedures.

A DR program is also an evolutionary and continuously adjusting process. One of its biggest challenges is keeping up with technology changes, technology refreshes, and configuration changes. If coordination of such changes does not factor in DR plans, then it is easy to end up with several worthless documents that are out of date and add no value.

BUSINESS CONTINUITY PLANNING (BCP)

Business continuity planning refers to the plans and preparations put in place by an organization to ensure that its critical business functions and operations can continue during and after a disruptive event. These plans are highly subjective as each business has its unique needs. The key elements that make up an effective BCP include:

- BIA – similar to a DR BIA, it is necessary to identify time-sensitive, mission-critical business functions and resources through analysis and assessment of risks covering potential scenarios. When performing BIAs it is important to cover as many angles of disruption as possible. They may span outside the space of cyber incidents and a CISO's involvement given a wider scope is an organizational culture issue. For example, if the CISO is seen as an expert in this space they will most likely be pulled into BCP functions outside of the cybersecurity space. Other areas to consider are:
  a. Natural disasters – fires, floods, tornadoes, earthquakes, hurricanes.
  b. Power outages – power grid failures, equipment malfunctions.
  c. Supply chain disruptions – supply shortages, transportation disruptions, supplier failures, global pandemic.
  d. Accidents – system misconfigurations, programming errors, etc.
- Continuity planning – this entails creating detailed response plans (documents) for scenarios that are foreseen. These are then practiced through simulations. The results of these sessions will expose areas of strength and weakness. They will also give you data points so that the team can address effectiveness, communications, high availability mechanisms, automated technology failovers, etc.
- Resilient resources – a large portion of BCP relies on designing high availability and redundancy into certain solutions.

- Testing, testing, testing – conducting continual readiness tests, testing of contingency plans, and staff capability are essential to identify and address weak links.
- Addressing external entities – supply chain challenges have surfaced as an area needing attention. The team needs to assess and collaborate with critical suppliers, vendors, and logistics providers. This is to ensure they have appropriate continuity programs on their end that will ensure continuity of deliveries through disruptions.
- Continuous improvement – analyzing gaps through testing or actual response experience will keep BCP plans up to date with evolving business needs.

The focus for BCP plans is on pragmatic and adaptive mechanisms that will prove resilient to operational disruptions, making for a continuation of critical business operations.

Ensuring that response and resilience capabilities as well as playbooks and such, actually work is a critical part of maturing these types of programs. Continuous testing and evaluation of the elements (IR, DR, and BCP) that make up a resilient ecosystem is critical. It cannot be assumed that having processes documented or programs existing equates to them being successful in the face of a negative event. While tabletop exercises and periodic failure tests are the norm, nothing can test effectiveness like real fault injections and exercises such as chaos engineering. With these types of exercises, the goal is to closely simulate real negative situations. This should lead to a state where environments are proactively built in a non-fragile fashion. If those environments exist, the goal is that they lose whatever fragility exists.

ANTIFRAGILITY

In cybersecurity, antifragility refers to designing and building solutions in a way that allows them to thrive under negative conditions, such as failures, attacks, and other potentially impacting forces. Antifragility goes beyond mere resilience. It actively improves an environment in the face of stressors, volatility, and even failures. Some key aspects of antifragility include:

- Benefitting from adversity – adversity is typically a negative in cybersecurity, something that represents potential problems. Pursuing a state of antifragility turns adversity around to make it something beneficial, a positive. This requires using crafted cyber-attacks, forced crashes, forced failures, exploit-driven attacks, and other events that simulate a nefarious condition. These conditions created by a security team create opportunities to rapidly identify areas that need improvement response capabilities. Often uncertainty comes along with adversity. Embrace this, expect, and prepare for those angles of attack that only a select few can think up.
- Experimentation and risk-taking – programs that have antifragility as a premise embrace risk-taking and controlled experimentations. New technologies and approaches, even if risky, allow for the discovery of innovative solutions, and expose potential weaknesses that can then be addressed

before they become problematic. Failures in controlled settings provide valuable learning opportunities.

- Understanding a margin of safety – contextually, a margin of safety means never being tight or short on resources, sizing cybersecurity teams, solutions, and redundancies well beyond the norm. Put simply, this means having more security controls and redundancy than any required minimums, providing a set of buffers against unexpected disruptors. This could include implementing highly available protective mechanisms, maintaining multiple backups across multiple locations, and employing layered solutions that can catch attacks that others may have missed.
- Leveraging options – this comes down to avoiding constraints and having a series of flexible options to increase system availability. This could come in the form of incident detection solutions, cloud and infrastructure configurations, or multiple cloud hosting providers serving up the same applications.
- Decentralizing decision-making – environments that were built to embrace antifragility empower individuals and teams to make autonomous decisions. Moreover, the focus is on those teams closest to issues to drive effective ground-level responses based on their domain expertise. This, in turn, fosters accountability, a sense of ownership, agility, and responsiveness. This also avoids single-point-of-failure situations, allows for quicker adaptation to fast-evolving situations, and bypasses process-driven bottlenecks.
- Redundancy and diversity – antifragility properties inherently eliminate dependencies on individual protective technologies that represent single points of failure. They utilize a diverse set of security solutions to cover various attack vectors and areas of vulnerability. This redundancy and diversity create a more complex and resilient ecosystem that's harder to negatively impact.
- Openness to criticism – this type of environment is built by people with a mindset that actively solicits feedback of the harshest form to build the best environment possible. These people welcome constructive criticism (even from known attackers) and use those data points to robustly improve defenses. This openness creates a continuous improvement loop and facilitates rapid learning from diverse perspectives.

Beyond those aspects, a CISO and team can pursue antifragility by embracing some of the following:

- Fail fast – encourage proactive discovery of security flaws through red/blue/purple team exercises rather than reacting to incidents. Failures represent data points to strengthen defenses so long as the team can learn and adapt fast.
- Attack technical debt – work toward continually paying down technical debt, update legacy systems, hunt down data stores that are no longer used but still available, find all data stores you are responsible for, hunt down obsolete infrastructure, and address all those head-on. Layering on new controls on fragile foundations is simply a formula that does not work.

- Creatively stress test – embrace the notion of chaos engineering and inject real-world faults into your environments. Then be agile in terms of rapidly incorporating lessons learned into practical defenses. See "Chaos Engineering" section.

In essence, antifragile systems are designed to stand up to chaotic situations, volatility, and stressors without just surviving but actually thriving under crises. A major part of building an antifragile environment is how testing is conducted, a humbly brutal approach is in order and found in the area of chaos engineering.

CHAOS ENGINEERING

Chaos engineering is the practice of intentionally introducing faults and failures into a solution to detect thresholds, uncover weaknesses, and then take those learnings to improve resilience. The goal is to create issues proactively and purposely during testing so that weaknesses can be addressed before they negatively impact customers. The benefits of chaos engineering exercises can be seen in several key areas:

- Testing resilience – chaos engineering creates situations that truly test the resilience of an organization's systems. The reason for the "truly" in that previous sentence is that chaos engineering stress tests under realistic conditions and synthetic or controlled ones. By simulating real-world failures or worst-case scenarios (loss of access to APIs, network outages, host/server crashes and shutdowns, traffic spikes, etc.) chaos engineers can observe and measure how a system reacts and then how it recovers from these disruptions. This real-world perspective helps validate the system's ability to stand up and adapt to anomalies and negative events without interrupting business operations.
- Identifying weaknesses – these types of tests help uncover hidden or unknown weaknesses in a system. These weaknesses may be old, accepted risks, or may just have never surfaced during normal operating conditions. By intentionally injecting faults and observing a system's response patterns, chaos engineers can identify areas of fragility, architectural deficiencies, performance bottlenecks, single points of failure, or other issues related to fault tolerance and error handling. These data points can then be used to pursue improvements and enhance overall resilience.
- Shifting to the proactive – chaos engineering takes a proactive approach to risk mitigation. It does so by forcing the identification, and addressing, of areas of weakness before they impact an organization negatively. In the case of cybersecurity-related events, this is obviously done by friendly entities before nefarious ones can. By proactively creating disruptions and measuring thresholds, organizations can discover potential issues early on and take appropriate measures to address them.
- Confidence building – this testing methodology removes the "what-if" questions. It provides teams with an unprecedented level of confidence in their systems' ability to withstand unexpected failures or attacks. By

actively testing and/or validating a system's resilience, organizations can gain assurance that graceful recovery and business continuity are possible.

- Collaboration – chaos engineering promotes collaboration among different teams. The planning and designing of an exercise require lots of coordination from software engineering teams, SRE teams, IT operations, and cybersecurity. This fosters cross-functional cooperation at the least, and knowledge sharing becomes possible as well. Collaboratively teams will have to come together to address system weaknesses and improve overall reliability. This makes for valuable learning opportunities, where teams can explore the intricacies of what others do and start to understand the complexity of some systems at a deeper level.
- Continuous improvement – continuous improvement is an obvious goal of chaos engineering exercises. By regularly introducing these chaotic conditions, and analyzing the results, teams can identify patterns, trends, and recurring issues. These can then be used to continuously improve resilience. This data-driven approach allows for targeted improvement and remediation efforts.

Here are some real examples of how chaos engineering is applied, some are more subtle than others:

- Killing live processes, running server instances (physical or virtual), or containers to analyze system reaction and confirm if restart policies work as expected. This exercise tests and validates recovery procedures.
- Injecting multiple responses to a single request (web application or API call). This scenario tests any systems monitoring network traffic for anomalies.
- Killing microservices (such as those hosting APIs). This exercise tests and validates the resilience and behavior of an application that is dependent on those APIs.
- Randomly shutting down servers from a live pool. This scenario tests if the system can handle the loss of capacity gracefully. This helps uncover bottlenecks or single points of failure.
- Injecting malformed data into an application or directly into a DB. This exercise will ensure input validation, data hygiene mechanisms, and error handling work properly.
- Inject well-formed data that abuses expected behavior. This scenario will ensure that certain conditions are not entered, for example, resource exhaustion scenarios.
- Deteriorating network quality by introducing noise, latency, or packet disruptions (fragmentation, loss, etc.). This exercise will test the boundaries of settings (timeouts, retransmissions, etc.).

As with most things in life, there are pros and cons with chaos engineering, some of the pros are:

- It is very effective at identifying weaknesses in complex systems. These are typically difficult to expose through regular functional or stress testing.
- Builds confidence that a system can withstand chaotic real-world conditions.
- Forces teams to proactively address potential failures, even if they are edge cases.
- Validates that high availability, redundancy, and fail-over mechanisms actually work.

Some of the cons are:

- Can be dangerous if the tests hit areas that are susceptible to the cause of systemic failures. The full outcome of the disruption may not be obvious at first.
- Requires many resources to think through the test design.
- Can be operationally disruptive. If it turns out there are weaknesses, then outages are inevitable.
- Needs mature engineers to make the exercises meaningful.

Overall chaos engineering is effective because it enables organizations to proactively test and enhance the resilience of their systems, identify vulnerabilities before they become critical issues, build confidence in system reliability, and foster a culture of continuous improvement and collaboration. By intentionally injecting controlled disruptions, organizations can better prepare their systems for real-world challenges and minimize the impact of failures, ultimately leading to more reliable and robust systems.

Being a first responder is more of a mindset than anything. A CISO will most likely not be in the incident commander role, for instance. But that same CISO needs to know how all these functions work and be educated so that they can properly scrutinize things with their unique perspective. Also, keep in mind that even though this is all documented and dedicated teams will likely deal with the operational components, senior leaders will not be going to those folks with hands-on keyboards for updates and answers. When communicating with those senior leaders, knowledge in this space will provide great confidence in the way the CISO presents data and answers questions.

REAL WORLD PERSPECTIVE

Managing a cybersecurity incident can be a challenging task for any CISO. We have three key points for CISOs to keep in mind:

- First, your initial role is to orient stakeholders to the situation. Your security team needs to understand the priority of the incident, executives need to understand the potential severity, external advisors need to understand the status, etc. You are the quarterback calling the plays and ensuring that everyone knows the score.

- Second, establish clear expectations for information flows. Lay out who is meant to tell what to whom, and by when to enable which decisions. Build the appropriate communication cadence for the situation and enlist others to help you capture, organize, and convey the proper information at the proper times.
- Third, develop a realistic resource plan. Don't allow a critical security engineer to spend 19 straight hours in troubleshooting mode. No one can be effective working that long without sleep. For large-scale events such as ransomware incidents, it's imperative to recognize that it will demand the organization's focus for several days or weeks. Burning out key staff, including yourself, in the initial phase of the response sets you back. A ransomware attack isn't the worst day of your career, it's the worst month of your career. Adapt your resource plan accordingly.

Having laid out this advice, here are some principles on how to effectively handle such situations:

- Preparation is Key: Ensure that you have an up-to-date and comprehensive incident response plan in place. This plan should outline the steps to take in the event of a cybersecurity incident, including roles, and responsibilities of team members, communication protocols, and procedures for containment, eradication, and recovery. This plan should include details on how you will engage DFIR support and how you will activate a claim under your cyber insurance policy. The plan should be sent to relevant stakeholders and used as a training guide during tabletop exercises. It should not sit until a major incident occurs.
- Establish Clear Communication Channels: Designate communication channels for internal stakeholders, such as IT teams, executives, and external stakeholders like DFIR, law firms, customers, regulators, and law enforcement. Ensure that these channels are secure and reliable. Have a plan to leverage out-of-band communications protocols such as Signal or WhatsApp should your email be compromised.
- Act Quickly but Thoughtfully: Time is of the essence during a cybersecurity incident, but it's crucial to act thoughtfully to avoid exacerbating the situation. Quickly assess the nature and scope of the incident, and then implement your incident response plan accordingly.
- Contain the Incident: Once you've identified the incident, take steps to contain it to prevent further damage. This may involve isolating affected systems or networks, shutting down compromised services, or implementing temporary mitigations. Immediately reach out to your MSSP, SOC, or a DFIR provider for assistance in detection and containment.
- Embrace the Inevitable: A cybersecurity breach will happen, whether a targeted APT attack or an opportunistic ransomware attack.

Choosing the right partners in advance can turn six months of chaos into six days of organized response efforts. Take time to review a cybersecurity insurance provider, a cybersecurity law firm, and, most importantly, an incident response provider. Understand how the interactions will take place and set expectations to create a robust response team.

- Engage Relevant Stakeholders: Involve relevant internal and external stakeholders, including legal counsel, law enforcement, regulators, and third-party vendors as necessary. Coordinate closely with these stakeholders throughout the incident response process.
- Maintain Transparency: Be transparent with internal and external stakeholders about the incident and its impact. Provide regular updates on the situation, including what is known, what actions are being taken, and any potential impacts on operations or data.
- Learn from the Incident: Once the incident has been resolved, conduct a thorough post-incident review to identify lessons learned and areas for improvement. Use this information to update your incident response plan and enhance your organization's cybersecurity posture. While reviewing incidents, it is also important to document "near miss" events where things could have gotten a lot worse (e.g., a threat actor had access to the OT environment and could have caused a production outage).
- Implement Remediation Measures: After the incident has been resolved, implement remediation measures to address any vulnerabilities, or weaknesses, that were exploited. This may include patching systems, updating security controls, tuning your EDR platform, and providing additional training.
- Stay Vigilant: Cybersecurity incidents are an ongoing threat, so it's essential to remain vigilant and proactive in monitoring for potential threats and vulnerabilities. Regularly review and update your security controls, policies, and procedures to stay ahead of emerging threats. By staying current on the threat landscape, understanding threat actor TTPs, and examining responses in your industry, you can gain an edge.

While CISOs generally have a good grasp of incident response strategies, there are several common pitfalls they may encounter:

- Underestimating the Importance of Preparation: Some CISOs may underestimate the importance of thorough preparation for incident response. This includes having a well-documented incident response plan, conducting regular tabletop exercises and simulations, and ensuring that the entire team is trained and aware of their roles and responsibilities.

- Lack of Clear Communication: Effective communication is essential during a cybersecurity incident, both internally and externally. CISOs may sometimes fail to establish clear communication channels, leading to delays in response efforts and confusion among stakeholders.
- Overlooking Legal and Regulatory Considerations: CISOs need to be aware of the legal and regulatory requirements related to cybersecurity incidents such as data breach notification laws. Failure to comply with these requirements can lead to significant legal and financial consequences for the organization.
- Neglecting Forensic Analysis: Conducting a thorough forensic analysis is critical for understanding the root cause of the incident, identifying the extent of the compromise, and preventing future incidents. Some CISOs may overlook this step or fail to allocate sufficient resources to forensic investigation in lieu of a quick recovery and return to business as usual.
- Focusing Solely on Technical Remediation: While technical remediation is an important aspect of incident response, CISOs should also consider broader organizational and procedural changes to improve security posture. This may include updating policies and procedures, enhancing employee training, and implementing risk mitigation measures.
- Not Learning from Past Incidents: Failure to learn from past incidents is a common mistake in incident response. CISOs should conduct post-incident reviews to identify lessons learned and areas for improvement, and then incorporate these insights into future incident response planning.
- Overreliance on Technology: While technology plays a crucial role in cybersecurity incident response, CISOs should not rely solely on technological solutions. Human expertise and judgment are also essential for effective incident detection, analysis, and response.
- Ignoring Third-Party Relationships: Many organizations rely on third-party vendors and partners for various services, and these relationships can introduce additional cybersecurity risks. CISOs should ensure that third-party relationships are properly assessed and managed from a security perspective, including incident response capabilities.
- Failing to Adapt to Changing Threat Landscape: The cybersecurity threat landscape is constantly evolving, with new threats and attack techniques emerging regularly. CISOs may sometimes fail to adapt their incident response strategies to address these evolving threats, leaving their organizations vulnerable to new attack vectors.
- Not Involving Executive Leadership Early Enough: Executive leadership involvement is critical during a cybersecurity incident, both for decision-making and for providing necessary resources and support.

CISOs should ensure that executive leadership is briefed on the incident promptly and involved in the response efforts as needed. Cyber is an important enough item on every organization's risk register that we should move on from fears of "crying wolf" during network intrusions.

In summary, CISOs have complex, multi-dimensional, and dynamic roles. Incidents are surely stressful and often damaging, yet they are also opportunities to be a fighter, to take charge of a situation, and to demonstrate that the hard day-in-and-day-out work to strengthen security posture can pay off.

– Billy Gouveia, Founder and CEO, Surefire Cyber, Inc. & Jason Ossler, Director of Advisory and Response, Surefire Cyber Inc

Some of the greatest challenges in security incident response come down to classification and procedures. As a first responder in the cybersecurity realm, you first need to determine if the present event is, in fact, an incident. If so, what kind of incident? Is it an IT incident, such as a single user unable to login to corporate IT systems or is it that multiple users are suddenly unable to connect? Could these connection issues be due to system availability, and if so, is it malicious in nature? These are important questions as you triage the situation at hand. While system availability creates an accessibility issue, as an IT issue the goal is to restore service and get back to status quo. A cybersecurity issue is much different. With a cybersecurity issue, there are a number of critical factors that require evaluation prior to returning services to normal. In the case of a cybersecurity issue, you want to understand the goal of the attack; was malicious activity detected, or a payload executed? Containing the incident allows the investigation to proceed without potential risk to other systems, or widespread infection. Additionally, valuable evidence needed about the security incident could be lost or corrupted in the process of remediation if not captured. Once an understanding of the incident is determined, eradication can be completed, systems tested for proper removal of any malicious activity/code, and new procedures can be documented in change controls.

– Patrick Hayes, Chief Security Officer, Third Wave

I have a favorite philosopher. I know that some of my friends are partial to the ancient greats, others the mystics and spiritualists. Some more contemporary. But for me, it has to be Tyson. Iron Mike Tyson. Mike quite rightly said: "Everyone has a plan until they get punched in the face". So here are the times in incident and crisis management when I have had a punch to the face and, of course, what I learned.

The first is of course at the very root of Tysonian philosophy. In essence, plans change, indeed in the Army, we used to say that no plan survives contact and so it is critical to be adaptable. Indeed, in the majority of the major cyber security incidents I have been involved in our original (nailed on and certain) hypothesis never ended up being what we thought as more data became available. Adaptability is critical as is language and temperament. Your job is to prove or disprove. To deal only in fact. There should be no adjectives in any report writing. Any hypothesis dressed in categorical terms (and which inevitably ends up changing) will lead to a loss of trust and even create another crisis of its own. Or another head to the Hydra.

Indeed, the Hydra is a perfect symbol for incident management. You have the original head but then, depending on how the incident is handled, others will appear. Senior Management, HR, PR, Internal Communications, and internal employees who take to Twitter (or X). As the incident leads it is critical that you are mindful of all of these potential Hydra heads and that they are cut before they outgrow the incident itself.

The first building block to incident management has to be tried and tested processes and plans. Those are rehearsed. And rehearsed. At all levels of the organization including senior management. It was not raining when Noah built the Ark. Cyber Crisis Management exercises have to be achievable and realistic.

The first hours of the incident are critical. Sadly, in my experience, a lot of time is often wasted in trying to apportion blame (or trying to) to rabbit holes, "Why didn't we . . ." the answer simply put is we didn't. And now we have a fire. And we need to put it out. Leave the "why" to the lessons learned.

I learned the following from a friend in Seal Team Six. When confronted with a problem they would often say: "Good (acknowledges the problem in a positive way), what's next (forward-looking to problem solve)". Once this mindset is established and the right teams are where they need to be, the incident management can begin.

From experience, during an incident, you should focus on the kill chain and its stages. There are two specific aspects that I always try and look out for (once these are blocked most of the attack is mitigated). Lateral movement and Command and Control (C2).

Once detected, the focus has to be on containment and eradication, but be careful, there is a punch to the face coming. You must understand your systems, what part of the business they serve, and their level of criticality. In shutting down a server or blocking x DNS, you might inadvertently do more harm than the attack itself.

After containment and eradication, you are in the recovery phase. Again, testing here is critical. Business Impact Analysis is not the same as business continuity plans and these are no good if they have not been tested or put through a disaster recovery process.

Now all of this is all well and good and contained with the singular – though rather sizable original head of the Hydra – but there are others, and this is where cyber incident management dovetails into Crisis Management. This is where the rehearsed crisis management plan with its clear escalation criteria comes into play.

Once you are in crisis management territory the focus shifts away from the technical incident to legal risk management and communications. And here comes another couple of punches to the face. In terms of legal risk management, it is critical to bring your legal team in as early as possible. The incident must now be driven at their direction. It is critical that the problem is understood in lay terms and not communicated in IT speak.

In terms of communications, internal should, as a rule, be the same as external. And must be limited to facts. Without conjecture or supposition, or as I mentioned above, adjectives. The relevant executives must be briefed so that they are on the same page. Further, there must be a singular source of truth that all are party to. There are a number of incidents I recall where the CEO was getting 11:00-hour news at 11:00, but then also 9:30-hour news at 11:00 as folk cannot resist their moment in the sun. A lot of this can of course be ironed out via exercising.

And finally (see the leadership chapter) lessons learned further to an incident must be held – in a safe place. And without, definitely without, the Director of Hindsight and their pal the Director of Well. Learnings must lead to a concrete action and remediation plan and, of course, feed into the incident and crisis management plans themselves.

Coming back to Iron Mike, being in an incident is not too dissimilar to being in the ring. Look after your team. Ensure that alternates are planned well in advance. That families are looked after and that different aspects are considered (childcare, food, accommodation, rest, and logistics, to name a few).

And if you get punched in the face, learn from it, and share the experience with others so that they are not knocked out in the first round.

So, in distilling this for leaders:

1. Plan and rehearse.
2. No plan survives contact and very few hypotheses stay as true at the start as at the end of the incident.
3. Deal only in facts.
4. Don't look back – look forward positively ready to solve.
5. Think kill chain to prove or disprove. Focus on C2 and Lateral movement.
6. Think of the other Hydras heads.
7. Learn – without judgment nor the Director of Hindsight.
8. Look after your team.

– Stuart Seymour, Group CISO. Virgin Media O2

TRUE STORY

In cybersecurity, the line between defense (such as incident response, blue team operations) and offense (ethical hacking, penetration testing, red team exercises) is often perceived not merely as a boundary but as a wall. To me, it's a line that MUST be crossed. Understanding the mindset of the attacker is crucial for anyone leading incident response efforts. Let me share a story from nearly ten years ago that injected this idea into my mind. A financial institution (name redacted) prides itself on its robust cybersecurity measures. They hired only the best of the best, seasoned blue team leaders, good technical people to operate the SOC, only top-class providers to help with the implementation of a SIEM, and so on. The bank successfully deflected numerous cyber threats. However, the blue team is just that, the blue team only. They are not an experienced red team. One ordinary morning, this bank's monitoring systems trigger an alert: an anomaly in the network traffic suggesting a potential breach. The blue team immediately put together an emergency response. They check all the logs, and everything seems ok. The SIEM was alerting about users paying their taxes. So, it must be a false positive, right? So naturally, the SOC engineer marked this as a false positive event. After a couple of days, several users were complaining about their accounts presenting some payments that they didn't perform. I don't want to bore you with the details but here's what happened: 1. Attackers, with the help of compromised internal users who colluded with them, stole all user account information. 2. With those credentials, they needed to take over the MFA. So, they created a phishing email, and they were also asking for an email password. Believe it or not, many people gave away their email credentials. 3. To increase the amount of users compromised, they also created a fake bank webpage. They also paid for some Google ads so the fake page could be pushed to users before the real one. 4. Now the problem – monetization. How would they take away the money without leaving any trail? Welp, paying taxes. They published marketing ads on social networks saying that they could pay any bill, any ticket, any taxes you wanted. You just needed to pay 50% of that in cash. Of course, they get the cash and pay with the compromised bank accounts. This well-known scam model in the offensive security community illustrates a critical oversight by the SOC. This incident is a real-world case and serves as a testament to the critical importance of blending offensive and defensive mindsets in cybersecurity leadership. By stepping into the shoes of an attacker, you can anticipate the breach and lead your team to a smooth and effective response, safeguarding your assets, the company, and its reputation. I know it's tacky to say this, but in cybersecurity, the best defense is a good offense. Leaders who embody the skills and tactics of both blue and red teams are indispensable in navigating the complex and ever-evolving landscape of cyber threats. The hallmark of effective incident response is the ability to think like an attacker and proactively implement defenses, moving beyond mere reaction. This scenario underscores a fundamental truth in cybersecurity: understanding the offense is key to fortifying the defense. In a world where cyber threats are becoming increasingly sophisticated, the ability to anticipate and counteract attacks is not just valuable, it's essential.

– Jose Alejandro Guinea Rivera

7 Be a Team Lead

It is generally sound advice to state, "Building a strong cybersecurity team is crucial for any organization in today's digital landscape". Contextually, a "cybersecurity team" does not have to mean a team of full-time employees. A good CISO will address this point head-on and make the determination as to whether they need a team of full-timers, or if they even afford a good team. Ultimately a CISO needs a team supporting their effort. It can be a team of full-timers, a team that is fully out-sourced, or a hybrid model. Outsourcing options can provide attractive alternatives for certain cases. For example, you are given a budget of $500,000 USD to build whatever support entity will support you in that organization. How many skilled and senior full-timers can you get for that amount? Compare that to having access to an external via an MSSP relationship. Make your decision considering all the elements you are working with.

This chapter will focus on the buildout and structure of a cybersecurity team staffed with full-timers. But, the same principles and roles can be used to gauge an MSSP if the decision is that model makes more sense. Irrespective, the need for cybersecurity personnel is not just a necessity but a vital component of any business's operational strategy. The task of building or structuring the team requires a strategic approach, an engaged and motivating leader, a deep understanding of cybersecurity principles, and a commitment to team health and continuous learning and improvement. In the case of using an MSSP, the team's health still matters even though you may not be directly overseeing that aspect. If that team is servicing your operation well, you owe it to them to address these types of issues with senior leadership at the MSSP.

ORGANIZATIONAL SIZE

The size of a company has an impact on focal areas and capabilities. As such, the process of building, and structure of, the security team is different for small and large organizations. The size and structure of the security team need to make sense for the organization at hand. For example, take a small company that focuses all customer-facing activities on SaaS products. They rely on those SaaS vendors to protect their data. While things like endpoint protection will matter to that organization, do they really need a data lake and an expensive SIEM?

Typically, a small business security team must be able to operate in these areas:

- Data backup and recovery.
- Endpoint protection (malware, possibly DLP, etc.).
- Password management.
- Phishing/ransomware protection.
- Employee awareness training.

To build an enterprise cybersecurity team, the following need to be considered beyond those areas of concern for a smaller organization:

- Defining the scope of responsibility.
- Building relationships with all relevant entities (legal, privacy, HR, IT, etc.).
- Managing policies (development, updating, etc.).
- Building an enterprise security architecture practice.
- Proactive threat hunting.
- Protecting data and systems through different security controls.
- Measuring maturity through different frameworks and/or methodologies.
- Pursuing active protection mechanisms (MFA, passwordless, zero trust, WAF, etc.).
- Limiting access privileges.
- Having a comprehensive resilience program (IR, DR, BCP).
- Ensuring adherence with regulatory or compliance requirements.

BUILDING A CYBERSECURITY TEAM

Building a cybersecurity team is not just about hiring individuals with certain certifications or technical skills. It involves finding the right people who will be a good fit for the organization; creating a culture that encourages collaboration, innovation, and growth. That culture must have room for growth through failure because there will be failures. Those should become learning opportunities. Here are some key steps in building a healthy and effective cybersecurity team:

- Role and responsibilities – the first step in building a cybersecurity team is to clearly define roles and responsibilities. This involves understanding areas of responsibility, what the team will be protecting, the relevant threat landscapes, and the desired outcomes in terms of results. Also, be clear on leveling as this will dictate the experience levels that recruiters focus on. This clarity helps in recruiting the right people and setting the right expectations.
- Scrutinize existing situations – unfortunately, sometimes a new CISO inherits some situations that are sub-optimal. Look for these as they will require tact in addressing them. For example, some organizations promote folks based on tenure or the need to get individuals into a specific compensation range. The latter is very dangerous because a team can end up with someone very technically skilled but horrible as a leader in a leadership position. In that case, you should consider a shift to a senior principal individual contributor that will not negatively impact the compensation package at hand. But accepting bad leaders is something that should not be tolerated. These types of situations should be resolved as soon as you sync up with HR.
- Hire the right people – first and foremost look for a good bi-directional fit. The candidate must be a good fit for the organization and the organization must be a good fit for the candidate. Otherwise, job satisfaction could become an issue. Hiring the right people is crucial for building an

effective and productive cybersecurity team. Look for individuals who have a deep understanding based on the role requirements, are passionate about cybersecurity, and have a strong desire to learn and grow. It's also important to consider diversity, as diverse perspectives can lead to an awareness of angles not previously considered as well as innovative solutions. Some other points to consider:

- Focus on skills not just certifications or degrees, experience is invaluable. It is a healthy stance to prioritize relevant experience and technical skills over traditional qualifications.
- Depending on the seniority of the role, don't just consider the technical skills required. The soft skills cannot be ignored. If for example, the person in a given role may ever end up speaking in front of senior leaders, soft skills will be more necessary than technical skills. Some of the relevant soft skills are the ability to communicate clearly and with confidence, critical thinking, problem-solving, and adaptability.
- Have realistic expectations. Unrealistic expectations can be the antithesis of mutual benefit where neither party ends up in a healthy positive state. For example, if a solid candidate does not meet all of your requirements but is clearly hungry to grow and has a track record of fast and adaptable learning, look no further.
- Create a culture of collaboration and innovation – a culture of collaboration and innovation is key to building a healthy and effective cybersecurity team. Many people get into the cybersecurity field for the challenges it brings. These types of folks would easily get bored in more traditional IT environments. Encourage team members to be creative in their approach to solving problems, share ideas, and collaborate.
- Stay in tune – where possible stay in tune with the team. There is a reality here regarding team size, but it is possible to periodically take a temperature reading of how things are going. Regular reviews can help improve a team's performance if the intelligence is handled properly. For direct reports, the traditional performance reviews and feedback loops are useful. It is also useful to gather feedback from the many peers that interact regularly with your direct reports, their perspectives can prove very valuable.
  - It would be wise to measure and track the performance of team members. To do so, a good practice is to establish clear and sensible KPIs. Based on those it is possible to evaluate team members effectively and identify areas for improvement.
- Inspire growth – continuous learning and development is important, given that cybersecurity is a rapidly evolving field. Regular training sessions, CTF challenges, conference workshops, and cross-training for further learning can help keep the team engaged and up to date with the latest cybersecurity trends and technologies. Further areas to consider:
  - Internal knowledge sharing is very powerful. It can also lead to organic team bonding. Informal sessions such as learning lunches, coffee chats, ask-me-anything sessions, presentations, and specific peer-to-peer sessions can be very valuable when considering team growth.

- External security resources are plentiful. Pay for access to knowledge bases where relevant, subscribe to industry publications, and research reports as they can all enhance the team's overall value. A plus here is that it also benefits the team members on a personal level.
- Participation in conferences and local events can be beneficial. Encourage attendance at relevant conferences and local security meetups.
- CTFs, hackathons, and bug bounty programs can all be very fun for those in this field. Support this culture of gamifying learning, experimentation, and proactive threat hunting.

Building a healthy and effective cybersecurity team is not simple but it is necessary. It requires active participation from multiple levels of leadership, but the main driving force is usually from the top, the CISO in this case.

STANDARD TEAM STRUCTURE

There are no formulas here, and the material presented here aims to give guidance, things to consider, and some real-world perspectives on the notion of a cybersecurity team. One thing to consider is whether your cybersecurity team will be made up of sub-teams. This decision comes with the risk of fragmentation creeping in over time, the notion of "us versus them" at a team level. The delineations across "teams" seem to be something that starts to get unofficially enforced by team members in that model. An alternative to consider is one cybersecurity team with multiple squads as those delineations tend to be perceived in a softer fashion. Put some thought into this, as a CISO you may be ok with the harder delineations. Or you may want everyone to operate as one team, this tends to work better for organizations with a smaller staffed cybersecurity team.

It should be noted that differentiation between people leaders and individual contributors is important. Avoid the mistake of putting people into leadership positions prematurely, or even when it is just not a good fit, as this can have a devastating impact on a team. There are instances of folks wanting to be leaders really badly, but they are just not leaders.

Many of the roles covered here can have manager and/or director variants. These include those with the senior designation as well. The manager/engineer/analyst relationship is depicted in the "Operations" section. The important areas to home in on are the capabilities and value-add to the organization. Generally, the structure comes down to a combination of these functions and roles (from the CISO perspective and not inclusive):

- Leadership
  - Steering Committee (Cybersecurity or Information Security)
  - Deputy CISO
- Architecture
  - Security Architect
  - Application Security Architect
  - SOC Architect

- Operations
  - SOC Manager
  - SOC Engineer
  - SOC Analyst
  - SIEM Engineer
  - Cybersecurity Incident Responder
  - Threat Intelligence Analyst
  - Vulnerability and Threat Management Program
- Engineering
  - Cybersecurity Engineer
  - Application Security Engineer
  - Cloud Security Engineer
  - Network Security Engineer
  - IAM Specialist
- Cyber GRC
  - Awareness and Training Specialists
  - GRC Specialists

LEADERSHIP

Steering Committee

Steering committees are a telltale sign of a mature security program. When used properly they can become one of the most important security management functions. Steering committees are advisory bodies empowered to address large problems, make organizational-level decisions, and make sure things are moving in the right direction. Keeping in mind these objectives, it should become apparent that steering committees need senior leaders to be part of them. Moreover, these senior leaders need to represent various organizational departments, such as legal, privacy, IT, compliance, sales, etc. The committee holds decision-making power, as such a subset of the members need to have voting rights. An example of voting would be a prioritization of what efforts the team needs to focus on now. Meetings should be held on some regular cadence to review the organization's cybersecurity posture, address current challenges, discuss emerging threats and trends, make recommendations on cybersecurity initiatives, and provide guidance on seeking cybersecurity funding, strategy, and governance.

Deputy CISO

Larger organizations bring on a Deputy CISO to augment the CISO. A Deputy CISO is a senior-level cybersecurity professional who tends to be more tactical and operational than the CISO. They play a crucial role in supporting the CISO in either overseeing an organization's information security program and/or in building new capacity. While their specific responsibilities can vary depending on the organization's business model, size, and structure, here's a general overview of a Deputy CISOs responsibilities:

- Supporting the CISO – Deputy CISOs support CISOs in analyzing, developing, implementing, and managing the overall cybersecurity strategy and related programs. This can involve tasks like application security, penetration tests, vendor selection and management, risk assessments, policy development, and budget management.

- Leading specific programs – they may take ownership of specific security programs such as application and API security, cloud security, operations (incident response, threat hunting, vulnerability management, etc.), and leading and managing teams focused on those respective areas.
- Being the CISO's representative – Deputy CISOs are typically empowered to represent the CISO in various capacities. This is important in larger organizations where a CISO may be spread very thin. These representational activities can be speaking with senior leaders, attending meetings, leading initiatives, and communicating security posture and risks to stakeholders.
- Driving projects – based on specific domain expertise or experience, Deputy CISOs may initiate and lead key security projects to improve control coverage and processes and enhance overall security posture.

ARCHITECTURE

Security Architect

An architect designs the organization's security infrastructure, systems, applications, integrations, and networks. They may work with security frameworks, standards, and best practices (where applicable), ensuring that the organization's technology and processes are aligned with business objectives and security requirements. They aim to add value by weaving in security concerns and, where possible, protective mechanisms into the very design of solutions that engineers will, in turn, build.

Application Security Architect

An application security architect focuses exclusively on introducing security matters into the design of web applications, mobile applications, and APIs. As an example of the value these architects add, consider a set of APIs hosted in conjunction with a web application. Let's say these APIs will use JSON Web Tokens (JWT) to hold sensitive data for transfers across TLS-protected streams. Many developers will consider the use of TLS enough from a security perspective. A good application security architect could suggest improving that model by adding native payload encryption by way of using JSON Web Encryption (JWE) for stronger data security (payload level encryption and decryption).

SOC Architect

This role can be part of Architecture or Operations and needs to exist where it makes most sense for a given organization. This is typically a senior, client-facing role that works toward recognizing organizational needs and translating those into actionable plans and practical security solutions. The SOC architect is responsible for the development of SOC services and processes that are customer-centric. Examples of the relevant responsibilities include ensuring alignment between technical deliverables and organizational strategy, reviewing components (VPNs, vulnerability scanning technologies, etc.) for proper configuration, developing project timelines for future tasks and system upgrades, overseeing the testing of security solutions, and regularly communicating with senior leadership to ensure things are being built for organizational value-add.

OPERATIONS

SOC Manager

SOC managers oversee and directly lead the operational activities of the operations team/squad. They supervise and manage operational activities, helping the operations teams/squads stay focused and on schedule where appropriate. This is typically a senior person who has come up the operator ranks and has deep hands-on experience. This is the type of person others go to when help and advice are needed. They may have experience in designing and implementing operational processes along with expert-level knowledge of SIEM, networking and firewalling concepts, cybersecurity practices, techniques, tools, and different operating systems, such as UNIX, Linux, and Windows.

SOC Engineer

SOC engineers mainly monitor and report events to SOC analysts. They are typically the earliest point of contact in a potentially dangerous situation. Beyond the monitoring of events and such, seasoned engineers build solutions for the SOC. Designing, supporting, troubleshooting, configuring, and upgrading products such as WAFs, FWs, IDS, and VPN all fall within their remit. SOC engineers must take time to properly research, develop, test, and support the tooling that all other SOC team members rely on.

SOC Analyst

SOC analysts are the eyes and ears, the watchdogs of an organization's ecosystem. They monitor the organization's security systems and tools, including log management systems, intrusion detection systems, active protection systems (WAF, etc.), and SIEM solutions. They analyze events, especially from disparate systems, and try to make correlations and/or establish patterns. They also investigate potential incidents and escalate or respond to threats as necessary.

SIEM Engineer

Many security operations programs revolve their efforts around the SIEM as a central component. A SIEM engineer is the one who makes sure that the SIEM is a useful tool for the entire operations program. They have relevant technical skills (might be product-specific) and a deep understanding of the organization's applications, security devices, and infrastructure components that comprise the data sources that feed a SIEM for it to function. SIEM engineers design, develop, maintain, and troubleshoot the SIEM environment(s) an organization uses. They also improve its value through rule and policy creation as well as the design and development of automation capabilities.

Cybersecurity Incident Responders

An incident responder works to handle incidents and analyze security events that may cause significant issues. They generally receive reports in varying forms (email, SIEM alerts, phone calls, etc.) and have the exclusive function of responding to these reports. With the information they get from the reporting source, they get to work and provide deep analysis that helps other team members know how they should act against the activity at hand. Since they get to know processes well, they often have a strong hand in the development of incident response plans and playbooks, conducting drills and tabletop exercises. They are typically part of a larger incident response team and in a mature program, they will also see things all the way through recovery efforts.

The incident response team has multiple members, most likely with multiple incident responders to avoid single points of failure. The key member is whoever has been designated as Incident Commander. An experienced incident responder can easily play the role of incident commander. In the face of a nefarious event, this person leads the incident response team and coordinates the respective organizational response.

Threat Intelligence Analyst

A Threat Intelligence Analyst is responsible for gathering, analyzing, and interpreting data from various sources (government sources, professionally crafted intelligence by professional researchers, OSINT, etc.) to identify potential security threats and vulnerabilities within a given ecosystem. Depending on experience, they may research emerging threats, vulnerabilities, and attacker tactics themselves. Their work is intended to feed a proactive stance and provide actionable intelligence to ensure proper controls exist before potential attacks come. They also collaborate with other security teams to develop strategies and countermeasures to mitigate risks. An example of this could be that a threat intelligence analyst discovers an exploit against a specific plugin used by the corporate Content Management System (CMS). This information needs to be brought to the attention of the application security team as well as the system owners of the CMS. At that point, proactive measures can be taken.

Vulnerability and Threat Management (VTM) Program

VTM refers to the ongoing and consistent process of identifying, evaluating, and reporting on cybersecurity vulnerabilities that may exist across applications, systems, and networks in a company's ecosystem (on-prem, cloud-based, etc.). These identified vulnerabilities offer an attractive opportunity for nefarious actors to perform cyberattacks. The members of a VTM program aim to get ahead of these vulnerabilities before they become an actual attack target.

The typical roles in a VTM program are:

- Vulnerability management specialist – this person is responsible for identifying, prioritizing, and addressing discovered security vulnerabilities within an organization's systems and networks. Their tasks typically include the use of commercial tools for vulnerability scanning, then analyzing those results, prioritizing, and coordinating with relevant teams to remediate any identified issues. The phases of analysis and prioritization cannot be undervalued as the data discovered can grow quite large and unmanageable. Most organizations end up with multiple disparate systems generating vulnerability data, and that data needs to be normalized and prioritized. Once that is complete, the specialist evaluates their severity and potential impact on the organization's security posture.

- Threat hunter – a professional who proactively searches for signs of vulner-abilities, potential areas for breach, or malicious activity within an organi-zation's systems and networks. They use a combination of manual work, tools, techniques, and expertise to seek out these areas of weakness within an ecosystem, especially those that have not yet triggered any alarms or alerts. They actively probe, pen test, analyze network flows, and system logs to uncover hidden threats or patterns of suspicious behavior. By actively seeking out these threats, threat hunters help identify security risks before they can have a negative impact on an organization's business operations.

The data generated by a VTM program is ultimately used in collaboration with rel-evant teams. VTM members work closely with IT teams, security teams, and system owners to ensure timely and effective remediation of vulnerabilities. By effectively managing vulnerabilities, members of the VTM program play a critical role in pro-actively reducing an organization's exposure to potential security threats, increasing that organization's resilience.

Part of the management aspect of a VTM program is the pursuit of applying security patches and other types of remediations. This is known as patch manage-ment. A patch is a specific software update that is applied to fix specific vulner-abilities or technical issues. Other remediations may not come in the form of a patch but are, in essence, performing the same function, an update to address a problem or risk area.

It should be noted that patch management has long been touted as a best prac-tice. Because of this many people in the field of security push for continuous patch management. The real world however is not so Boolean. Patches may fix a security problem but introduce a regression elsewhere or even create new prob-lems. As such, before patches get applied to production-level systems, it is opti-mal that they be tested properly on non-production mirrors. Unfortunately, some environments just don't have these mirror environments, and applying patches either requires risk acceptance or not applying them. Contextually, risk accep-tance means the risk introduced by the patch itself, as it can potentially be prob-lematic as already mentioned.

ENGINEERING

Cybersecurity Engineer

An engineer builds solutions to problems. Cybersecurity engineers are skilled pro-fessionals capable of working on a myriad of challenges and their respective solu-tions. The folks in this role are more generalist in nature, especially compared to some of their highly specialized counterparts. They tackle challenges by analyzing a problem space, researching the appropriate tooling (commercial products, FOSS, etc.), and then building relevant solutions. This typically involves analysis, design, possibly development, and researching and procuring products where appropriate, and possibly invention of the most effective and efficient solution. Depending on the team structure and size this role may also conduct assessments and vulnerability scans.

Application Security Engineers

Application security engineers specialize in securing software applications (web applications, mobile applications, APIs). Typically, these are folks with coding backgrounds who can speak the same language as software engineers and developers. They may conduct analysis of architectures, help design effective penetration tests, conduct code reviews (where possible and applicable), vulnerability assessments, and possibly perform penetration tests to identify and remediate software security flaws. In a mature program, they will also be designers of an organization's Secure Software Development Lifecycle (SSDLC). This often puts them in a position where they will work closely with software development teams to implement secure coding and automated build (CI/CD, DevSecOps) practices (resources allowing of course).

Cloud Security Engineer

A cloud security engineer is responsible for designing, implementing, and maintaining security measures to protect cloud-based environments and the data they store from cyber threats and breaches. This role requires knowledge on multiple levels. On the one hand, these engineers need to have a standard cybersecurity skillset but on the other hand, they need to have very cloud provider-specific knowledge. This is compounded by the fact that many organizations do not play in the cloud space homogeneously and an engineer may have to become knowledgeable in the nuances of multiple cloud offerings. Beyond this, cloud security engineers also own the responsibility of ensuring security of multiple SaaS solutions and the related integrations that typically come with SaaS usage. This SaaS-centric work typically takes the form of reviewing vendor capabilities and ensuring their best security configuration is actually in place.

Network Security Engineers

Network security engineers generally focus on securing the organization's network infrastructure, most likely including where the network spans out to cloud-based ecosystems. They design and implement WAF configurations, load balancers, network segmentation, micro-segmentation, firewalls, IDS/IPS, zero-trust implementations, and other network-enforced security controls.

IAM Specialists

IAM specialists manage user identities, the solutions that house and control user identities, and access control of an organization's systems and applications. They design, implement, and maintain solutions to ensure that only authorized users have access to the resources they need as well as ensure proper provisioning and de-provisioning based on specific events (hiring, termination, promotion, etc.). Other areas where IAM specialists are focused are developing and implementing IAM policies and processes, conducting access reviews and audits, integrating IAM solutions with other systems, and monitoring and responding to security incidents related to identities.

Oftentimes, Privileged Access Management (PAM) and access control fall within the scope of IAM. Those who have special access privileges need special attention because a breach of those accounts can instantly become problematic in comparison to a user who doesn't seamlessly have access to important resources. The IAM experts have the responsibility of designing working access control and management solutions that allow for business functionality but prevent unauthorized access to protected resources. Some examples of areas where IAM specialists may focus are adopting a zero-trust approach to security, enforcing MFA, and creating just-in-time access policies.

Cyber GRC

Awareness and Training Specialists

This role focuses on educating employees about resilience to threats, cybersecurity best practices, internal policies, and relevant regulatory requirements. They develop training materials, conduct security awareness programs, test the effectiveness of these programs, and help employees understand their role in maintaining a safe work environment.

GRC Specialists

GRC Specialists, also known as auditors, ensure that the organization adheres to industry standards, relevant regulatory requirements, and internal policies. They assess, measure, and track the organization's compliance posture and maturity levels as well as coordinate audits. Typically, these are the folks who perform the bulk of the work when an organization seeks out things like SOC2 reports, ISO 2700X certifications, PCI-DSS compliance, etc.

Other Possible Roles

The following are other roles that may be found on a security team. These are based on need and an organization's business model. The "specialist" part is being used generically as these roles can take the form of engineer, architect, or specialist.

AI Security Specialist

AI security entails protecting systems that are either providing AI features or are integrated with systems that do. AI security specialists are responsible for identifying and addressing potential security risks in these applications, developing policies, leveraging frameworks, and staying up to date on emerging threats and best practices in the field of AI security. The analytical component of this role requires one to think beyond just standard attacks because, for example, there is the possibility for misuse via crafty wording that fools a GPT application into exposing sensitive data.

AI security specialists must perform analysis and design protective controls around many different attack scenarios, such as:

- Prompt injections – a type of attack where an attacker injects misleading or incorrect prompts into an AI system in order to manipulate its behavior and output. This type of logical attack can lead to biased outcomes and undermine the reliability and trustworthiness of the AI system.
- Poisoning attacks – a type of attack where the attacker manipulates model training data in order to distort the learning process and cause an AI system

to generate inaccurate outputs. Poisoning attacks assume the attacker does not actually have access to the target model. If the attacker does have access to the model, this is an attack variant known as a "trojan" attack.

- Inference attacks – these attacks exploit information leakage from AI systems to infer sensitive data (e.g., PII, PHI, etc.) about individuals or organizations.
- Evasion attacks – a type of attack that involves manipulating input data in order to deceive the AI system into making incorrect predictions or classifications. A specific form of evasion attack known as "adversarial" aims to achieve the same objective by modifying input data in a way that is not detectable to humans.
- Extraction attacks – these attacks probe an AI system in an attempt to learn information about the internal workings of an AI model in order to reconstruct it or steal it.
- Backdoor attacks – a type of attack that involves inserting malicious code during model training. The code could activate specific behaviors in the AI system, such as providing disinformation, incorrect predictions, or classifications.

Operational Technology (OT) Security Specialist

OT, Industrial Control Systems (ICS), and Supervisory Control and Data Acquisition (SCADA) are terms that may be used interchangeably within the security world. Irrespective of the title, these folks are focused on protecting critical infrastructure, manufacturing, robotics, and the entire space of non-standard computing devices (PLCs, motors, turbines, etc.). Their main duties include all the standard security functions (vulnerability assessments, penetration tests, etc.) generally practiced with the caveat that many of the OT communication protocols (Modbus/TCP, DNP3, etc.) are radically different from those known in the IT space (HTTP, SMTP, FTP, etc.).

Another major caveat is that IT security practices have limited value in OT/ICS environments. Some of the areas where there is overlap are in air gapping, network segmentation, network-level access controls, and IDS solutions. But, there are simply differences between IT and OT environments that can complicate the effectiveness of these IT security practices. Some of the considerations that OT security specialists must face are:

- Legacy systems: Many OT systems run on older, legacy equipment and operating systems that may not be compatible with modern security tools and updates.
- Real-time operations: OT environments require real-time monitoring and operation, making it difficult to implement security measures that could potentially disrupt operations.
- Limited resources: OT environments often have limited resources and expertise to implement and maintain complex security measures.
- Complexity: OT environments are highly complex and interconnected, making it difficult to fully understand and secure all components.

- Human error: OT systems are often operated by non-technical personnel who may not have the necessary training or awareness of security best practices.

Data Security Specialist

A data security specialist is responsible for protecting an organization's data (inside of files, stored in DBs, etc.) from cyber threats and unauthorized access. Protection within this context basically means avoiding data leakage and unauthorized exfiltrations. Data security specialists operate at multiple levels (DB, cloud, attack surface, etc.) and design and implement security controls, native protective mechanisms, conduct regular security audits, and sometimes provide training to employees on best practices for data protection. This role requires an understanding of data at multiple stages through its lifecycle, creation, storage, classification, in transit, and in use. It also requires being very comfortable with storage models and structures, such as text-based data formats, structured data, and unstructured data.

Intimate knowledge of certain products is necessary. For example, if a relational DB stores PII, it would be optimal to natively (at the DB level) encrypt that data at rest. The encryption is likely targeting the specific column within a given table. "Encrypting a database" is a questionable notion and that term often gets used incorrectly. Plus, the performance of a DB of any substantial size would be negatively impacted if the entire thing was encrypted. But, encrypting a column may be possible depending on the DB product. This requires knowledge of the DB product at hand. It also requires interacting with all known and authorized touch points (application, scripts, etc.) so that they can be taught to effectively decrypt the data when it is needed.

Resilience Specialist

Resilience specialists focus on availability. Their approach is usually balanced between the proactive (high availability, redundant systems, BCP) and the reactive (DR). They typically perform some analysis of existing BCP/DR plans and architectures followed by recommendations if any are in order. They are also very involved with tests, such as chaos engineering exercises, that validate the effectiveness of existing resilience solutions (geographic load balancing, automated failovers, elastic cloud elements based on load spikes, etc.).

RED, BLUE, PURPLE

Red, blue, and purple teams can be put together in very productive ways even though they don't need to be permanent entities. The three terms typically refer to groups of individuals, made up of the roles already covered here, within an organization who are responsible for different aspects of cybersecurity offense and defense.

- Red team – the red team represents the offensive side of cybersecurity, the attackers. They are responsible for simulating cyber-attacks to test the effectiveness of the organization's defenses. This helps proactively identify weaknesses in the cybersecurity posture, allowing the blue team to improve protective mechanisms. Red team members often include threat hunters, penetration testers, ethical hackers, and security consultants.

- Blue team – the blue team represents the defensive or protective side of cybersecurity, the defenders. They focus on actively protecting the organization's resources from cyber threats. The active part is important because this is not about incident response after some damage has been done. Blue team members typically include security engineers and analysts who work to prevent and detect incidents.
- Purple team – The purple team is a combination of the blue and red teams. It represents a collaborative effort between offensive and defensive cybersecurity practices. Purple team exercises involve joint efforts between the two teams to improve overall protective effectiveness. This is also a very effective way to get offensive and defensive-minded folks to cross-train and push toward a well-balanced team.

Regarding the roles that have been covered here, be aware that there are times when some roles do not cleanly fit into the traditional structure. Take for example an organization that is a holding company, a parent company that owns many other businesses as business units. The parent company will most likely not have a large software engineering function as opposed to the business units that are building customer-facing applications. The cybersecurity function at the parent company level has application security experts. Do they fit into the architectural function to influence early development and SDLC efforts? Or do they fit into an operational role where they focus on application security after those applications have already been written and deployed? These are the types of decisions that security leadership needs to make with an understanding of the business and its organizational culture and needs.

CERTIFICATIONS

Opinions vary regarding the landscape of security-related certifications that are available and surely there will be more to come. Like so many things there are pros and cons.

Pros

- Credibility – customers and others in the business may view certified professionals as more credible, and more reliable in their ability to handle cybersecurity challenges.
- Skill validation – cybersecurity certifications can demonstrate that an individual possesses the knowledge and skills needed to effectively perform a job in security.
- Networking opportunities – certification programs often include access to networking events, forums, and communities. This provides your certified team members opportunities to connect with other professionals in the field. This can be beneficial by way of bringing back insights from other's experiences and perspectives.

Cons

*   Cost – obtaining cybersecurity certifications can be expensive and employees may expect the company to pay for them.
*   Time – studying for and obtaining certifications can be time-consuming, taking away from the responsibilities you have placed on these folks.
*   Rapidly changing landscape – the cybersecurity landscape is constantly evolving, which means that certifications may quickly become outdated and require recertification.

The real-world value of security-centric certifications requires the coupling of the certification itself with a valid, scrutinizing interview process. It is the interviewer's job to probe past the textbook knowledge required to pass an exam. The certification needs to be backed up with real knowledge and, better yet, experience. Focusing on an individual who does possess real knowledge and experience, certifications provide tangible evidence of this knowledge. Moreover, certifications represent a personal commitment to the field of cybersecurity.

MAINTAINING A CYBERSECURITY TEAM

Team maintenance is an often-overlooked area. Without a healthy and productive team, a CISOs ability to succeed starts to diminish. As such, ensuring a security team is engaged and caring should be a goal (even if a silent one) for any CISO. This comes down to being committed to the team, engaging with them, and building a security culture with the right mindsets. Here are some considerations:

KEEPING THE TEAM ENGAGED

Aim to have a positively engaged team. This is a stressful field, and making everyone satisfied at work is an unrealistic goal. But some of the following recommendations can help:

*   Keep them challenged – most people in cybersecurity fear boredom more than anything. Aim at keeping them challenged and personally growing with interesting projects.
*   Take them out of their comfort zones – many people dislike public speaking, but it is an essential soft skill. Motivate team members to speak in public settings, even if internal company events.
*   Rotate roles – move folks around so that they get to experience different areas of cybersecurity. These diverse challenges and learning opportunities can prevent boredom and stagnation.
*   Promote autonomy and ownership – most professionals don't appreciate being micromanaged as they take it as a sign of distrust. Empower team members to take ownership of solutions, projects, and decisions.

- Offer paths for growth – create career development paths for those who want to grow. A CISO can create these paths for progression and possibly specialization within the team.
- Recognize achievements – publicly acknowledge and reward individual and team successes.
- Create a fun environment – encourage some fun at work with interesting challenges that will foster collaboration and team building.

CONTINUOUS LEARNING

Enabling continuous growth via learning is mutually beneficial. Consider some of the following:

- Subscription to security resources – provide access to expert/industry advisory services, professional publications, and analyst research reports.
- Participation in conferences and events – encourage attendance and speaking engagements at relevant conferences and security meetups.
- Career coaching – where you feel there is value, sponsor career and/or executive coaching.
- Regular training and workshops – invest in industry-recognized training programs and specialized workshops.
- Hackathons – foster a culture of curiosity, experimentation, and proactive threat hunting.
- Internal knowledge sharing – organize lunch and learn sessions, presentations, and peer-to-peer presenting/learning opportunities.

Beyond that, consider starting things like an annual Cyber Summit (or whatever you decide to call it) to bring many people from disparate functions together around cybersecurity themes. The goals could be:

- Education of security team – bring in industry experts to cover existing and expected challenges.
- Enable dialogue and partnerships – interactions that bring together different perspectives are always valuable and can lead to smarter policies, controls, and more effective user awareness training.
- Inspire innovation – consider creating opportunities for sponsoring innovations. For example, put some budget aside to fund some invention the team comes up with and make it a committee-voted decision as to which idea will get funded.
- Provide diverse professional networking – if enough variety is introduced in the audience this could be bi-directionally beneficial for leaders across public, private, and academic spaces.

Properly structuring a cybersecurity team can take time. The age-old advice of hiring slowly is very valid as some people are great talkers yet produce very little. It is your job to seek out truly talented and productive people for your team. A CISO has comprehensive control and authority over who ends up on the team. But remember that best practice for one organization may not translate equally as what is best for your organization. The team (internal, MSSP, hybrid) you put together has to make sense for your particular organization.

EXPERT ADVICE

I recently spoke at a Technology conference on the subject of leading high-performing teams. I was preparing my speech and reflecting on my career while doing so. I wanted to share some of my learnings. In crafting my key-note, I immediately came to a choice, I could highlight some of the great teams and leaders that I had come across and juxtapose them against some of the bluntly terrible ones I had had and of course what made them terrible.

So, I guess the first lesson is that you have a choice. And this is critical to leadership and leading teams. One of the most impactful prayers I learned at school (all boys Jesuit boarding – but that is another story in its entirety for another day) was the prayer of St. Thomas Aquinas – or the Serenity Prayer. "Give me the Serenity to understand those things I can change, those things that I can't, and the wisdom to know the difference".

As a leader, there are things you can change. You can change how you come to work. You can own, as opposed to passing down a problem. You can shield your team from turbulence as opposed to distributing it. So, in writing this piece I chose only to focus on the positives. Like this choice, there are others that a leader has: what you accept, what you tolerate, what standards you set, what you prioritize; "the what" or "the how".

I had the privilege to serve in the British Army for 12 years and there I took two critical things with respect to leadership which are still with me. Have a "North Star" and ensure that your team knows what this is and buys in.

This North Star can change and you need to adapt it as the situation changes. Our threat is dynamic and evolves. The key aspect is that as the North Star (or mission) changes the team must be fully read in and also fully bought in. If everyone is clear on their objectives, knows where they have to get to and why they have to get to, the team operates at a higher level. Further, once this understanding is reached, then other critical aspects like empowerment and "mission command" (I want you to take this hill, but I won't interfere in how you do it) come into play.

The second important aspect I took from the Army was Servant Leadership. Indeed, it was the motto on our cap badge at Sandhurst "Serve to Lead". That, to me, means that you are in the service of your team. In a log run, you are first on the log. You lead by example.

I had an interesting discussion with a "top leadership coach". His argument was you should never be on the log. That job is for others. I think I must have been ineloquent in my arguments, as there was no changing his mind. It is all about example and doing the hard yards with the team, not micromanagement or doing their job for them but showing them that if there is going to be some hard work, simply, you are the first in and last out. Others will then follow. You eat last in case the food runs out. You shun the executive dining room and join your team in the canteen, you are first to an incident and the last to leave. You leave your executive office and walk the floors. I firmly believe that though there are many others, having these two pillars (North Star and Servant Leadership) as your foundation you will not go far wrong. In moving from military to commercial life, there were other aspects of leadership that I learned. I teased it in the second paragraph.

I learned that the How is as important, if not more so, than the What. There is no point in delivering all of your objectives and projects if no one will want to work with you and if you leave a dozen broken people behind you. I initially found some of this hard to discern. Some of this is hidden in the hierarchical nature of the military and of course the necessary inflexibility of some missions due to the peril or jeopardy that they inherently contain.

However, in civilian life, these are clearly rarer. Indeed, as the proverb says: to go fast you go alone, but to go far you need to go together. If you do not concentrate on the How I firmly believe that all that will be achieved is a Pyrrhic victory at best. You will only be followed out of fear and neither respect nor buy-in. An objective will be achieved but the cost will be significant, it will unlikely be repeatable, and malicious compliance will follow. The focus on the "How", combined with Servant Leadership ethos, will soon develop a fertile ground for other important concepts to develop. I remember working at a major US defense and aerospace company and looking at the criteria to achieve an "outstanding" rating. One initially surprised me which was "this person is not afraid to fail". I was initially taken aback; our work was mission-critical, surely failure was not an option. But then thinking about it more and reflecting on how some of the world's amazing "moonshots" have landed, they are nearly all grounded in failure. No one has landed their shot the first time. It is all about trying, failing, learning, adjusting, and trying again. A leader cannot fall for Wylie Coyote syndrome – giving up on an idea after the first failure.

Being allowed to do this is not only great for innovation but also creates psychological safety within your teams. It breeds curious people, ones that want to solve problems and achieve, stretch goals, as they know that there will be no punishment, loss of face, or finger-pointing. Further, this attitude fosters a culture where mistakes are not covered up, which means the team can move faster together knowing that having all the same aims they are safe with each other. And if you think about it, this is second on Maslow's hierarchy of needs (safety) only being beaten by the physiological (eat, sleep, breathe, etc.)

Finally, a leader (and not a manager) is a role model of these behaviors. Teams copy the behaviors of their leaders. A fish rots from the head and if the leader is rotten then so will the team.

So, distilling this into a playbook for leaders:

1. You have a choice. There will be things you can control and things you cannot. Focus on the ones you can.
2. Align your teams to a North Star and get their buy-in – but this can change.
3. It is a privilege to serve your team. Be the first on the log and the last to eat. Make sure that everyone is taken care of before you look after yourself.
4. The "How" is more important than the "What" – be aware of the Pyrrhic victory.
5. Build a culture of psychological safety where your team is not afraid to fail. This will unlock the keys to innovation and also transparency.

– Stuart Seymour, Group CISO, Virgin Media O2

8 Be an Executive Leader

A CISOs main goals are to protect what a business has gained (revenue, etc.) and to facilitate a business pushing forward and growing. This clearly implies that a CISO is an executive leader, one that needs to operate and carry themselves as such.

EXECUTIVE QUALITIES

Here are some general qualities and/or goals for an executive leader in any capacity:

- Personal growth – a good executive understands the value of constantly learning and growing. Executives need to be in the right headspace in order to effectively lead others. Being at this level does not mean one has all the answers, but one does carry a lot of responsibility. As such, it is an executive's responsibility to always seek improvement. Embrace continuous learning and work hard to be up-to-date on industry trends, best practices, and emerging technologies.
  - As part of this personal growth journey, humbly and actively seek feedback from peers, colleagues, mentors, and stakeholders to identify areas for improvement. Embrace constructive criticism as a gift and an opportunity to improve.
  - Be self-aware to avoid burnout. Prioritize and make time for your well-being. This way you can sustain your leadership effectiveness. A disengaged or burnt-out leader adds no value to anyone. Ensure you have outlets so that a balance with work can be achieved. Also, make time for rest, relaxation, and other personal pursuits.
- Selflessness – consider the creation and raising of other leaders as part of your personal leadership mission. While there are different camps when it comes to assessing the value of this, raising the next generation of leaders comes with various benefits. These include: succession planning, positively impacting someone else's life, and setting up the current organization with leaders that are already in tune with the organizational culture at hand.
- Vision – effective leaders are strategic thinkers who have a clear vision of where they want to take things. These leaders think long-term and set out a clear path for where they want an organization to go.
  - Along with a solid vision be aware of the need for flexibility and agility. Most businesses are continuously dealing with changing market landscapes. A CISO needs to constantly adapt and be prepared to adapt to these evolving market conditions. Moreover, be prepared to adapt to continuous technological advancements. The assets a CISO is tasked with protecting are most likely technological. With that remit comes the reality of staying on top of technological evolutions. As such, you

DOI: 10.1201/9781003477556-8

must continuously assess and refine your strategy to maintain or gain business/competitive advantage.

- Communication – following through from the point about having and setting a vision, communication of said vision is just as important as the vision itself. Effective leaders can communicate vision, strategy, and direction in a way that inspires others to follow. This requires people that are clear communicators of organizational goals, priorities, and plans. A good executive leader will listen to understand the needs of those they lead. Then when the time comes, they tailor communications for their audience.
  - Along with being an effective communicator, an executive must exercise transparency via openness and honesty. To be clear here, this must be genuine. One should aim to foster a culture of trust and transparency, and this requires honesty, even when delivering difficult news.
  - Communication needs to be bi-directional. This means taking the time to actively listen to feedback. A common complaint in the corporate rank and file is that they have no voice, a good executive will give them one whenever possible.
    - Embrace diverse perspectives, especially while engaging in communication. Apply value to diverse opinions and viewpoints as they may open possibilities not encountered before.
  - Create a safe space for disagreement and constructive criticism. So long as this is focused on healthy growth it will prove its value over time.
- Emotional intelligence (EQ) – effective leaders are in control of their emotions. Moreover, they have the ability to read others' emotional cues. This gives them the ability to build rapport and human connection by demonstrating empathy, vulnerability, and a sense of humor when appropriate. This ability can take a leader far by motivating and influencing others in a positive way.
- Integrity – leaders with integrity build trust by being ethical, honest, and consistent in their actions. They make decisions, especially the difficult kind, based on core principles and values. Leaders who display a lack of integrity tend to build toxic environments and end up with no credibility and no one willing to follow them.
- Accountability – effective leaders are not afraid to own mistakes and/or take personal responsibility for their decisions and/or actions. When mistakes happen, good leaders confront those situations decisively before they spiral out of control. They don't blame others as they know ultimately a leader is responsible.
- Decisiveness – effective leaders act. They may wait to have sufficient data to make informed decisions, but they display strength and confidence by making decisions swiftly and firmly. Procrastination and indecision often make for situations where followers have no faith or confidence in a given leader, or team of leaders (e.g., a C-Suite, etc.). Leaders need to be comfortable making the best decision they can with the information at hand.
  - Seek out balance between risk and reward. Most business decisions carry some risk. Own that. But use data points to weigh the potential

consequences of each decision carefully. As an executive, you should aim to identify and mitigate potential risks while pursuing opportunities for growth, revenue, or the pursuit of a mission.

Homing in on cyber and/or information security executive leadership, some added, more focused, qualities start coming to light:

- Vision – cybersecurity leaders need a vision based on proactivity. For too long the cybersecurity industry has operated in a purely reactive state. This vision needs to span across the following areas: enabling safe business to happen, technological innovations, the handling of emerging threats, continuous personnel/team skills development, and process improvements. This vision clearly touches many different areas but should closely map with business goals and objectives.
- Staying current – cyber and information security are incredibly fast-moving, volatile domains. Leaders need to stay on top of the latest exploits, APTs, threats, technology developments, and regulatory developments. Continuous learning is a priority for leaders and their up and downstream teams. This helps inform proactive measures, incident response functions, and strategic plans.
- Proactiveness – the cyber landscape is always evolving. Reactive security, while necessary and a reality, will never compare to proactively having defenses that work. This means advancing cyber resilience through advanced techniques (predictive analytics, moving target defense, disinformation, honeypots, intelligent systems), architectural upgrades, training employees in up-to-date tactics and techniques, continuous penetration testing, live disaster recovery testing (e.g., chaos engineering, etc.), and more. Complacency and reactivity are dangerous things of the past.
- Communication – clearly conveying cyber risk to boards and C-Suite to obtain support (priorities, budgetary, human resources, etc.) for cyber-related endeavors is crucial. Leaders need to be able to translate cybersecurity priorities into business objectives, and cybersecurity risk to potential financial impact, such that they resonate across the organization.
- Collaboration – cyber and information security are both team sports, and this makes collaboration a key executive quality. Breaking down silos and facilitating collaboration between security and other departments is vital for security to become part of an organization's culture. Effective cyber leaders actively work to have themselves and their teams work cooperatively with others.
- Accountability – effective leaders create accountability structures and use things like metrics reporting and audits to measure and track progress. Those structures should aim to not create an environment of micromanagement. A good CISO aims to empower the security team leaders through trust, giving them autonomy and ownership of responsibilities. In this case, success and failure are fairly the responsibility of those being held accountable.

Irrespective of whether a CISO is part of the executive team, a CISO occupies a unique position in most organizations. The uniqueness is obvious by way of all the things a CISO needs to be in order to pursue success. One of those areas is where a CISO must manage relationships with both superiors (managing up) and subordinates (managing down). Mastering this delicate balancing act is critical for success as an executive but especially so for a CISO. With robust strategies for managing up and down the hierarchy, CISOs can transform into influential business leaders who align security with business goals.

MANAGING UP

A core part of the role involves managing up to the C-Suite and the Board of Directors. Part of managing up involves regularly interfacing and effectively communicating with these organizational leaders. During these interfacing sessions, the notion of managing upward becomes real, the following tips are helpful to succeed:

- Know your audience – study and learn what excites or worries your C-Suite and member of the board. Learn their priorities and concerns. Meet with key stakeholders early on and have candid conversations to understand their business objectives, challenges, and pain points related to security. Then make this a continuous process. On each iteration aim to gain insights that you can keep top of mind during future communications.
- Speak in business terms – learn the data points that resonate with your target audience. The C-Suite is generally concerned with anything that keeps a business in a healthy state. If you are addressing risk, don't just present it, quantify it as well and then present that in business terms, in terms of how said risk can negatively impact the business. Executives generally respond best to risk assessments quantified in dollars and potential impact to the business. Hence, a CISO needs to translate cyber risks into concepts like loss of revenue, loss of customers, fines and penalties from regulators, and legal exposure.
- Ensure alignment – always aim to align security strategy to business objectives. It is imperative that a CISO direct a security program clearly. Once support and alignment are in place, business objectives like improved operational efficiency, reduced expenditures, reduced risk exposure, and increased competitive advantage become very possible. If a CISO can achieve some of these objectives a set of executives cannot deny the business value of that security program.
- Demystify cybersecurity – educate leadership in simple terms about the real cyber threats facing the organization. More importantly, make it personal. Subjects like cybersecurity almost always resonate with an audience when it is presented in terms of how it can impact them. Many executives have limited security expertise, so awareness building and education are key. Real-world stories are generally impactful, so weave in examples of how your team has successfully detected and prevented threats in the past. Concrete success stories build confidence and support amongst executive leaders.

- Set regular touch points – establish a cadence of quarterly updates, monthly reports, or even weekly (formal or informal) check-ins to keep leaders and stakeholders regularly informed and invested.
- Present options, not mandates – frame security recommendations as options. It is always best to have willing partners, rather than force someone into a partnership. Link options to risk management such that the audience is invested in an outcome. Fairly and neutrally present and/or discuss pros, cons, costs, and trade-offs of each option.
- Manage third-party security vendors – oversee external security vendors diligently to ensure they meet contract obligations and any standards set by the security team. Vet them thoroughly and seek validation of any claims.
  - For example, ask a SaaS vendor how they protect your data once it is in their ecosystem. Have this vendor prove their claims to your team rather than accept claims at face value.
- Conduct tabletop exercises – for these to be effective they must be conducted with both the technical teams and with leadership. Run simulated breach scenarios with stakeholders, incident response teams, security team members, and system owners to test and improve processes and plans at varying levels of the organization. Some of the teams mentioned here are not necessarily included in the notion of "managing up" but in the face of a negative event, a CISO needs to ensure these team members have some experience directly interfacing with executive leaders.
  - As an example, those with hands-on keyboards during an incident response may be very technical and have limited communication experiences with executives. Some executives feel the pressure of incidents and can be demanding or ask open-ended questions. The pressure these executives put on incident responders can take a toll. Open-ended questions can be a problem to some folks who are more pragmatic and linear thinking, leading to frustration, confusion, and possibly a derailing of response efforts. It's better to catch this before it happens as a real event.
- Stay calm under pressure – during high-stakes security incidents, keep leaders regularly updated with facts, next steps, and reassurances in a calm, competent manner. During stressful situations, such as high-stakes budget negotiations, keep things unemotional, neutral, and factual. Stick to data points and manage both your and their anxieties.

The principle of managing up is all about understanding. It's about you understanding your leadership. By gaining awareness into what their goals, motivators, and operational modes are, you can build a healthy relationship that is mutually beneficial but also benefits the larger organization. Ultimately, remember that the folks you are managing up can have a substantial impact on your career trajectory. Consistently delivering value-add helps this audience easily notice your talents, qualities, and abilities.

MANAGING DOWN

Besides interfacing effectively with executive leadership, managing down to build a high-performing security team is equally crucial for a CISOs success. Some strategies for effectively managing down are:

- Lead by example – this cannot be understated. One of the best ways to gain the respect and support of the people reporting to you is to lead by example. If you are seen as an ivory tower-type leader your position may be feared but you will not be respected. Lead in a style modeled with strength, ethics, and commitment. Roll up your sleeves when necessary and avoid asking the team to do anything you would not.
- Clearly define roles and responsibilities – create clear-cut role definitions and delineations (boundaries) detailing each team member's role, duties, decision rights, and metrics of success. Often, team members want to know exactly what they are responsible for and being evaluated on. The crossing of boundaries does happen of course but organizational culture plays a strong role here. If for instance, a given organization clearly frowns upon blurred boundaries most employees will be respectful of this.
- Hire wisely and strategically – be very picky with your hiring. Unfortunately, in some organizations, once someone is an employee, they are difficult to get rid of. There is truth to the old business concept that a leader should hire slow and fire fast. This means that one should take their time when finding the right person and bringing them into the organization. Conversely, if things are not working out, let that person go quickly. Ultimately, aim to build a balanced cross-functional team with complementary technical and soft skills. Assess candidates thoroughly for culture fit, and fill roles based on real organizational needs and not "best practice".
  - As an example, take an organization that outsources its security operations to a Managed Security Services Provider (MSSP). Do they really need SIEM experts on staff? Maybe they do based on volume. Maybe they like having someone directly managing the MSSP staff from within the organization. But maybe they don't need that role filled. The point is to hire wisely based on real needs.
- Empower the teams/squads and delegate – it is fair to say that most people dislike being untrusted. As a leader, part of your job is to grow those under you structurally. Foster trust by pushing decision-making authority down to the appropriate levels. Also, delegate strategic initiatives to help team members grow. Nothing teaches like real experience so allow your team to get some. This means expecting, accepting, and learning from failures along the way. Failure is a great teacher. Failure is inevitable. Failure will ultimately empower your team members to go forth with confidence.
- Maintain open communication – encourage open dialogue in both directions. Solicit input proactively and regularly. Respond to concerns transparently. Share context and explain the rationale behind decisions. This will

help build bi-directional trust. A lack of communication can be the death sentence of working relationships.

- Be transparent and be consistent. Hidden agendas, or even the perception of them, can make for an unhealthy or toxic work environment. Within the realm of what is not violating any laws, communicate openly. Admit mistakes honestly to the team and show resilience, don't just talk about it. Showing the team mistakes and failures are ok and they are just hurdles that can go a long way in building team confidence.
- Don't stop at just communication, promote collaboration. Fragmented and siloed teams can make for a toxic work environment. Work to break down silos by facilitating collaboration, knowledge sharing, and networking. Security-specific collaboration can be achieved by building security champion programs within business units. These programs can be very successful but they take time and energy to build. Be ready for some pushback from leaders within the targeted business units because they may see this as a time suck on employees that could already have a maxed-out workload. These situations are very real, and oftentimes require a lot of collaboration and influence at the leadership level in order to put them in motion.

- Set clear goals and metrics – Collaborate to define specific, measurable, achievable, relevant, and time-bound (SMART) goals. Make sure these goals are aligned to business objectives and then track progress relentlessly.
- Don't dictate, motivate – cultivate passion and drive rather than give orders. Part of this is connecting work functions to a compelling vision. Aim to motivate team members to want to do their best. Recognize and reward contributions as this reinforces when someone has performed in a positive way.
- Develop the team – continuously keep yourself looking for skill gaps and invest in technical and soft skills training as needed. This requires being very connected to at least the leaders directly reporting to you. It is important for a leader to uplift team members. This needs to be done based on organizational needs but also with a keen eye on personal development.
  - Sometimes an early start toward leadership is in order, and you should look to identify future leaders as soon as possible. Enable their professional development and growth via training, education, and executive coaching.
  - Become a coach and mentor yourself. For both team members and young candidates outside your organization, it is important that you help raise up the next generation of leaders. This includes providing developmental assignments and regular constructive feedback tailored to individuals. The goal is to help them continuously improve and develop while taking on greater responsibilities.
  - Part of team development is being sensitive to burnout. Support work-life balance and respect personal time. Unless necessary you should

discourage excessive out-of-hours work. Here again, you can lead by example, and show the team that maintaining a healthy work-life separation is possible.

- Budget adequately – it is the CISO's job to fight to secure an adequate budget and headcount to execute a strategy. An important part of this budget is the justification of business cases for a healthy team size with proper tooling.
- Monitor workloads – actively keep watch over workloads and morale. Be ready to step in at signs of excessive overtime or unrealistic workloads that can lead to burnout. Have regular skip level 1:1s to spot issues.

By mastering the acts of "managing up" and "managing down", CISOs can become truly strategic business partners. This while also fostering an empowered, motivated, and aligned cybersecurity team. Enable your team(s) with radical candor, clarity, empowerment, and development. With this up/down balance, CISOs can transform into credible, effective business leaders delivering value, beyond just protection, to an organization.

EXPERT ADVICE

In today's intricate digital terrain, the paramount importance of prioritizing cybersecurity within an executive's strategic commercial framework cannot be emphasized enough. The safeguarding of intellectual property and sensitive information is a cornerstone of success in the Information Age where the material repercussions of cybersecurity breaches on stakeholder trust and consumer confidence can be both immediate, severe, and tangible. It is incumbent upon executives to lead the charge in cultivating a cybersecurity-conscious culture within their organizations. This entails ensuring that each employee is not only aware of but also actively participates in the protection of the company's strategic assets and reputation. By doing so, executives can turn their workforce into a formidable first line of defense against cyber threats.

Moreover, executives should not shy away from seeking external expertise to rigorously evaluate their cybersecurity posture. Welcoming outside perspectives can serve as a powerful catalyst for critical self-assessment, helping to mitigate the risks of myopia and complacency that can endanger an organization's cybersecurity defenses. Engaging with specialists from outside the organization to scrutinize and challenge the existing cybersecurity strategy fosters an environment of continuous improvement and innovation. This approach not only enhances the resilience of cybersecurity measures but also ensures that strategies remain adaptable and responsive to the ever-evolving landscape of digital threats.

**– Surinder Lall, SVP Global Information Security Risk
Management, Paramount**

REAL-WORLD PERSPECTIVE

In 1997, David Ghantt's audacious heist of over $17 million from the bank he worked at remains a gripping tale. However, beyond the sensational headlines lies a narrative of workplace dissatisfaction and the ramifications it can have in today's ever-evolving professional landscape. Ghantt, once a loyal vault supervisor at Loomis, Fargo & Co., found himself disillusioned by grueling 80-hour work weeks for a paltry wage, setting the stage for the daring act of embezzlement.

Fast forward to the present day, and the contours of discontent within the workplace have taken on new forms in the era of hybrid work environments. No longer confined to traditional expressions of dissatisfaction, such as outright resignations or strikes, modern discontent can manifest in subtler ways. Employees may become disengaged, resort to passive-aggressive behaviors, or even engage in acts of insubordination or workplace bullying.

However, the implications of such discontent extend far beyond mere disruptions to workflow or team dynamics. Disgruntled employees, particularly those entrusted with critical assets, can pose significant monetary and reputational risks to organizations. Whether through intentional sabotage, inadvertent negligence, or exploitation of digital vulnerabilities, the fallout from employee dissatisfaction can be profound and not always manageable by the tried-and-true security apparatus.

In an era marked by rapid technological advancement, the nature of threats faced by organizations has evolved. While traditional bank heists may capture headlines, the real danger lies in the digitized secrets that organizations hold. Intellectual property, sensitive customer data, and proprietary information are all coveted targets for cybercriminals seeking to exploit vulnerabilities in a modern digital infrastructure.

While security leaders often prioritize safeguarding high-value digital assets such as intellectual property, it's the seemingly mundane data and digital resources that often fly under the radar. Personally identifiable information (PII), for instance, may seem innocuous until mishandled by an employee with access privileges. The ramifications of such lapses can be severe, ranging from breaches of privacy, facilitating identity theft, government fines, or corporate espionage.

Ranging from disgruntled employees, distributed infrastructure, rapid prototyping with sensitive data, or traditional corporate environments, one thing has always remained true – without the full support of the executive community within an organization the task is an uphill battle. How does one step into the shoes of the executive mindset? What drives them? What keeps them up at night? What headwinds are they considering for the next month, year, decade? Do you have a seat at that table to understand the ramifications of your decisions?

Here is a high-level point of view with a few practical lessons for driving positive momentum in a security program to support this changing landscape.

1. Harness the Power of Storytelling – I always considered this a soft approach to serious security challenges, however, reflecting on a past role overseeing technology, I've learned that executives and employees alike require more than just training – they need awareness campaigns and safeguards to operate within. I remember encountering resistance to security investments until I illustrated the risks vividly, even beginning a presentation with a striking image of handcuffs. While such tactics may seem drastic, what matters is conveying the monetary, reputational, and personal risks convincingly. Executives are not concerned with how the "Blowfish algorithm will replace Triple DES encryption"; they care about safeguarding intellectual property from potential threats and bringing with it loss of business and ruined reputations.

   When faced with this situation in a previous life, we realized that we were framing the challenge all wrong. So, to simplify communication with this type of target audience, we developed a security program called RM2 (Risk Mitigation and Management). The acronym itself conveyed the essence of our message without repetitiveness. We initially kept the full meaning under wraps but gradually expanded the program into six distinct components. One innovative aspect of the overarching program was certification: access to certain data or applications required RM2 certification. This not only ensured compliance but also instilled a sense of pride among those who attained certification. This raised the level of general awareness quite significantly from remote markets to the boardroom.

   The program's success led to global word-of-mouth promotion that exceeded our training capacity. Additionally, it fostered open dialogue with clients who appreciated our transparency, thereby strengthening our partnerships.

2. Foster Operational Flexibility – Security should integrate seamlessly with an organization's core purpose, rather than existing as a disconnected vertical. Bridging the gap between technologists and operational employees is essential to prevent friction and inefficiencies.

   To address this, we implemented a program that resonated with the organization's many functional groups. We created the "What's Your Minor" program, a model commonly used across several industries under different guises. The program involved placing technology employees in various business roles and vice versa. By immersing employees in different departments for a few hours each week, we promoted mutual understanding and collaboration. This initiative resulted in reduced noise, enhanced operational flexibility, and a more cohesive workforce.

   With subject matter experts embedded in business teams, policies were reshaped to treat data as a strategic asset. Notably, the presence of these experts mitigated risks associated with urgent responses to requests for proposals (RFPs), as teams had access to the right information and resources. This approach takes time and commitment across functional leaders and is a key area for building lasting executive sponsorship. The result was truly gratifying and well worth the effort, it also supported an unexpected retention outcome across key roles where employees found opportunities to enhance their careers.

3. Embrace Trust with Verification – As Ronald Reagan famously said during nuclear treaty negotiations in the 80s, "Trust but verify". This principle holds particularly true in security programs, where tactical and technological controls are crucial for safeguarding intellectual property.

    In today's hybrid work environments, where organizational perimeters are blurred and access to systems from around the globe is the norm, the risk of data breaches from internal or external sources is heightened. Balancing trust with verification is challenging but essential.

    While modern technologies can provide many tactical capabilities to allay concerns in this area, trust is a top-down relationship dynamic as well – Executives must trust their Chief Information Security Officers (CISOs) as partners in navigating these complexities. The CISO on my team at the time emphasized a layered approach to security, blending a robust exterior defense with a flexible, trust-based core. This approach facilitated many late-night discussions on capital investment, operational costs, and risk management strategies. This led to a better understanding of potential limitations and still allowed for significant progress.

    Ultimately, the goal was to mitigate risks effectively while maintaining trust and collaboration within the organization. We ensured that it was not a "feel good" security program operating within its own echo chamber.

4. Managing Operational Responses – The realm of security within organizations often operates in the shadows, its significance only fully appreciated when a crisis strikes. The ethos of Murphy's Law permeates through every layer of security planning and implementation – "What can go wrong, will go wrong" – reminding us that unforeseen challenges can emerge at any moment, demanding swift and decisive action. Two scenarios, at two different companies, bring to life the power of good operational responses.

    In the first scenario, set in Asia, the specter of a data breach threatened to unravel the delicate fabric of trust between the supplier organization and a prospective client. The suspected leakage of sensitive client data onto the unforgiving expanse of the internet sent shockwaves through the suppliers' operational structures. Despite meticulous preparations and exhaustive risk assessments, the reality of the situation caught the team off guard, highlighting the sobering truth that no amount of planning can completely inoculate an organization against the unexpected.

Navigating through the many corridors of digital forensics and strategic communication, the suppliers' team unearthed a narrative that diverged from the initial assumption. Rather than a grave and potentially unforgivable misstep on their part, a rival entity had inadvertently put them in the crosshairs by releasing an earlier version of the same information they had. The forensic processes in place were able to identify the subtle differences between the released versus the protected information and prove that the suppliers' organization had maintained the extensive confidentiality they signed up to. A detailed response with supporting proof points strengthened the partnership for years to come; a shared crisis with sound operational response helped further build trust.

Similarly, in a parallel narrative unfolding in a different market, the sanctity of intellectual property came under siege in the unforgiving landscape of social media. A meticulously crafted packaging design found itself thrust into the public domain, threatening to undermine months of arduous work and strategic planning. While the knee-jerk reaction may have been to attribute blame internally, a deeper examination revealed a narrative quite different from what the team imagined but still had the same debilitating consequences.

The dissemination of the sensitive package design across digital platforms was not the result of a systemic failure but rather a member of the client's own team attempting to get feedback from an acquaintance who, in turn, shared it across a prominent social platform. A single impulsive gesture, fueled by enthusiasm and devoid of malicious intent, served as the catalyst for a cascade of repercussions that reverberated across that organization – from the delay of a product launch, combined with the loss of an industry-first design concept, to a drop in share price, the ramifications were far-reaching.

In both instances, the overarching lesson remains clear: the efficacy of security measures lies not solely in their design but in their adaptability and operational resilience in the face of adversity. As organizations traverse the challenges of an increasingly digitized world, the imperative to cultivate a culture of vigilance and transparency has never been more pronounced. Beyond the realm of financial considerations, the true currency of security lies in the preservation of trust and integrity, assets far more valuable than any monetary sum.

From the corridors of power to the front lines of digital defense, responsibility rests with everyone across the organizational ecosystem, including vendors and partners. This, however, requires a significant commitment and appropriate messaging from the executive bench. Achieving executive buy-in takes time and effort and some of the most successful organizations in the world have this critical relationship nailed down. They include updates and feedback loops at the Board level and Audit Committees. Their policy, legal, talent, audit, controls, training, and business functional leads are regularly updated on the progress and risks facing the company. These relationships will help tremendously when things go sideways, as they always do.

It is not a matter of IF security challenges will arise but rather when, and it is during adversity that all the efforts over time, from technology to tactical responses and executive relationships will all play a role in mitigating the challenge.

"Knowing where you stand is half the challenge solved".

– **Yuri Aguiar**

The role of the CISO/VP Cyber Security (IT/OT) is to provide TRUST and RESILIENCY in an organization to ensure the stakeholders are reassured that the appropriate systems and capabilities are in place and fully operational. In P&G I was responsible for the cyber security capabilities across 116 manufacturing plants, 200+ distribution centers, and, with limitation, our top supply chain critical suppliers (TPRM program) – I was accountable to the global supply chain president (Global Product Supply Officer) – my "compelling business need" (CBN) reflected the expectations of my role.

CBN: To protect the company and its stakeholders, including employees, from a business and reputational loss due to a security breach incurring loss of critical information or an impact to operations.

Essentially, the CBN should state on what basis you will be fired!

Top of the list of CISO qualities is the ability to provide a risk-based measurable strategy to strengthen the organization's capability appropriate to the risk appetite of the company leadership and BoD, leadership needs to see an RoI on the investments ($ and people) that are assigned to the cyber security program.

Within P&G the measures included:

1. IT Systems (NIST CSF).
2. IT/OT Systems (Department of Energy C2M2).
3. Security Operations reports and trends.
4. Incidents addressed.
5. Compliance from governance bodies (2nd and 3rd lines of defense).

In many conferences where I'm on panels, I hear the CISOs complain that they are not heard – essentially they are "victims" – I dispute this as I believe that they are lacking in leadership skills to provide a compelling reason why the cyber security investments are needed – this requires the CISOs to look to internal data AND external benchmarks (with peer companies – preferably those that have suffered breaches (in P&G's case I leveraged the breaches with Reckitt Benckiser and Clorox).

CISOs need to be great CONNECTORS across an organization – their success is dependent on engaging the whole organization to adopt the cyber security Policies, Standards, and Controls (PSC) – if they can embed these practices in how an organization works (versus cyber security being perceived as something the IT department does) then you have a huge win in your capacity to enable a step change. In P&G my role included governance PSC across all sites, in the first 28 years with P&G I was an engineer (VP for different business units) and at one time Capital Systems Manager, so in my following eight years as global cyber security VP I was also able to bring this to the 2000+ engineering community – I changed the capital appropriation process to include cyber security investments within appropriation requests (P&G annual capital spend is $4 billion) – so this is a wonderful opportunity to get cyber security investments undertaken ahead of installations (e.g., OT network renewal, patching of OT MS devices and provision of network threat & vulnerability tools). I was lucky – with 36.5 years with P&G I knew the company and how to get things done – all CISOs need to be equally smart to leverage the ecosystem they live in!

COMMUNICATION skills to upper leadership/stakeholders also need to be complemented with methodologies to engage the collective organization to be ACTIVE participants in the program, within manufacturing plants the secret is to leverage the synergies with SAFETY and QUALITY systems where the pyramid of escalation applies (e.g., for quality a product recall – serious quality incident – typically reflects poor standards and practices on a daily basis on production lines, for safety – if the culture isn't embedded to take safety seriously at a basic level such as cleaning up oil spills and locking out machines before entering, then a serious incident, even a fatality, is likely. If the CISO can get into the daily work of people and provide examples (that also relate to their at-home lives = good cyber hygiene and practices within their families), the CISO will capture the "hearts and minds" of an organization.

Well-thought-through TABLETOPS with senior leaders (CEO, CFO, CLO, etc.) makes a BIG difference, I provided a Tabletop following our launch of Ariel Pods and Tide Pods across the globe (a $700 million capital project I led as the Engineering VP) – which is worth $1.4 billion in annual sales – I simulated a Rockwell Automation firmware update that was infected – the story involved SEC filing and external media communication requests as the sites started to shut down – a real case that prompted questions at the end on "this could really happen to us . . . what do we need to do better"? A heaven-sent conversation as you look to forward-looking budgets!

Finally, I want to reinforce the value of MEANINGFUL – INSIGHTFUL DATA, often a huge missed opportunity by CISOs is the real data available in the SOCs. I was responsible for the two P&G SOC operations in Manila and Cincinnati. I coached the tool owners and SOC team to provide data (less false positives) on sites, such that when I went to a site I could show the plant leadership and employees what was happening on their turf (PCs reimaged, blocked transactions/URLs and payloads discovered) – this made it real versus a conversation on "this could happen".

– Geoffrey Kerr, former VP of global cyber security,
Procter & Gamble Corporation

The continuing evolution of the 21st-century CISO/Risk Executive: I call CISOs Risk Executives because they manage more risk than most people at their corporations and do so with increasing responsibilities and liabilities. They are responsible for protecting the data, IP, brand, and shareholder value of a company and many times these corporations are part of critical infrastructure which is a fabric of our national security and economic security and inherent right to privacy. They deserve and should see themselves having a seat at the table along with the other officers and the respect that comes with this title. The CISO role from twelve years ago has changed from when they were seen as cost centers, reported to the CIO, rarely, if ever, briefed the board, and were somewhat seen as a security person. Today's tier one CISO/ Risk Executive is one who understands the business objectives, is seen as an enabler and driver of the business enterprise-wide, can articulate complex matters to their boards and briefs their boards on a quarterly basis if not more.

– Robert D. Rodriguez, Chairman SINET &
Partner at SYN Ventures

TRUE STORY

I worked for someone years ago who told me, "You hire most of your problems" and that certainly has proven true to me over the past 40 years. Most of my career has been working my way up on the Go-To-Market side of the business until I got the chance to lead a company.

Often, I noted that 5% of all teachers, doctors, lawyers, judges, engineers, etc., probably aren't successful at their roles but on the GTM side the failure rate can come close to 50%. There are many reasons for this, from the obvious that many people think Sales is all sunshine and rainbows of taking people to lunch and golf to the simple fact that many small tech companies have products that don't have a ready market for a number of reasons.

The trick in managing a sales team is making sure they understand that the person they are most likely pitching to actually doesn't have a good grip on everything that has to happen internally to actually buy a product or service. Companies don't put their general staff through training of "Here's how you spend our money", it's quite the opposite.

But the real trick is knowing when to hold em or fold em when evaluating a team member who isn't making their numbers. The story that comes to mind is a salesperson I had working for me years ago, Rob. Rob worked almost primarily on a deal with the Social Security Department for the first nine months of his employment. It was an all-encompassing process, as a small company we were competing against IBM, Unisys, and Verisign.

At the end of this nine-month process, we were selected as the technical winner, a huge accomplishment given our size and a testament to our technology and Rob's tenaciousness and understanding of the sales process.

There was one thing we all missed, the random purchasing agent we were assigned to for the procurement process. We quickly found out that the number three company was to be awarded the contract by the purchasing agent. Incredulous, I asked Rob to set up a meeting with this gentleman. We flew across the country to meet with him in the bowels of the Social Security Administration.

We were quickly told by the purchasing agent that GSA rules allowed him to assign the contract to vendors one to three at his discretion. We pointed out that vendor three didn't even have their own technology, they were licensing it from a third party and had little experience in the space which is why the technical team awarded us first place.

While he acknowledged that he then said, "We have a contract in place with vendor number three and since they are in the top three, I am awarding the contract to them because it's less work for me". He then went on to tell us we could go to his boss, but we wouldn't get anywhere because he didn't want the extra work either.

After leaving the building Rob and I stopped on the sidewalk to chat. Rob is a tall athletic guy and he looked at me and said, "Look, if you need to let me go, I understand". "Let you go"? I replied. "Did you know you would end up with this idiot at the beginning of the purchasing process? Of course not". I continued, "Look, Rob, we ran into an idiot, there was no way you could have predicted that, you won the technical bake-off over nine months against three huge companies, don't quit, I'll try to move some money to you so you can pay your bills".

Rob didn't quit and he became our number two salesperson in the company and helped propel us to a nice exit. Sales is a lot like baseball, sometimes your best pitcher can't get anyone out. The skill is to know when it's time to exit someone from the team and that I think just comes with time and dealing with many people in different situations and understanding the threads of success and failure that you see that run through an individual.

– Kevin Senator, CEO, Constella Intelligence

9 Be a Governance, Risk, and Compliance (GRC) Advocate

A CISO may or may not own the GRC space within a given organization. Organizational culture and maturity play a big role in that structural makeup. Irrespective, a CISO must advocate GRC initiatives in order to help organizations prove, and track, maturity as well as navigate complex regulatory environments, be able to compete for business opportunities, mitigate risks, and foster a culture of integrity and accountability. GRC initiatives used to be very compliance-centric but, in the world of today, these initiatives are also a pathway to business opportunities, relationships, and partnerships. These benefits provide real-world business value, but a CSIO needs to enter the GRC space with eyes wide open.

Typical cybersecurity-related GRC initiatives are:

- Security Information Gathering (SIG) questionnaire.
- Cloud Assurance Questionnaire (CAQ).
- Software Assurance Maturity Model (SAMM) processes.
- NIST CSF assessments.

It is naïve to assume that any of these compliance processes, or certifications, equate to secure, protected, or resilient. Some CISOs make this mistake and it is one to avoid. An effective CISO will look, and move, beyond compliance requirements and actively contribute to the overall protection and resilience of the company being protected. This is not to say there is no value to these GRC functions, there absolutely is. But that value does not make an organization secure, protected, or resilient. There is a fundamental flaw in most of these models, or processes. Unfortunately, the reality of this is that most of these models are based on the honor system. Simply put, either there are questionnaires used or interviews performed. Often, these questionnaire and interview answers are taken, and accepted, at face value.

Accepting these data points at face value is a personal decision for a CISO. But the CISO is the one who would most likely have to answer for any accepted inaccuracies or deception. Even worse is the reality that a CISO will most likely carry the burden of handling breaches in environments where these types of answers were just accepted. Given this liability, the notions of "trust but verify", or "trust nothing", become very important. As such, a CISO should become an assessor of truth and build an Information Assurance program to scrutinize and validate (true or not), the information that has been provided by system owners and such. This can be done

DOI: 10.1201/9781003477556-9

independently as part of the overall cybersecurity program, or it can certainly be tied in with an effective GRC program.

INFORMATION ASSURANCE

Information assurance programs represent a systematic approach to protecting an organization's assets from threats. It involves a combination of people, processes, and technology systems working together to identify risk, detect threats and vulnerabilities, deter, and respond to attacks.

The Need for an information assurance program is relatively self-evident. With the modern state of digitization of business operations, the threat landscape has expanded. Moreover, successful cybersecurity-related events and incidents have reached a point where entire companies can be taken out of business. These threats, including data exfiltration, malware, phishing, and ransomware attacks, are on the rise in terms of volume and sophistication. They can lead to significant financial loss, damage to reputation, and even legal consequences.

Without an Information Assurance Program, organizations are at risk of falling victim to these threats. This type of program represents a systematic way of establishing maturity with proof by way of control validations. Furthermore, not having this type of program could lead to non-compliance with regulations, such as GDPR or HIPAA, which can result in unnecessary financial losses (e.g., fines, etc.).

Some of the key components of an Information Assurance program are:

- Risk Assessment
- Risk Management
- Information Security Policies
- Security Controls
- Validation Processes
- Incident Response Plan
- Continuous Monitoring and Improvement

RISK ASSESSMENT

Risk assessment consists of identifying, analyzing, and evaluating risks to an organization's systems and assets. The assessment may also include risk quantification processes. A good assessment will include data identifying the potential impact of a threat and the likelihood of it occurring. Potential impact is typically represented in some estimated dollar amount so that business leaders can understand it. Typically, presenting risk alone to C-Suite members has a varied impact. But when that same risk is presented with potential negative financial impact attached to it, the message will most likely resonate better.

As an example, an organization might identify a risk area around users processing (clicking and/or submitting data) content from a phishing attack. The risk assessment could involve analyzing the potential impact of such an attack (e.g., financial loss, data leakage, etc.) and evaluating the likelihood of it happening (e.g., based on patterns of users failing phishing simulations, etc.).

RISK MANAGEMENT

Given discoveries from the risk assessment processes, risk management processes focus on reducing the possibility of actualizing those discovered risks. This stage of an assurance program involves the pursuit of risk-mitigating activities and controls, pursuing risk acceptance or rejection, and, possibly, the pursuit of risk transference or avoidance.

As an example, because of a risk assessment an organization might be facing weak controls around data stores housing sensitive data. They may decide to mitigate this risk by pursuing different mechanisms. One could take the form of isolating the data store at a network level and move toward a model where only specific entities (relevant applications, database administrators, etc.) can communicate with that data store. Another mechanism could be an analysis of exactly what users have access to in that data store, what their access patterns (source addresses and times of access) are, and what typical query response sizes are. Closely scrutinizing some of these data points could help identify anomalous behavior moving forward. These exercises could help reduce the likelihood of sensitive data being exfiltrated by unauthorized actors.

INFORMATION SECURITY POLICIES

Information security policies have already been covered in Chapter 2, they hold the rules that define how business should be conducted, for example how information should be handled within the organization.

As an example, an information security policy might state that customer data needs to be adequately protected. It can go on to say that sensitive data (PII, PHI, credit card data, etc.) must be classified as such. It can go further to state that data classified as sensitive must be encrypted both at rest and in transit. A policy could also potentially go into detail outlining how the organization defines encryption at rest. This type of policy could help ensure the confidentiality and integrity of data where an organization is considered the custodian.

SECURITY CONTROLS

Security controls are mechanisms that enforce the rules defined in the information security policies. Policies without actual controls cannot truly be enforced. They could be technical controls (like WAFs or intrusion prevention systems) or administrative controls (like access controls or incident response procedures). Many options and examples of control frameworks were covered in Chapter 3 ("Controls" section).

As an example, a technical control could be a WAF that blocks traffic from known Tor exit nodes (IP addresses). An example of an administrative control could be a policy that requires employees to never take data classified as sensitive outside of the boundaries of the corporate network.

VALIDATION PROCESSES

Often a CISO must operate with data provided by others without direct access to be able to validate what has been provided. This is often the case where an organizational structure consists of autonomous business units. The business units may have to provide answers to compliance or regulatory questionnaires and sometimes even provide evidence backing up the claims. A CISO's function should be given the authority to validate such claims to limit unnecessary liability for the organization. When this authority is granted a set of validation processes can provide results either validating or invalidating a series of claims.

As an example, let's assume a control claims that it is encrypting sensitive data at rest, inside of a relational DB. A validation process for that control could be a process that runs on a certain cadence (or at random assuming it is regular enough to catch regressions). This process could query the DB to read data from the appropriate column inside a table. Then there could be an iteration on the returned data and multiple validation checks could be performed. Examples of those checks could be looking for non-ASCII characters or checks against strings that are valid words in a dictionary.

INCIDENT RESPONSE PLAN

Incident response was covered in Chapter 6. By way of a simple summary, an incident response plan is a predefined set of actions to be taken in response to a security event or incident. It includes steps like identification of the activity that makes up the event/incident, containing the activity, neutralizing the threat, recovering from the event/incident, and then learning from it.

As an example, if some malware detonation is detected on a host (e.g., users' laptop, etc.) an incident response plan will get put into action after endpoint protections provide the detection and hopefully stop the nefarious activity. The plan may call for isolating the infected host, creating an image of the host (for evidence and forensics), removing the malware from the end user's machine, conducting a thorough investigation to try and identify lateral movement and such, and then taking measures to prevent future incidents.

CONTINUOUS MONITORING AND IMPROVEMENT

Most business environments are quite agile and ever-changing. In order for an information assurance program to succeed it must keep pace. Continuous monitoring involves regularly checking the state of the relevant information systems as well as the effectiveness of the security controls. When many changes are made (e.g., multiple software releases, automated software builds, etc.), regressions can take place and previously working controls can start to fail. The information assurance program is responsible for catching these regressions and having these situations rectified. This could involve techniques like penetration testing, vulnerability scanning, or log analysis looking for outliers or known bad detections.

Continuous improvement involves using the results of the monitoring to consistently pursue enhancements to the information assurance program. This could involve creating new policies, updating existing policies, improving controls, or even entirely changing out protective mechanisms.

BENEFITS

The benefits of an information assurance program are many. It can significantly reduce the risk footprint within a given organization. By implementing, validating, and continuously checking robust security controls and conducting regular risk assessments, organizations can be proactive in their overall security posture and actual ability to prevent security incidents.

An information assurance program can also have indirect positive impacts across an organization's ecosystem. One area is on the resilience side. The benefit here is the reduction of the risk of system unavailability, or downtime, due to security incidents. Seamless business continuity will be viewed in a positive light by most organizations, knowing that their systems are available when needed. Another example is that by demonstrating a commitment to data protection, organizations can increase customer trust and compliance with regulations.

CHALLENGES

There are challenges with building and implementing an information assurance program. Some of them are:

- Technical – implementing, integrating, and/or replacing security controls with existing systems can be complex. In some cases, a value-add from a security perspective will negatively impact features or functionality. This is especially true for organizations with legacy systems or complex solutions. While this is on the technical front, make it a business decision regarding how this is handled. Non-technical business stakeholders should take part in these types of decision-making processes, they have a strong stake in the outcome.
- Organizational – getting support from stakeholders can sometimes be difficult. This is especially so when competing interests are fighting for a limited budget. An information assurance function can be seen as a luxury, additional cost, or a hindrance to business operations. This is where being influential becomes imperative, educating stakeholders on the value of security can prove to be challenging.
- Budget – implementing a successful information assurance program can be expensive. This includes the cost of new security tooling, technical controls, bringing in expertise from the outside, and continual maintenance and improvement.

STRATEGIES

There are some strategies for overcoming some of these challenges:

- Technical – organizations can overcome technical challenges by leveraging modern technologies and bringing in external experts. Very often an external perspective can add a lot of value since these experts have probably solved similar challenges elsewhere. Regarding the use of modern technologies, an example is the use of AI-powered automation tools. These pieces of software can analyze volumes of data that would be challenging for humans. The end result of that could be a simplification of processes around implementation and management of security controls.

- Organizational – organizational challenges can be overcome mainly by education. Tactfully pushing security best practice knowledge and awareness for stakeholders is key here. If key stakeholders or decision makers understand the value at hand directly, gaining support for programs, such as information assurance, starts to become possible. This can also foster a culture of security within an organization, making security just part of company values.
- Budget – organizations can overcome budget challenges by seeking funding from multiple sources. Assuming positive relationships have been built, having senior allies put supportive pressure on decision-makers can prove very beneficial. Most folks simply need to be made aware of risk, business impact, and cost-benefit in order to understand the value of the program.

A solid information assurance program can prove invaluable to a GRC function, but more importantly, can become a critical component of modern-day business functions. It targets protection in a space that can potentially impact an organization all the way to taking out of business. While the CIA triad is a bit of an academic notion, it does provide guiding principles that are sound. Information assurance plays right into this space with a focus on protecting the confidentiality, integrity, and availability of data, technical crown jewels, and business-critical systems. Collectively these elements targeted for protection comprise the cornerstones of most modern organizations.

Clearly, there are challenges when designing and building an information assurance program. One size does not fit all and customizing the program to fit a specific set of needs compounds the challenges. But the benefits far outweigh the challenges. By proactively managing security risks, organizations can increase their odds of survival in the modern digital age. Information assurance will play a vital part in that digital landscape for organizations of varying sizes.

CORPORATE GOVERNANCE

Corporate governance plays a crucial role in shaping the overall effectiveness of a CISO within an organization. Moreover, it plays a crucial role in the way an organization manages risk and protects itself. Given the systemic risks that many companies face, it is imperative to:

- Have a dedicated executive focused on cybersecurity risks and matters; one whose experience and singular focus is on managing the potential impact of cyber incidents.

- Ensure that this dedicated executive has the necessary support, resources, and independence to effectively address cyber risks.

Beyond a dedicated executive, consider that the US SEC at one point included a dedicated security resource on the board of public companies as part of the disclosure rules they were trying to provide the industry. This is a clear message about the importance of this type of knowledge at corporate leadership levels.

From a cybersecurity perspective, corporate governance refers to the policies, processes, and oversight mechanisms that an organization has, or puts, in place to address and/or manage cyber risks in an effective manner. This involves delineating authority and decision-making ability at the highest levels of the organization. It also involves holding those entities accountable for the necessary attention cyber risk should be given. Here are some key elements of corporate governance to consider either validating or pursuing as a CISO:

- Board oversight – the BoD should play a crucial role in overseeing and supporting strategic cybersecurity initiatives. This includes establishing a level of risk appetite, providing input on strategies, and ensuring that adequate resources are allocated to cybersecurity and risk management. If your situation is such that the BoD is disengaged or simply not operating at the level of risk engagement, then it must become part of your mission to get in front of these folks. Given an organization's culture, this may require patience, tact, and perseverance. Irrespective, creating this level of engagement is part of your responsibility as a CISO. One recommendation is to reach out to each board member individually and establish rapport one-on-one. This could yield great results with the overall BoD if you show them the value of interacting with you.
- Steering committee – many mature organizations establish a dedicated cybersecurity steering committee. This can also come in the form of an advisory board. Whatever form they take, these bodies need to report to the C-Suite and directly to the BoD. Steering committees were covered in Chapter 3.
- Communication – when interacting with boards and steering committee members communication is the key component. Regular reporting and clear communication channels need to be established to keep the relevant audience informed about the organization's maturity, risks, and ongoing events and initiatives.
- Alignment – corporate governance should be a mechanism that can ensure a CISO's initiatives are aligned with the overall business objectives of the organization.
- Cybersecurity risk management framework – a comprehensive risk management framework should be established to identify, assess, quantify, and prioritize cybersecurity risks. This was covered in Chapter 4.
- Roles and responsibilities – clear delineation of the roles and responsibilities related to cybersecurity needs to be established and documented. This

ensures accountability and avoids confusion and/or overlaps regarding responsibilities based on role.

- Incident Response (IR) and Business Continuity Planning (BCP) – corporate governance should ensure that robust IR and BCP plans are in place to effectively manage and recover from cybersecurity incidents. These areas were covered in Chapter 6.
- Security first culture – effective corporate governance includes embracing of security across the culture of an organization and promoting cybersecurity awareness, not just to employees but contractors and third-party vendors as well. Make it known that you and your organization are serious about this, and you will be able to establish a strong cybersecurity ecosystem, hopefully reducing the risk of human-caused incidents.

Specifically, for a CISO effective corporate governance represents opportunities to:

- Establish authority and accountability – when there is a clear definition of roles, the authority of a CISO will become apparent. The corporate governance function will solidify this by ensuring that a CISO has support from the appropriate levels; the authority to implement security policies, make decisions, and hold other departments accountable for risk management and compliance.
- Establish independent reporting structures – given the way many organizations are structured it is dangerous and sub-optimal to have the CISO function controlled by entities that need to be held accountable in various ways. Objectivity avoids conflicts of interest, and it is difficult to hold the person you report to accountable. To combat these scenarios, it is essential for a CISO to have an independent reporting line to the BoD or somebody who can act when the target is someone at the executive level. This independent reporting structure, detached from the operational structure, allows a CISO to escalate critical security issues without fear of retaliation.
- Establish a proper level of oversight – the BoD, as an independent body of oversight, should provide objective guidance to the CISO regarding risk management strategies, risk appetite, and acceptable levels of risk exposure. The C-Suite may be too close to matters or have their own agendas, and so oversight simply must take place at a level above and outside of them.
- Seek proper resourcing – a corporate governance mechanism that has an objective viewpoint and the best interest of the organization at heart should ensure that a CISO has access to proper resources, including budgets, personnel, and technology.

By implementing effective corporate governance practices, organizations can empower their CISOs to effectively manage cybersecurity risks, make informed decisions, and contribute to the overall success and resilience of the business. Beyond pursuing effective corporate governance and building an information assurance program, here are some practical ways a CISO can serve as an effective advocate for GRC in an organization:

- Educate – a CISO could make themselves accessible to provide education, targeting an organization's leadership and possibly their board as well. While this type of education could cover some cybersecurity areas, the target audience would probably benefit more from education focused on threat awareness, cyber risks, and their potential impact. The goal is to communicate risk exposures clearly and simply to financial and reputational impact terms.
- Align – work toward aligning security objectives with business objectives. This is of great importance because showing how a stronger security posture directly enables business objectives to position the CISO role and function, as a business entity as opposed to a technical one. Focusing on business operational resilience, customer trust, and growth through safe/secure operations, is key.
  - A major part of alignment is collaboration with strategic entities. Actively promoting collaboration with internal audit, legal, finance, and IT will prove invaluable. Pushing collaborative efforts, such as risk analysis and/or policy reviews, in a cross-departmental way will help balance perspectives and obtain support.
- Be policy-driven – become the known champion of comprehensive policies and related enforcement controls. The CISO should become this advocate pushing for company-wide information security policies, proposing priority areas for control improvements based on identified areas of risk.
- Be compliance-driven – aim to streamline the processes and tooling necessary to achieve regulatory compliance. Part of the success in this area is staying on top of changing compliance rules and regulations. Being on the cutting edge of this information will give a CISO the ability to proactively adapt technical controls and awareness training that will improve audit preparedness.
- Be team-driven – make the necessary investments in automation and team development. Automation aims to make things smoother for your team members, freeing them up to focus on other tasks. This includes time to upskill based on organizational needs. In order to empower your team, allocate resources toward integrated GRC platforms, tools that automate manual processes, and continuing team education to enable an up-to-date risk-aware culture.
- Measure – monitor maturity, progress, and effectiveness with meaningful metrics. Leverage key risk indicators that are aligned with your relevant organization. Not all metrics are a generic fit so a focus should be applied on subjective metrics. Use these data points to measure and track business impact. Ultimately, metrics are a tool for a CISO to demonstrate GRC program maturity and/or progress toward a mature state.

The CISO sits at the intersection of business and organizational risk, cybersecurity, information security, privacy, IT governance, and compliance/audit functions. By embracing this key role as either a GRC leader and advisor, or an advocate for those leading in the GRC space, a CISO can positively influence protection, resilience, trust, innovation, and growth.

EXPERT ADVICE

Being a Governance, Risk, and Compliance (GRC) advocate transcends mere acknowledgment of its importance; it demands a nuanced understanding and a commitment to aiding organizational compliance in the ever-evolving landscape of cybersecurity. GRC is not a static strategy but a dynamic practice requiring constant adaptation, measurement, and refinement. It's akin to tailoring a custom-made suit for organizational compliance, where every aspect needs meticulous adjustment for a perfect fit, not just the sleeves or the pants. As a GRC Advocate, navigating stakeholder dynamics, balancing security imperatives with business operations, and fostering a continuous improvement and innovation culture is paramount. Challenges abound, from articulating the value and urgency of GRC compliance to various stakeholders to ensuring sustainability and continuous monitoring of security controls. However, through innovative problem-solving, effective communication, and stakeholder engagement, GRC advocates can overcome these hurdles. The journey as a GRC Advocate is replete with rewards – increased compliance, risk reduction, federal audit accreditation, and recognition as a catalyst for change and cybersecurity innovator. It's not just about understanding regulations; it's about driving meaningful change and making a lasting impact in cybersecurity.

– Nia F. Luckey, CIO Advisory Services Sr. Consultant, Infosys

Governance for CISOs also includes a need to understand and execute against their expanding role in the corporate boardroom. With the US Securities and Exchange Commission's new cybersecurity disclosure rules, the CISO's role is both expanding and rising in importance in the eyes of regulators and the corporate boardroom. Cybersecurity and corporate governance are coming together for the first time in these new regulatory requirements. CISOs now have a heightened responsibility to understand and articulate cybersecurity risk in the context of both an incident and its materiality on investors and cybersecurity risk disclosure for corporate reporting. These are new responsibilities and challenges for the CISO, and ones that create a leadership moment that can both elevate the role and individual.

– Bob Zukis, Digital Directors Network Founder and CEO

REAL WORLD PERSPECTIVE

The adage "compliance does not equal security" has never been more true and is clearly apparent by the long list of ISO27001-certified organizations that have suffered devastating breaches in recent years. That being said, a CISO should never underestimate the value of using compliance as a tool to drive security maturity. Attempting to recruit sponsors and stakeholders with security technicalities, acronyms, and FUD will often end in a futile pursuit. On the other hand, offering your BOD something tangible and a shiny accreditation that the sales team can slap on the brochure increases the likelihood that security initiatives are sponsored and supported. Why not then use that support to improve the areas within an ecosystem most at risk? Fundamentally compliance and security are not the same thing, their ultimate objectives are completely different. But used symbiotically compliance and security have the potential to be the perfect "sword and shield" combination.

– **Dennis Partridge**

The necessity for organizations to enhance their governance, risk management, and compliance (GRC) frameworks as we move from 2025 to 2030 is crucial. This period calls for a focused effort to merge these traditionally separate processes by utilizing the capabilities of artificial intelligence (AI) and automation not just as add-ons but as fundamental elements of the GRC strategy. The transition toward anticipatory risk management marks a significant shift in how organizations handle potential threats, calling for a flexible and proactive approach to operational and strategic risks. The swift changes in regulatory requirements, especially in key areas like data privacy, cybersecurity, and environmental responsibility, demand companies to be watchful and adaptable. A deep-seated culture of compliance, backed by strong data security measures, will establish the foundation of organizational trustworthiness and ethical soundness. Simultaneously, addressing the urgent need for skilled GRC professionals is vital. Companies might have to explore beyond conventional talent pools, making substantial investments in training initiatives and potentially seeking external expertise to fill these critical positions. This strategic emphasis on training, coupled with the implementation of advanced technologies for real-time risk evaluation and compliance management, will be essential in maintaining a competitive advantage in an increasingly intricate regulatory and threat environment.

– **Aric Perminter**

10 Be a Measurer

Measuring and communicating the effectiveness of cyber and/or information security programs is essential for CISOs to showcase value-add, gain support, identify gaps, and make data-driven and strategic improvements. When a set of metrics are properly crafted and communicated, they comprise a way of proving effectiveness to an organization. Stakeholders like the C-Suite and the board of directors need to have cyber risk and security data presented to them in relevant business terms. Cyber risk quantification plays a big role regarding business terms as it is a way of attaching estimated and potential financial impact to some identified risk.

Regarding presentation, certain points are key. One point is that metrics need to paint a picture, they need to tell a story. If a metrics program simply presents folks with acronyms, graphs, and statistics it may not be getting the right message across to the target audience. Understanding that target audience is another point. Most C-Suite executives, board members, and general stakeholders are not technologists or security professionals. They simply look at the world through a different lens. To effectively relay a message a metrics program, and the delivery of such data need to cater to the views and perspectives of the audience.

Regarding the actual metrics themselves, there should be a focus on metrics that matter, that the target audience can digest. This introduces the subjectivity factor since each organization is unique. What matters to one organization or target audience, may just not matter to another.

BUILDING A SUCCESSFUL METRICS PROGRAM

There is a high level of subjectivity in the actual metrics that a CISO uses. Depending on the goals and organizational size/culture a CISO may choose to design a metrics program around something formal like the NIST CSF functions. But, for instance, if you work for a startup and you have a security team of three, that may not make sense. Metrics still play a role in both those scenarios, regardless of organizational size/culture there are some fundamental principles that can apply when building a successful metrics program.

- Alignment with business objectives – ensure that the metrics chosen align with an understanding of the relevant organizational culture, stakeholder goals, definitions of success, and business objectives demonstrating the value of cybersecurity investments.
- Select relevant metrics – aim to choose metrics that are directly relevant to your organization's needs. Don't focus exclusively on security posture as that may be seen as only relevant to security, or counter to some business goals. The point of posture can be used so long as it is facilitating business

DOI: 10.1201/9781003477556-10

growth. Relevance here will rely on your knowledge of the organization and the relationships that you have built with stakeholders.

- Establish baselines – each metric needs a starting point. Develop baseline measurements for each metric to understand the normal performance levels and more easily identify anomalies. These will serve as the foundation of future measurements and progress.
- Automate data collection – many security teams find themselves scrambling when it is time to put together metrics-based presentations. Those usually lack automation. Leverage tools and technologies to automate the collection of data for metrics, reducing typical last-minute scrambles and possible errors.
- Continuously improve – these are not static sets of data. Moreover, members of your audience may change over time. The program must adapt to such changes in order to remain effective. Periodically review your set of metrics to ensure they remain relevant and adjust them as needed.

A successful cybersecurity metrics program is not static; it requires ongoing scrutiny, honest questions, and adaptation to remain effective. By focusing on metrics that offer clear insight into business value through security, and alignment with business objectives, organizations can significantly enhance their ability to operate in the most secure fashion possible.

METRICS

Here are some examples to consider regarding areas of metrics:

Cost Savings

Just about every business that is active aims to lower debt, increase revenue, and improve its overall financial health. As a CISO, you can build part of the metrics program to speak to some of these goals, especially when cost savings can be proven. When providing data points to stakeholders, it's essential to focus on high-level, impact-driven metrics that directly relate to business outcomes. These metrics should prove the value of cybersecurity investments. Here are some examples that effectively communicate that importance to a non-technical audience:

- Cost savings via contract consolidation. For example, in an organization that is made up of autonomous business units, there may be multiple contracts for the same product. Negotiate with the vendor and try to create an enterprise contract that introduces discounts, possibly with longer terms.
- Cost savings via product consolidations. For example, in that same organization (made up of autonomous business units) there may be multiple EDR products in use. Find one that meets all the functional needs and create an enterprise contract with that vendor. Then work with all the business units to get them standardized on one product with negotiated savings.

- Cost savings via the addressing of technical debt. As an example, perform analysis on backup strategies and archival policies. Maybe a policy states that three years' worth of backups are required but that policy has become outdated. A modern review could, for instance, show that two years is enough, and the relevant cleanup will save money by way of using less storage.
- Cost savings by automating IAM provisioning/de-provisioning. As an example, perform analysis to unearth orphaned or stale accounts. Set a policy that accounts that haven't logged into systems for over six months (stale) automatically get removed. Then look for orphaned accounts that were once provisioned and not automatically de-provisioned. A cleanup of those may also translate into savings on software licenses. This could also show the value of automation.
  - For example – "by implementing an automated discovery process that validates user accounts against a master global directory, we de-provisioned inactive accounts by X%, generating $Y in software license savings".

Where possible, quantify hard cost savings in dollar amounts. The savings can come from different efforts such as reducing unnecessary redundancies, leveraging AI and automation, and the removal of security products that are adding no real value. Any of these types of efforts that lead to cost savings will strongly resonate with stakeholders and executives.

Financial Loss Protection

Given a typical, non-technical, audience for metrics data points, two areas of importance come to light.

- Cyber Risk Quantification (CRQ) – attaching estimated financial impact to areas of risk is a solid approach. The financial estimation process is explored further in the "Cyber Risk Quantification" section of this chapter. These values will resonate with the appropriate audience as they will understand the numerical value of financial loss that will be prevented if risk is properly addressed.
- Financial loss avoidance – showcasing active protection solutions that have taken action and linking a numerical value of protected financial resources to the performed action.

Financial Loss Avoidance

The value of active protection controls implemented by the security team is not proven exclusively by metrics such as the number of attacks blocked. The proof of this value is how much financial loss was avoided by blocking some number of attacks. To focus on metrics that make sense regarding financial loss avoidance, quantify estimated losses avoided due to blocking of security attacks. These block actions typically avoid incidents through protective controls such as WAFs, firewalls, IPS, and endpoint detection and response platforms.

Cyber financial loss prevention is a critical aspect for an entire business, not just as related to cyber risk. This includes losses from fraud, theft, or damage to digital assets, as well as indirect costs such as downtime, reputation damage, legal fees, and regulatory fines. This is one area where a risk-aware CISO can start adding business-level value outside of the boundaries of just cyber or technology-centric risk. Here are some examples of cyber financial loss avoidance, along with an explanation of the math used for quantification:

- Cybersecurity awareness training and tests – "Regular cybersecurity awareness training, coupled with randomly scheduled tests, reduces the incidence of data exposures caused by employee error by 40%, yielding a loss prevention of $500,000 USD".
  - This example will place an annual cost of data exposures, due to employee error, at $1,500,000 USD.
  - At a 40% reduced rate, the new annual cost of a data exposure becomes $1,500,000 * 60%, or $900,000 USD.
  - If the relevant awareness training program costs $100,000 annually, then the loss avoidance is calculated as such: original annual loss – (reduced annual loss + cost of training program), or:
    - $1,500,000 – ($900,000 + $100,000) = $500,000 USD.
- Deploying EDR to reduce malware infections – "Our organization deployed an advanced EDR solution that has decreased malware infections by 80%, resulting in a loss prevention of $1,450,000 USD".
  - This example will place the cost (detection, recovery, loss of productivity) of a malware infection at an average of $100,000 USD per incident. The organization experiences 20 incidents per year. This means annual losses before the EDR solution are $2 MM USD (20 * 100,000).
  - After deployment of the EDR solution, the reduced number of incidents per year became four (20 incidents * 20%). The 20% is due to the reduced infection rate of 80%. At this reduction rate, the new annual loss becomes $400,000 USD (4 incidents * $100,000).
  - If the EDR solution costs $150,000 USD annually, then the loss avoidance is calculated as such: initial annual loss – (reduced annual loss + cost of EDR solution), or:
    - $2,000,000 – ($400,000 + $150,000) = $1,450,000 USD.

The math behind quantifying cyber-related financial loss prevention involves calculating the savings in losses due to specific protection measures, subtracting the cost of implementing those measures, and determining the net loss avoidance.

SECURITY AWARENESS

This area is important due to the impact of the human factor on an overall cybersecurity posture. These metrics should measure the effectiveness of the organization's security awareness program. Typically, these metrics will come about via the results of simulations you put your organization's employees through. KPIs that are metrics-driven, such as the following, can help the organization track its health in this respect:

- The number of awareness training sessions conducted over some cadence.
- The number of employees who completed the training, or the percentage of employees that completed them.
- The number of employees (and/or assessment scores) who fell victim to a simulated attack even after training, or the percentage of them.
- The number of actual security incidents caused by employee negligence.
  - Possibly to factor in before and after training.
- The number of times employees report suspected phishing attempts or other security threats (indicating their vigilance).
- Security culture surveys – use statistics from employee feedback about security's impact on productivity and experience.

These metrics will also help identify areas of improvement and provide a sense of how to get the message across that employees are key in protecting the organization from cyber threats.

Leverage metrics like phishing click-through rates, simulation failure rates, and engagement rates to evaluate and demonstrate program effectiveness. Other metrics that can provide a sense of the efficacy of the awareness program are:

- Phishing failure rates – track improvements over time.
- Reported threats – the number of potential incidents reported by employees across some period. Those numbers rising could indicate improved employee awareness and engagement.
- Policy attestations – the number of employees accepting and acknowledging security policies annually. Trends here can be revealing as well with a rise possibly indicating positive shifts in the workforce.

Here is an example of a metrics-driven story:

> The security team has migrated the awareness training software to an AI-driven one that factors in individual behavioral patterns. In the first quarter after the update employees now report X% of actual phishing attempts versus an average of Y% in previous quarters. This showcases substantial improvements in our employees' identifying and resisting real-world attacks.

This example assumes X > Y.

Another example could be:

> After refreshing the security awareness training program, simulated phishing click rates dropped from X% of users to Y%. Individual user training test scores also increased from A% in Q1 to B% currently, demonstrating a stronger level of awareness content retention.

This example assumes X > Y and A < B.

VULNERABILITY AND THREAT MANAGEMENT

These metrics aim to measure the effectiveness of the VTM program in identifying vulnerabilities. Time may be a factor you can consider but be careful because activities like threat hunting take a lot of time, presenting those metrics may create a situation where the data is misunderstood. KPIs that are metrics-driven, such as the following, can help effectively relay relevant messaging and help identify areas of improvement and risk:

- The number of vulnerabilities discovered, especially critical and high.
  - The number of vulnerabilities discovered over a specific time frame.
- The time taken to get discovered vulnerabilities remediated.
- The percentage of known vulnerabilities that have been patched or mitigated.
- The percentage of identified critical and high vulnerabilities that have been addressed.
- How quickly a security incident is detected after it occurs (incident detection time)
- The percentage of alerts that are determined to be false positives after investigation.
- The accuracy of threat intelligence in predicting or identifying actual threats.

Effective VTM metrics are prioritized based on risk, and risk areas need to be classified in a sensible manner.

One key aspect to keep in mind is that the security team will likely not be in control of remediation actions, priorities, or cycles. For example, vulnerabilities can be discovered that impact a specific version of an OS. But that machine runs an application only certified to run on that specific version of the OS. This cannot arbitrarily be patched or upgraded as it may negatively impact the application in question. In this case, the lack of remediation itself can be used as a metric to showcase the need for more support on some other team and that can indirectly have a positive impact on security matters.

Here is an example of a VTM metrics-driven story:

> The team implemented automated vulnerability scanning in Q1 to cover 100,000 hosts. Compared to the legacy solution (non-automated) this created an increase in detection of critical and high vulnerabilities by N%. This led to an increase in focused remediation efforts that improved the rate of critical and high vulnerabilities patched within a 7-day period from X% to Y%, positively impacting our attack surface.

This example assumes $X < Y$.

THREAT DETECTION

These metrics are generally more operational in nature and related to activities outside of the proactive threat-hunting scope. But, they do aim at measuring the effectiveness of the organization's operational threat detection capabilities. KPIs that are metrics-driven, such as the following, can help you identify areas of operational improvement:

- The number of alerts generated.
- Mean Time to Detect (MTTD).
- Dwell time or the number of days threats go undetected before discovery.
- The time taken to perform forensics, investigate, and respond to alerts.
- The percentage of alerts that, after investigation, are deemed not to be actual threats (false positive rate).
- The percentage of alerts that are investigated by the security team out of all the alerts generated.

An example of a threat detection metrics story is:

We have used AI and ML to tune our SIEM this quarter. These improvements to the threat detection analytics engine have positively impacted the MTTD for insider data exfiltration attempts. The MTTD has been lowered from X hours to less than Y hours. This improvement enables rapid incident response and minimizes the impact of data leakage and/or theft.

This example assumes X > Y.

INCIDENT MANAGEMENT

These metrics aim at measuring the organization's effectiveness when responding to cybersecurity findings, events, and incidents. KPIs that are metrics-driven, such as the following, can help you identify and gauge the effectiveness of your controls and incident management program:

- How many events took place?
- How many of those events turned into incidents?
- Mean Time to Respond (MTTR).
- The time taken to contain an incident.
- The number of incidents handled per some interval of time.

An example of a story driven by incident management metrics:

Optimization of the SIEM has been accomplished via the use of AI and ML. The positive impact was introduced into the advanced behavioral analytics engine. This engine was enriched with threat intelligence creating a reduced MTTR against insider threats from a previous average of over X hours to less than Y hours currently.

This example assumes X > Y.

RISK MANAGEMENT

These metrics aim at measuring the effectiveness of the organization's risk management program. KPIs that are metrics-driven, such as the following, can help the organization become streamlined in regard to risk management:

- The number of risks identified.
- The status of each risk.

- The average time taken to identify new risks from the moment they emerge.
- The time taken to mitigate each risk.
- The tracking of hurdles to risk mitigation.
- The potential financial loss from identified risks (in financial terms).
- The percentage of identified risks that have been mitigated or resolved within a specified timeframe.
- The number of blocked attacks against critical assets.
- The adherence to established risk management policies and procedures.

The goal here is to demonstrate management of, or reductions in, cyber risk. Optimally this is correlated with quantification data and feeds security program maturity improvements across multiple domains (IAM, data protection, vulnerability management, etc.).

An example of a story driven by risk management metrics:

As per the information security policy, all customer-facing applications, or those classified as critical, must have MFA enabled and in use. The pursuit of this by the business units has created a reduction in the likelihood of account takeover by N% given that X% of all relevant applications are now in compliance with the policy. Based on historical assessments, this control lowers estimated financial loss by $Y MM.

The example presented represents decoupled data points that comprise a solid story when used together. This is especially so with the added quantification point outlining projected savings without the stated changes.

COMPLIANCE

These metrics are intended to measure an organization's adherence to whatever regulatory measures apply. KPIs that are metrics-driven, such as the following, can help the organization ensure that it does not end up in a negative situation (fall out of compliance, miss a regulatory deadline, etc.):

- The number of compliance audits expected.
- The number of compliance audits completed/passed.
- The score against some known framework.
- Posture improvements stemming from compliance efforts.
- The number of times the organization fails to comply with laws, regulations, or internal policies over a specific period.
  - The time to resolve these compliance failures.
- The number of issues or gaps identified during compliance audits.
- The rate of repeat compliance violations.

Regarding compliance metrics, the goal is to show progress toward, or evidence of, compliance to internal security policies and external standards. These metrics can apply to compliance with a corporate information security policy. For example, the following metrics-driven story can effectively relay a message of progress:

\

Based on our quarterly information security policy audit, systems that currently cannot support MFA saw a user-initiated adoption of long passphrases. The user base in question created an improvement from X% in Q3 to Y% in Q4, significantly lowering risks from brute force authentication attacks. This progress was driven by a strong awareness campaign along with technical enforcement mechanisms put in place by the IAM team.

This example assumes X < Y.

An example of compliance being driven from an external perspective is the pursuit of some certification that mandates/requires MFA to be in place across all critical applications. Many certification processes created by government entities have these types of requirements built into them. The decision to pursue one of these is typically a business-level decision but it gives a CISO the ability to demonstrate improvements based on the external requirements. Areas such as data classification, access reviews, use of MFA, backup redundancy, etc., are often included in the requirements.

An example story that is empowered by compliance metrics: "Compliance with certification X created an improved state of MFA adoption across business units. In Q2 X% of critical applications were using MFA, in Q3 the adoption rate is Y%". This example assumes X < Y.

Ultimately, metrics can be challenging. The metrics a CISO focuses on should be relevant, measurable, and aligned with the organization's objectives. But they should also be subjective, and they should matter to your organization; "what matters" is generally subjective to four entities:

• The organization.
• The organization's C-Suite.
• The organization's varying board members.
• The organization's cybersecurity leadership.

One of the enemies the industry must contend with is our indoctrination to always strive for 100%. Over time an effective metrics program will show what actual percentage is good enough for your organization, realizing that 100% of anything is most likely unrealistic in the cyber or information security space.

In some cases what is effective is a small, tight, set of metrics that are representative of real-world elements of importance. This comes with a fear alert because in some cases measuring these areas will show results that come off as some type of failure. You need not feel like this is reflective of your work, you are merely reporting the facts to those who need them. "Those" would generally be the board and the C-Suite. They will probably have a hard time initially understanding some of these areas and admittedly they are very difficult to measure/quantify.

It is the job of an effective CISO to make sense of these difficult-to-understand areas and educate those folks. But the education aspect is not just about understanding them, but to extract value from them. This is where courage comes in because a lot of people have a hard time accepting that which is different from what they are accustomed to.

Subjectivity is important here. There are few formulas in the world of cybersecurity, and what matters to one organization may have little relevance elsewhere. Organizations need to tailor their goals and, in turn, the measuring mechanisms, based on what matters to them. This, of course, has a direct impact on what risk areas come to light, which ones need to be addressed with urgency, and those that can wait. Hitting these subjective goals (that should be defined by the metrics) could also bring about ancillary benefits. For instance, this could force the issue of addressing technical debt or force a technology refresh.

One recommendation is to be super consistent in the metrics you choose. Stick with them and show changes over time. The changes can be negative, that's ok. No one should expect total positive momentum all the time. Your presentation of the metrics you choose, will be an investment and in time the board and the C-Suite will start to see the value, and that you are one persistent individual.

ALTERNATIVE METRICS

Here are some suggestions with respect to non-standard metrics (some may be difficult to measure but valuable nonetheless):

- Effectiveness of active protection mechanisms – this one seems obvious at face value. Grab some statistics after the implementation of some solution, for instance, a WAF, and show how many awful things it has prevented. But, this is a very fragmented perspective that may provide a false sense of security. What about your machine-to-machine communications deeper in your network (VPC or otherwise)? How are you actively protecting those (API requests/responses, etc.) entities?
- Reproducibility – the "X as a Service" reality is here and quite useful. "X" can be infrastructure, it can be software, it can be many things depending on the maturity and creativity of an organization. From the software perspective, what percentage of your build process exists within a CI/CD pipeline, or process? This strongly sets a reproducibility perspective. Within a CI/CD process many areas, such as security, resilience, and DR, can be covered in an automated fashion. Vulnerability management, and patching, can be included here as well.
- Repeatability – how repeatable are key functions within your organization? Measuring repeatability is super difficult and yet this is a foundational aspect of mature cybersecurity programs. Playbooks exist for this exact reason, and we invest resources into creating and maintaining them. This means repeatability is undeniably important but how do we quantify this?
- Budgeting – how do you know if enough is being funneled into a security program? At the end of the day, you can't plug every hole. One strategy could be analyzing budgetary investments against areas where there have been security problems. Insufficient budget obviously reduces the ability of a security team to implement protective mechanisms. The metrics you focus on need to push for clarity in terms of what becomes possible. There's most likely no correct amount of budget. But the budget itself needs to be

treated as a metric. Think of it this way, if you don't get enough budget to cover the areas you know need attention then there will be gaps that are directly attributable. Real world point – sadly a lot of budget increases come about because something bad has happened. But this (the fact that something bad happened) means more work needs to be done.

- All-out MTTR – imagine the absolute nightmare scenario that your entire organization is decimated somehow. Imagine you are brought back to the stone age of bare metal and have nothing but a few back-ups to recover from. How long will it take you to get your organization back to an operating business? Some organizations are well-positioned to recover from isolated incidents, like a ransomware-event. The more typical all-out scenarios you may encounter focus on operational areas. For instance, if all servers become unusable, there is a DR plan that has been designed, tested, and tweaked to reach acceptable MTTR.
- Strategic – strategic metrics can show how well security enables business objectives. Examples include:
  - Contribution to revenue – showcase revenue from new products/services enabled by security improvements. This pushes into the space where security unlocks innovation.
  - Revenue protection from the third-party perspective – showcase lowered audit deficiencies and fines through supply chain risk reduction. Use examples where third parties have been the source of problems, yet your TPRM program has not vetted these vendors.
  - Improved cyber insurance rates – demonstrate how mature security lowers insurance premiums.
  - Mergers and acquisitions (M&A) supported – provide assessment report statistics to validate the value of security posture assessments when M&A deals are at play. This showcases security support for business growth enablement.
  - Backup and recovery testing – count of successful BCP/DR tests against some time variable (monthly, annually, etc.). This is strategic to business operations in terms of continuance and recoverability.
  - Data protection – shows the percentage of sensitive data that is encrypted at rest, in use, and in transit. Tie this to documented crown jewel analysis to showcase protection of the most important business data elements.
- Productivity – productivity improvements and efficiencies realized through automation showcase operational business value. Track metrics like hours saved using automation, reduced resolution times, faster response times, and improved analyst ticket throughput times.
- Distance vector – how far into your ecosystem can an attack get before it is detected and handled (whatever handling means to your organization)? The logic here is simple, the longer it takes to detect something the more you need to pay attention to that area. Think of APTs and how long some of them exist inside a network before there is detection and response.
- Time vector – who is faster, you, the defender, or the attackers? There is a reality to the time factor, and every time your organization is targeted, there

is a bit of a race that takes place. Where you end up in the final results of that race dictates, to an extent, the success factor of an attack. This is very hard to measure. But, spending time figuring out ways to measure this will yield an understanding of the threats you face and how well you will fair up against them. One great benefit of spending time assessing your time vector is that it will force you to measure your ability to successfully address entire families, or classes, of attacks. Having the macro focus, as opposed to the typical micro focus may bring about an interesting level of discipline with your technical teams. Basically, they will be forced to think big and not exclusively on edge, or corner cases.

- Attack surface – ASM has already been covered. But it is an area worth of metrics as well. Is there some great deviance in terms of open world-facing ports for a given time period? What does your organization look like to an outsider? What does it look like to an insider? What does it look like when you factor in ephemeral entities (such as elastic cloud resources)? Does your attack surface data factor in all assets in your ecosystem? What about interdependencies? Asset inventories are seldom accurate and so possibly, your attack surface is a snapshot in time as opposed to something holistic.
- Software security – the maturity of software can certainly be measured with techniques like OWASP SAMM. Even tracking simple roll-up scores from a SAMM assessment can become a valuable metric.
- Technical debt – this area is complex as it can contextually refer to software that needs to be refactored or it can refer to legacy systems (stagnant or otherwise). Regardless of the context, how does one measure the level, or severity, of technical debt within an organization?

From a positive vantage point, the very act of trying to measure some of these admittedly challenging areas of operation will likely reveal many areas of improvement. That in and of itself may prove valuable to your organization in the long run. On the negative end, there is an enormous challenge in that board and the C-Suite might not understand these metrics. There are probably many IT leaders that won't understand some of these metrics. But these are not reasons to shy away from the challenge of gathering the data points and educating folks.

CYBER RISK QUANTIFICATION

Cyber Risk Quantification (CRQ) is a process designed to translate cyber risk into financial terms. This is a key component of any risk management strategy because these data points will enable organizations to understand risk in the context of business impact, make informed decisions about investments in cybersecurity, and prioritize risk management efforts. It represents a shift in mindset from the qualitative (e.g., high, medium, low) to a more objective, data-driven one. Simply put, the data generated by CRQ processes explain the likelihood and financial impact of cyber risk in a language understood by stakeholders and business executives.

CRQ KEY CONCEPTS

These are key concepts regarding CRQ:

- Likelihood – the probability of some event occurring within some given time frame.
- Impact – the potential financial loss resulting from some event. Impact can include direct costs such as penalties, operational disruptions, and data recovery costs, and indirect costs such as reputational damage and lack of contract renewals.

ANNUAL LOSS EXPECTANCY

The generally accepted formula used in CRQ exercises is for an Annual Loss Expectancy (ALE). The ALE represents a value that a company can expect to lose, on average, during some time period (annually, bi-annually, etc.) due to the referenced risk. This is a foundational formula used in risk quantification, calculated as the product of the Annual Rate of Occurrence (ARO) and Single Loss Expectancy (SLE), or ALE = ARO × SLE.

- When an asset is at risk, it is necessary to estimate the portion of that asset that would be negatively impacted if some threat became actualized. The percentage of that asset value that would be impacted is the Exposure Factor (EF). The monetary amount that would constitute the impact is then the Single Loss Expectancy (SLE), or SLE = Asset Value x EF.
- Likelihood comes into play when calculating ARO. Some threats are simply more likely to actualize than others. ARO refers to the frequency of those threats per year.

Some details covered in this example data:

- Data breach (PII) – for an asset valued at $5,000,000, with a 100% exposure factor, the SLE is $5,000,000. If such breaches are expected to occur three times per year, an organization can expect to lose $15,000,000 USD (the ALE) annually.

TABLE 10.1
An example of some quantitative risk assessment calculations.

Risk Event	Asset Value	EF	SLE	ARO	ALE
Data Breach (PII)	$5,000,000	1	$5,000,000	3	$15,000,000
Data Breach (no PII)	$1,000,000	0.3	$300,000	0.2	$60,000
Ransomware Attack	$2,000,000	0.6	$1,200,000	0.1	$120,000
Phishing Attack	$500,000	0.4	$200,000	0.3	$60,000

- Data breach (no PII) – for an asset valued at $1,000,000, with a 30% exposure factor, the SLE is $300,000. If such breaches are expected to occur 0.2 times per year, the ALE is $60,000 USD.
- Ransomware attack – for a $2,000,000 asset with a 60% exposure factor, the SLE is $1,200,000. Occurring 0.1 times a year, the ALE is $120,000 USD.
- Phishing attack – a $500,000 asset with a 40% exposure factor has an SLE of $200,000. With phishing expected 0.3 times a year, the ALE is $60,000 USD.

If a risk management program is mature there should be a good historical base of data to use for more advanced quantification. The data points in question are the asset value, EF, and ARO. Given a solid history of these variables, a level of certainty can be assumed of some risk areas. The opposite, or uncertainty, can be leveraged to further impact an ALE calculation as such: ALE = ARO × SLE × Uncertainty.

Generally, uncertainty values range from one to represent complete certainty an event will take place, to values higher than one for higher likelihoods. For example, an uncertainty of two means that the ALE is likely to happen twice as much in a given year. As an example, take the risk "Data Breach (PII)" from Table 10.1, apply an uncertainty of two and the ALE would become $30,000,000 USD.

In the case where there is no good historical base of data (asset value, EF, and ARO) there is another way to hypothesize an uncertainty value. Given the lack of baseline data, incorporating uncertainty into ALE calculations requires acknowledging that both the SLE and the ARO can vary due to a wide range of factors. This leads to the use of low and high values to establish a range of potential outcomes rather than a single fixed uncertainty value.

As an example, a company wants to calculate the ALE for a potential data exfiltration attack that could expose sensitive customer information.

- Uncertainty factors – the cost of each data exfiltration attack can vary significantly based on the type of data in the breach. This represents the SLE. The frequency of attacks, or ARO, can fluctuate based on changing threat landscapes and/or improved protective mechanisms.
- Estimates:
  - SLE – estimated between $50,000 USD (non-PII) and $200,000 USD (PII) per exfiltration.
  - ARO – estimated between 0.5 (once every two years) and two (twice per year).
- ALE calculations:
  - ALE (low/low) = $50,000 * 0.5 = $25,000 USD
  - ALE (low/high) = $50,000 * 2 = $100,000 USD
  - ALE (high/low) = $200,000 * 0.5 = $100,000 USD
  - ALE (high/high) = $200,000 * 2 = $400,000 USD

Irrespective of the model used, these examples provide a sense of how CRQ can help in preparing for the financial impact of various risk events. When this data is understood and relayed properly to stakeholders this allows for data-driven decision-making in risk management.

CRQ MODELS

CRQ models are clearly essential for organizations to assess and manage their cyber-security risks by translating them into financial terms. There are multiple models that can be used for this purpose, and one should be picked based on the fit for a given organization. Among the various models available, Factor Analysis of Information Risk (FAIR) is one of the most popular. There are other models and approaches, consider the following:

Factor Analysis of Information Risk (FAIR)

- Overview – FAIR breaks down risk into two main components: the frequency of events and the extent of the impact. It uses a structured, quantitative approach to assess probabilities and financial impact. Some key aspects are:
  - Loss Event Frequency (LEF) – how often loss is likely to happen.
  - Threat Event Frequency (TEF) – how often a threat event is expected to occur.
  - Vulnerability (Vuln) – a percentage representing the probability that a threat event will result in a loss.
  - Contact Frequency (CF) – how often a threat actor is expected to come into contact with an asset being protected.
  - Probability of Action (PoA) – the probability that a threat actor will act in a way that could result in a loss.
  - Loss Magnitude (LM) – the estimate of potential loss from a threat event.
- Strengths – it provides a mature, detailed framework for understanding and analyzing cyber risk in financial terms. It also supports data-driven decision-making with a focus on economic elements. At an industry level, it is widely recognized and used. One of its greatest strengths is the facilitation of risk communication to non-technical stakeholders, including the C-Suite and board members.
- Weaknesses – FAIR requires a certain advanced level of training and knowledge to be effective, it can also be complex to implement. Some of the data points that FAIR needs can be difficult to obtain. Gathering accurate and relevant data for the desired analysis can be challenging.
- Practicality – given its prevalence in the industry it is used and known. It is the basis, and under the hood engine, for other CRQ models and has developed a common language for discussing and assessing cyber risk.

CyberInsight

- Overview – CyberInsight is basically a mathematical model that leverages ML techniques to quantify and predict cyber risks in financial terms. Estimating potential monetary losses, or potential costs associated with cyber incidents, are goals of using CyberInsight.
- Strengths – it factors in many elements that simulate real-world conditions, such as vulnerability data, business context, and threat intelligence.

- Weaknesses – CyberInsight relies heavily on the quality of input data. It is also proprietary and requires specialized expertise and resources to implement and maintain.
- Practicality – it is particularly useful in environments where a quantitative and data-driven approach to CRQ is desired. Because its implementation and maintenance may require significant resources and expertise, it is more suitable for larger organizations with mature cybersecurity programs and access to comprehensive data sources.

Operationally Critical Threat, Asset, and Vulnerability Evaluation (OCTAVE)

- Overview – OCTAVE is a suite of tools, techniques, and methodologies for risk-based strategic assessment and planning. It focuses on organizational risk and strategic, business operational concerns rather than technical risk.
- Strengths – it considers subjective elements, such as organizational context and operational risks. It also encourages cross-functional collaboration and provides a systematic approach to identifying and managing risks. OCTAVE is particularly well suited for organizations with a strong emphasis on cybersecurity. It offers well-defined but flexible and adaptable assessment and mitigation techniques.
- Weaknesses – it is more qualitative than it is quantitative. The framework can be resource-heavy and may require significant collaboration and integration with broader ERM frameworks.
- Practicality – OCTAVE is practical for organizations seeking to strengthen their security risk management capabilities, especially with a focus on cybersecurity. But, this is not a fit for smaller organizations, the analysis and implementation requirements are intensive and will take a great deal of time.

Threat Assessment and Remediation Analysis (TARA)

- Overview – TARA is based on a process of identifying the most significant threats to an organization's critical assets and business operations. It evaluates both external and internal threats.
- Strengths – it facilitates a thorough analysis of a threat landscape, offering a holistic view of an organization's security posture. It also helps in prioritizing threats based on potential impact and likelihood. The methodology supports data-driven decision-making and can be tailored to the specific needs of an organization.
- Weaknesses – TARA is resource intensive and requires significant time and human resources, including specialized skills and knowledge. It has a tendency to need constant attention and become quickly out of date based on rapidly evolving cyber threat landscapes. The process can also be complex, especially for large organizations and it relies on sensitive data requiring stringent measures to protect implementations.

- Practicality – TARA is a solid technique if the proper resources can be assigned to its implementation and maintenance. So long as the complexity can be managed, it is particularly useful for informing the development of a cybersecurity strategy that aligns with business objectives.

Monte Carlo Simulations

While Monte Carlo simulations may not be considered an actual CRQ modeling technique in their own right, they play an important role in many CRQ modeling techniques. As such they are worthy of being part of a CISO's foundational knowledge base.

- Overview – Monte Carlo simulations use random samplings and statistical modeling to estimate and simulate the probability of varying outcomes. It does so for processes that cannot easily be predicted due to the reality of random variables.
- Strengths – it can model the uncertainty and variability of risk. The technique is applicable to a wide range of risk scenarios and not limited to cyber risk. A key strength is that this technique yields multiple possible outcomes rather than a singular one.
- Weaknesses – Monte Carlo simulations require large data sets and powerful computational resources. Depending on complexity the modeling may require advanced statistical knowledge to interpret results. The accuracy of a set of results relies strongly on the quality of the data inputs provided. Low-quality inputs will yield simulation results that can be inaccurate.
- Practicality – Monte Carlo simulations are particularly useful in environments where there is high complexity, uncertainty, or randomness. Simpler environments may get better results with other techniques.

NIST SP 800-30

The publication, NIST SP 800-30 is not a CRQ modeling technique, per say. But it is worth mentioning as it does cover the quantification function.

- Overview – 800-30 is a risk management guide that provides a structured approach to conducting risk assessments. It includes guidelines for identifying, estimating, and prioritizing information system risk. Quantifying risk involves a process that factors in likelihood and impact.
- Strengths – it does provide a systematic and comprehensive approach to risk management that is suitable for industry-agnostic organizations of varying sizes. It does focus on technology while offering comprehensive guidance that facilitates the mapping of vulnerabilities and threats, making it easier to understand the relationships between seemingly disparate elements involved in a risk assessment process.
- Weaknesses – 800-30 is comprehensive and resource intensive, making it potentially complex and time-consuming to implement. Smaller organizations may find it challenging to conduct assessments using this framework.

Another weakness is that it does strongly focus on technical vulnerabilities and threats, limiting its ability to provide a holistic view of an organization's overall risk landscape.

- Practicality – this framework is practical so long as skilled resources are available. It may not meet the needs of organizations seeking very granular CRQ data points but for those needing some quantification as part of a larger risk management process, it may be appealing.

The choice of CRQ model/technique depends on an organization's specific needs, the type of risks being assessed, the availability of resources (human, time, data, etc.), and the desired outcome of the process. It's sometimes beneficial to combine the results from multiple models to capture a comprehensive view of cyber risk from both technical and business perspectives.

When metrics are put together based on an understanding of the target audience and organizational culture, they are indispensable for proving security program effectiveness. The most important aspect is translating metrics into relevant business terms and translation needs to be based on a common ground of understanding, and financial impact. The examples provided demonstrate how to position security metrics to resonate with corporate leadership and boards. By quantifying cyber risks CISOs can create a layer of understanding and effectively convey the value of their critical function.

EXPERT ADVICE

In the fast-paced world of cybersecurity, mastering metrics is essential for effective decision-making and risk management at the executive level. Just as a well-tailored suit enhances one's confidence, precise measurement empowers organizations to protect their digital assets with certainty. As a security operations manager at Cisco, I spearheaded the development and implementation of key performance indicators (KPIs) and key risk indicators (KRIs) to measure the effectiveness and efficiency of our security operations center (SOC). Our journey involved understanding organizational objectives, conducting risk assessments, and selecting metrics aligned with our goals and risk profile. Through clear communication and buy-in from stakeholders, we emphasized the benefits of tracking metrics, such as improving security performance and ensuring compliance. Utilizing reliable data sources and appropriate tools, we measured KPIs and KRIs accurately, driving actionable insights and continuous improvement initiatives. By embracing a data-driven approach to cybersecurity metrics, executives can confidently navigate the complexities of the digital landscape and safeguard their organizations against emerging threats.

– Nia F. Luckey, CIO Advisory Services Sr. Consultant, Infosys

A cybersecurity regulation revolution is quietly reshaping the global economy – from the US Securities and Exchange Commission (SEC) to the European Union and beyond. Consequently, measuring and communicating cybersecurity risk is now imperative.

In today's interconnected digital economy, cybersecurity extends far beyond a company's own attack surface. The 2023 MOVEit vulnerability serves as a stark reminder that cybersecurity is dependent on the collective strength of the entire digital ecosystem. In other words, the responsibility of maintaining robust cybersecurity goes beyond individual companies. Any supply chain dependency could result in an incident that gets your company on the front page of a national newspaper. Yet, historically, there have been no key performance indicators (KPIs) in the security world that could effectively measure third-party risk.

Consider this: If you drive a car, you have the speedometer. At a doctor's office, you have a scale. Yet, with cybersecurity, many companies are still flying blind.

Some companies opt for "security by obscurity" in an attempt to shield their cybersecurity from scrutiny. This practice involves withholding information about their security measures, believing that if potential attackers don't know how a system is secured, they won't be able to exploit its vulnerabilities. However, this strategy is ineffective and leads to a false sense of security.

True cybersecurity leadership demands a proactive approach beyond response protocols, focusing on bolstering cyber resilience to maintain trust with customers, partners, and the broader public. Cybersecurity ratings serve as a universal measurement, enabling board members and security practitioners to communicate effectively. Just as credit ratings guide financial decisions, cybersecurity ratings provide clear, standardized benchmarks for cybersecurity.

Progress starts with precise measurement. And until recently, cybersecurity lacked effective measurements. Security ratings are a critical security tool rapidly gaining respect and acceptance in light of the surge of third-party-related breaches and remote work environments. Security ratings grade an organization's security performance by how well it protects information while providing key indicators of their internal and third-party risk, enabling companies to be more cyber resilient. By establishing clear KPIs we can enhance cyber resilience, and ultimately renew trust in our digital ecosystem. As companies communicate their cybersecurity through quantifiable metrics, customers, partners, and regulators gain confidence in the organization's ability to safeguard their business. The only path forward is to build a culture of cybersecurity transparency, trust, and accountability.

"You can't fix what you can't measure. Quite simply, metrics matter".

– Dr. Aleksandr Yampolskiy, CEO, and Co-Founder,
SecurityScorecard

REAL-WORLD PERSPECTIVE

"We tried addressing that before". "We want to do this, but it is not a priority". More than once in my experience, I've heard something like this when attempting to remediate a risk. The problem was not the severity of the issue, but rather the lack of clear data showing its importance. Vague statements about potential risks or best practices do not get projects prioritized. Concrete metrics and data, on the other hand, are much more likely to get attention and buy-in. For example, a team I worked with had been unsuccessful for years in creating a policy that would address a particular risk. To solve this problem, I presented the dollar amount this was costing the company annually. It was immediately prioritized and resolved within a few months. In a similar case, a request to restrict permissions within a tool had previously been denied. After gaining further insight into the problem and presenting simple metrics on how various staff were misusing the tool, we easily obtained approval to adjust. Metrics and data are key to clearly communicate risk and minimize resistance to resolution.

– **Christine Tornabene**

11 Be a Communicator

Effective communication is hardly a characteristic unique to the role of a CISO. But, it is a skill, ability, and characteristic that can have a profound impact on the success or failure of a CISO. A CISO often must be a translator, helping non-technical business-focused stakeholders understand cybersecurity needs and concepts.

EFFECTIVE COMMUNICATION

There are numerous factors that come into play when one is being a good communicator, some are:

- Curbing your ego – when communicating, the goal should never be showcasing your intelligence or anything of the sort. The goal should be effectively relaying a message such that the target audience walks away with insights they did not have prior to interacting with you.
- Use simple verbiage – when communicating, assume that the target audience is not technical. When addressing a non-technical audience, it is important to use simple and plain language that anyone can understand. Avoid using technical jargon or intricate-sounding terms that the target audience may not be familiar with.
- Use visuals – the use of visuals can be a helpful technique to explain cybersecurity concepts to a non-technical audience. Moreover, some research published by the National Library of Medicine (www.ncbi.nlm.nih.gov/pmc/articles/PMC4340450/) has shown that a large percentage of humans are visual learners. The study claims that, in the general population, the distribution of the three main learning styles is: 65% visual, 30% auditory, and 5% kinesthetic. Here is a simple breakdown of these three learning styles:
  - Visual learners supposedly retain information best by viewing graphical material (pictures or images). Visuals could include infographics, illustrations, diagrams, and/or cartoons.
  - Auditory learners should retain most information after hearing it.
  - Kinesthetic learners learn by doing. They are all about doing things physically. Role-playing or carrying out some action physically can help them learn things better.
- Be patient – it is important to be patient and empathetic when communicating with an audience to whom the material is not native, for example, cybersecurity material to a non-technical audience. One cannot assume that a target audience is quickly absorbing the material being presented. In some ways when we are communicating, we are teaching, remember that the audience at hand most likely does not have knowledge of the material being covered, this is why they are your audience.

DOI: 10.1201/9781003477556-11

- It is important to patiently explain cybersecurity risks and threats to non-technical audiences. The material must be relayed in a way that they can understand. This will increase the likelihood that a given audience will see themselves as part of the equation toward better security. Moreover, this can help the audience absorb the importance of cybersecurity to a business and give a CISO a new set of supportive allies.
- Be open – be open to both questions and varying perspectives from a given target audience. This will help you, the communicator, connect with the audience in order to help them understand the material better. Particularly for a CISO, this can lead to the audience feeling more engaged with security matters and confident in their ability to do their part in protecting their organization.
  - Varying perspectives – varying perspectives and/or different ideas generally require a diverse group of minds coming together for some common cause (solve a problem, design a solution, etc.). Our mindsets are molded by our personal lives and experiences. A lack of diverse mindsets when tackling cybersecurity matters can be detrimental. Diverse cybersecurity teams can analyze problems from different angles, unearth unique solutions, or factor in risks that were not considered in the past.
- Understand your audience – depending on the size of an audience it may be possible to do some up-front reconnaissance. Whenever possible, understanding your audience is important because it will give you the ability to tailor your message and delivery style accordingly. When you do gain an up-front understanding of your audience, you can:
  - Do research – before speaking, dedicate some time to learn whatever you can about your audience.
    - What are they focused on professionally?
    - What are they focused on personally?
    - What are they openly concerned about?
    - What is their level of knowledge about the topic at hand?
      - If your audience is familiar with the topic, you can go into more detail. If your audience is not familiar with the topic you will need to provide higher-level information.
    - What is the age range of your audience?
    - What is their gender?
    - What is their educational level?
  - Divide and conquer – if the audience size is manageable. And the audience members are known, use this to your advantage. Reach out to audience members individually prior to the communication session. Speak with these members of your audience before you speak to the entire group. Ask them questions about their interests and concerns as well as seek answers to some of the points presented in the research bullet point. This will give you an edge in better understanding what they are each looking for in your presentation.
  - Use appropriate verbiage – this will help you to communicate your message in a way that will resonate and stick with the audience. For example, if your audience is deeply technical, as opposed to business-centric, you will need to go deep technically in order to add value to that audience.

- Build rapport – aim to connect with the target audience on a personal level. Again, the size of the audience is a factor. But when this is possible it will make the audience more likely to engage in active listening. It may also provide an advantage if one of your goals is to influence or persuade some of the people in the audience.
- Continuously read the room – it is essential that you gauge reactions when certain things are said. This will help you to determine whether your message is resonating with the audience and whether you need to adjust the message and/or the delivery style. The importance of this cannot be overstated. If this is an ability you do not possess, please seek out professional training as it is invaluable. Here are a few things you can do to accomplish this when speaking:
  - Be observant – while speaking, pay attention to audience reactions when you say or do certain things. This could help you to gauge how well your message and/or delivery style resonates with them.
    - Are they engaged?
    - Are they head down on their cellular phones?
    - Are they nodding off?
    - Are they talking to each other?
    - Are they asking you questions?
    - Are they asking each other questions?
      - This one is especially of interest. There are cases where audience members have questions but will not pose them to the speaker. You can proactively inject yourself into these scenarios and add immediate positive value.
- Understand the setting – the setting and purpose of your presentation will help you to determine what kind of information your audience needs and wants.
  - Where will this speaking session take place?
    - Is it a boardroom? Is it in a restaurant? Is it at a conference where there will be lots of noise?
  - What is the context for your presentation?
    - Is it a regular board session? Is it an all-company call? Is it a session with financial analysts from an external firm? Is it to an audience of auditors looking for answers?

These tips should be able to guide you to understand your audience and effectively deliver a powerful presentation.

EXPERT ADVICE – EFFECTIVE COMMUNICATION

The CISO's Guide to Playing Nice With Others:
Tools for Stakeholder Wrangling

In the world of a CISO, where the art of persuasion meets the science of security, and your "customers" range from the enthusiastic IT intern to the finance team wondering why "we're spending so much on these firewalls again"?

Deploying tools used in product management, to prioritize requirements and understand customers, are clutch tools for a CISO. It all starts with knowing your customers. For CISOs, almost all your stakeholders are internal or external customers.

Mendelow's Matrix: Prioritize Like a Boss

Like most things in cybersecurity, success means prioritization. Enter Mendelow's matrix, your secret weapon. Once you have identified your team's customers by function, the next step is to gain an understanding of both how much a customer group can influence your team's results and their interest in your team's mission. Enter Mendelow's matrix, which will help you know where to prioritize your communication, what success looks like, and the frequency of communication. Most cybersecurity teams will struggle to make everyone happy, so being intentional with where you do not focus may be more important than deciding where you do focus. With my teams, I often use the mantra "If it's not a hell yes, it's a hell no". Showing up with kindness and empathy for all internal customers is non-negotiable, but deciding who to spend time with needs to be carefully assessed.

Table 11.1 is a starting point for a Mendelow Matrix for CISOs. Individual organizations vary based on structure, offering, and individual power, so it's worthwhile to spend time tuning your matrix for your organization and adding any specialized functions. For example, CISOs supporting utility companies providing electricity, natural gas, and water, may add functions like community relations that would not be relevant for an industrial product company CISO.

TABLE 11.1
Starting point for a Mendelow Matrix for CISOs.

Leader	Power	Interest	Quadrant
Executive Management	High	High	Manage Closely
IT Department	Medium	High	Keep Informed
Employees	Low	High	Keep Informed
Regulatory Bodies	High	Medium	Keep Satisfied
Customers	Variable	Variable	Monitor/Keep Informed
Suppliers/Partners	Low	Medium	Monitor
Legal Department	High	High	Manage Closely
Risk Management	High	High	Manage Closely
Engineering	High	High/Medium	Manage Closely/Keep Informed
Compliance Function	High	High	Manage Closely

Personas: Know Your Key Customers Like You Mean It!

Understanding your stakeholders means knowing how they experience cyber-security as work: what is important to them, their pain points, how they look at risk, and how their success is measured. The goal of this exercise is to be able to speak to the stakeholder in alignment to their worldview and to know where your joint efforts can support their success.

Table 11.2 is an example of a user (fictitious) persona template for the head of engineering.

With this understanding of engineering leadership, a CISO can focus meetings on metrics around what concerns Alex most related to cybersecurity. Aligning with Alex on these metrics, showing a positive trend around these metrics, and most importantly, contributing to Alex's team's success will significantly enhance the cybersecurity team's ability to minimize product cybersecurity risks and minimize attack surface.

Metrics That Matter to Your Customer

Let's go back to Alex. Without Alex's support, your team will be unsuccessful. Without Alex's engagement your mean time to respond, the age of your

TABLE 11.2
Example of a user persona template.

Alex Rivera	
Position: Head of Engineering	
Company Type: Mid-sized B2B SaaS Software Company	
Years in Role: 5	
Interests:	Passionate about technology innovation and product design.
	Sees cybersecurity as a necessary component but not a primary focus.
Pain Points:	Views extensive cybersecurity measures as potential impediments to rapid product development and deployment.
	Struggles with balancing the demand for quick market releases with the need for adequate security checks.
	Often sees cybersecurity requirements as a hurdle in achieving optimal user experience and system performance.
Goals:	To lead the development of cutting-edge products that dominate the market.
	To streamline engineering processes for maximum efficiency, integrating cybersecurity measures with minimal impact on productivity.
Success Metrics:	Product innovation and market success.
	Efficiency in development cycles and product deployment.
	Meeting minimum required cybersecurity standards without compromising product performance and user experience.

vulnerabilities, and your security debt will expand like summer wildfires in the High Sierra. Convincing Alex to prioritize product cybersecurity is all about spotting mutual goals and driving your team's efforts to favorably impact those metrics. Let Alex know how the development cycle has been moving in a positive direction due to your team's focus on automating cyber-related scope. Conversely, if your team has negatively impacted Alex's priority metrics, own it. If you can acknowledge you understand the negative impacts your team has had, Alex will work to find a path forward more rapidly.

With this understanding of engineering leadership, a CISO can focus meetings on metrics around what concerns Alex most related to cybersecurity. Aligning with Alex on these metrics, showing a positive trend around these metrics, and most importantly, contributing to Alex's team's success will significantly enhance the cybersecurity team's ability to minimize product cybersecurity risks and minimize attack surface. Here are some examples of the metrics that matter the most to a stakeholder like Alex.

Development Cycle Time: Monitor the time from development start to completion, noting extensions due to security tasks.

Issue Resolution Time: Measure the speed of addressing and resolving security issues.

Automation Ratio: Assess the percentage of security tasks automated versus manual, aiming for higher automation.

Deployment Frequency: Track how security requirements affect deployment rates, aiming to minimize negative impacts.

Team Productivity Metrics: Observe general productivity indicators (feature completion, bug fixes, velocity) for indirect insights into the impact of security tasks.

In Conclusion: Focus will set us free.

Being a CISO isn't just about warding off digital doom; it's about turning the cybersecurity narrative from a dreaded lecture into a shared view of the future where your key stakeholders are the heroes. It's about making cybersecurity the cool kid everyone wants to have a beer with. So, grab your Mendelow matrix, craft those personas, and remember that you can only succeed if you prioritize the success of your key stakeholders.

– Susan Peterson Sturm, Sr. Director, Wabtec Product Security

TRANSLATION

Proficiency in translation for a CISO is essential. This does not mean from one language to another (e.g., Spanish to English, or Russian to Japanese), but technology and/or cybersecurity talk to business speak. The CISO's role has become more and more business-centric. Moreover, for mature companies, cybersecurity risk and resilience are now legitimate boardroom and business matters. This means that the ability to perform effective translation is essential if a CISO is going to succeed in a modern-day business setting.

Communication can be focused on strategic initiatives but needs to cover risks and threats and how they relate to business risk. The CISO needs to be a translator such that risk is translated into financial language which is what most business-centric stakeholders speak. An important aspect of translation is that the translator must be versed in the target language. Most board members and most members of the C-Suite see the world through a lens very different from that of technologists and cybersecurity experts. These types of target audiences generally think in terms of financials, top and bottom lines. In essence, a CISO needs to make cybersecurity matters something digestible by businesspeople. It is all about conveying a message and if that message gets lost in translation, communication has not been successful.

Here are some tips for a CISO when the time comes to be a translator:

- Be clear about goals – this must be done up-front so that the tone is set with the audience. This way the audience already has a sense of what you want them to take away from your messaging. Also, if relevant let the audience know what action items are expected from them after they absorb the material.
- Use analogies – analogies can be a helpful way to explain complex concepts so long as they can bring a topic to a level of common understanding. The point is to demystify the topic and make it easy to understand.
- Use humor – depending on the audience and setting, humor can be a great way to make cybersecurity concepts more engaging and memorable. Tread carefully here since humor is a very subjective area.
- Be a storyteller – stories can be a powerful way to communicate many concepts, cybersecurity included.
- Be confident – some people may be resistant to change, and if you take them out of their comfort zones there may be reactions. This is especially so when it comes to cybersecurity because some feel there is no hope and that the "bad guys" will always win. Be prepared to confidently address their concerns while exercising empathetic understanding that some people don't do well with change.

STORYTELLING

Stories are powerful. They can unionize an abstract or foreign idea with a basic human emotion. In our youth, most of us have been the recipient of messaging via listening to stories. We have also probably read fiction books, seen movies, and attended theatrical plays. All those mediums tell stories. The good ones do so by telling a compelling and engaging story. In those cases, information is weaved into the overall experience, arousing our attention, emotions, and energy.

Storytelling is a powerful tool that a CISO can use to communicate complex and foreign concepts in a way that is engaging and memorable. In the field of cybersecurity, storytelling can be used to justify funding requests, educate, and inform people about the risks of cyberthreats, and to encourage folks to take steps to protect an organization and themselves personally.

Here are some tips that can be used to tell effective cybersecurity stories:

- Connect on a personal level – make the experience personal. The most impactful stories are the ones that create a personal connection with the audience. When telling stories related to cybersecurity, focus on the impact on human life. This could take the form of impact to quality of life or, for instance, some end result involving financial loss. Humanize those who were affected by some cyber event such that the audience can empathize and relate.
- Use real-world examples – people are more likely to feel connected to stories that they can relate to. Also, a connection takes life when it is related to an event the audience is aware of; maybe use a cybersecurity event that made the news and a lot of people heard of it. If the event impacted normal people, this will most likely resonate with the audience.
- Use humor – where appropriate use humor, it can be a great way to make cybersecurity stories more engaging.
- Be to the point – cybersecurity stories should be clear and concise. Avoid using technical terms that the audience may not understand. Engaging in technobabble could easily lose your audience.
- Make a call to action – every cybersecurity story should end with a call to action. Engage the audience in making cybersecurity a collective endeavor, a team sport as it is often referred to. Explain to the audience what they can do to protect themselves, their family members, and their organizations from cyberthreats.

Effective storytelling can be a powerful tool for a CISO to communicate cybersecurity concepts, gain support from important entities, and encourage people to be active in the pursuit of more protective states.

Specifically, when speaking to board members and/or members of the C-Suite, storytelling can be used to:

- Explain complex concepts in simple terms – board and C-Suite members are often faced with complex concepts that can be difficult to understand. This is especially so considering that most modern-day board members are not versed in cybersecurity. Storytelling can be a great way to break down these concepts into smaller, more digestible, and understandable elements.
  - Without being disrespectful or demeaning try to explain complex cybersecurity concepts as if doing so to a young child. That level of simplicity will go a long way.
- Build supportive relationships – storytelling can help to build relationships between you and those entities whose support you will need in the challenging business of cybersecurity. When you effectively share a story, you are giving that target audience a glimpse into the life and experiences of a

CISO, someone they will come to rely on during both good and difficult times. This approach can help to create a sense of connection and trust.
- Motivate action – storytelling can be used to motivate board and C-Suite members to take supportive action. When a CISO effectively shares a story about the impact of actual work performed, you are giving them a reason to care about your cause.

The point about motivating action cannot be understated. Sometimes this could make a difference at crucial moments. One example is when a board is choosing where to spend dollars from a tight budget. That story a CISO once told could sit in someone's memory and be the difference between the cybersecurity team getting budgeted or not. As such a CISO needs to choose the right stories to tell. Not all stories will have equal impact. When speaking with a board or C-Suite, a CISO wants to choose stories that are relevant to their interests and concerns. This touches on many points that have been stressed throughout this book where knowing your audience is critical.

To augment the point about knowing your audience, consider the following factors:

- The audience's interests and concerns – what are the board members passionate about? What is the C-Suite concerned about? What are their biggest challenges? Keep in mind that typical board and C-Suite members are not concerned about cybersecurity or risk. They are generally concerned about the negative impact (financial, reputational, etc.) of cybersecurity incidents or actualized risk events.
- The audience's level of understanding – how much do the board members know about cybersecurity? How much do they know about your work in particular? Do they need a basic overview, or can you go into detail?
- The audience's decision-making process – what kind of information does the board need to make decisions? What kind of stories will resonate with them?

By carefully considering these data elements, a CISO can choose stories that will be effective in relaying messages to board and C-Suite members alike.

Here are some examples of stories that you could tell a board or C-Suite:

- A story about a time where your work directly stopped some nefarious actors. This not only speaks to the effectiveness of your work, but it also instills confidence in you as a battle-hardened CISO. Experience counts for a lot in this industry.
- A story about a time when you solved difficult problems while overcoming some challenges. This type of story can show your levels of resilience and resourcefulness. This will also instill confidence in you as a CSIO capable of handling difficult situations.
- A story about a time when you positively impacted someone's life through your work. This type of story can showcase your passion for the job. And most can't deny that making a positive impact on the world is generally seen in a good light.
- A story about a time when you learned something valuable. This type of story can show the audience your level of humility and that you are open to feedback and looking for ways to improve.

EXPERT ADVICE – STORYTELLING

It is critical to develop your storytelling skills as a motivational speaker to your team, but even more so for communicating with senior leadership and the Board of Directors, so you can take the data and problem statement to transform that information into a consumable format. This is paramount so non-technical, or business-focused leaders can understand the importance of your situation. Most senior business leaders and board members understand very little about cybersecurity and the risk these threats and issues pose to the company or organization they oversee from a governance perspective. Creating a digestible and relatable story helps to ensure your success in getting these important situations funded and/or prioritized based on importance.

When creating these analogies and stories, please remember to replace acronyms and industry-specific vernacular with understandable and relatable words that demonstrate the threat and importance of the situation. I also recommend doing a practice run of your presentation with a non-technical audience to get feedback on whether or not your intended message is being conveyed. It's also important to know what your ask is and make sure you weave that into the closing statements of your message. Lastly, be clear and concise so you don't lose your audience.

– Brian Arellanes, Independent Director, Board of Directors for Lynx and North Bay Steel Recycling

Storytelling is an effective tool for communicating ideas, teaching lessons, and inspiring action.

But why? The answer lies in science.

Numerous scientists have proven how stories can affect people. One research study discovered that when we're presented with facts (e.g., PowerPoint bullets), two areas of the brain related to the production and processing of language and words, Broca's area, and Wernicke's area, respectively, are activated. When we listen to or watch a story, other parts of our brain spring to life. Incredibly, parts of our brain that are related to different aspects of a story are triggered when we hear the story. As an example, if the story describes an active event, such as "Chester punched the pillow" or "Rebecca kicked the ball", the motor cortex part of our brain becomes activated. Even more amazingly, the brain activity is concentrated in different parts of the motor cortex depending on whether the action described in the story is related to the arm or to the leg.

Another incredible phenomenon that scientists have discovered is how the sensory cortex is activated when stories containing highly descriptive metaphors such as "The singer had a gravelly voice" or "She had silky hands" are used. That is not observed when less descriptive phrases such as "The singer had a rough voice" and "She had soft hands" are used. Another well-known research study led by Uri Hasson at Princeton discovered that a subject can plant thoughts, emotions, and ideas in their listeners' brains by simply telling a story. Using functional MRIs, the scientists discovered that the brain patterns of the listeners were identical to the storyteller's when they told them their story!

What are the practical uses of this research? Start using stories in business! Regardless of the role you have, the power to convince your audience is already within your reach! The second thing you can do is to keep your stories interesting and more persuasive by using detailed, descriptive language. Whether you're trying to convince a board, an employee, or a collaborator, the power of storytelling can simplify your efforts to motivate changes in thought and behavior.

– Brandon Hoe, Founder/Chief Content Officer, Elevating Cyber

In the evolving landscape of cybersecurity, the role of a CISO extends beyond traditional tasks like managing firewalls and securing network perimeters. A distinguishing trait of a successful CISO is the ability to be an adept communicator, capable of articulating complex cybersecurity threats in terms understandable to non-experts and tailoring these communications to align with the business objectives of various stakeholders.

For instance, when engaging with the Chief Financial Officer (CFO), a CISO frames discussions around financial impacts, illustrating potential savings from averting data breaches, the cost-benefit analysis of security investments, and the financial implications of regulatory non-compliance. Similarly, dialogues with the Chief Operating Officer (COO) focus on operational resilience, highlighting how cybersecurity measures mitigate disruptions and enhance business continuity. Through examples like preventing downtime from ransomware attacks, the CISO underlines cybersecurity's integral role in operational efficiency and its alignment with the COO's priorities.

The CISO's relationship with the Chief Executive Officer (CEO) further underscores the need for strategic alignment, presenting cybersecurity not as a cost center but as a strategic asset that fosters business innovation, protects the company's reputation, and secures customer trust. By demonstrating to the CEO how investments in advanced threat detection can differentiate the market and enhance customer loyalty, the CISO aligns cybersecurity strategies with the company's overarching vision and growth objectives.

Additionally, effective communication with non-technical leadership and the board is crucial for a CISO. This entails translating technical risks into business risks and demonstrating how strategic security initiatives protect and enhance business value, such as reducing the potential for brand damage from data breaches. Mastering this art of communication enables a CISO to secure the organization's digital assets and become a pivotal figure in driving the business forward.

Ultimately, a CISO's success hinges on aligning cybersecurity objectives with the broader business goals. This necessitates excelling in storytelling through metrics and reporting, converting abstract security concepts into compelling narratives that highlight their impact on the business. Presenting cybersecurity metrics within the context of business outcomes – like reduced risk exposure, improved compliance posture, and enhanced customer trust – allows a CISO to effectively communicate the value of cybersecurity investments. Such an approach not only facilitates informed decision-making but also fosters a culture where cybersecurity is seen as an indispensable pillar of the business strategy. Through strategic communication and alignment, a CISO significantly contributes to the organization's resilience and success in an increasingly digital world.

– Ramin Lamei, Cybersecurity Expert & Founder @ TechCompass –
Helping Companies Navigate Technology Securely

REAL-WORLD PERSPECTIVE – STORYTELLING

Being a storyteller is an invaluable skill for a CISO, particularly in high-stakes environments where cybersecurity intertwines with physical safety and operational integrity. A few years ago, I conducted a comprehensive penetration test (pentest) in a compound operating within a region with terrorist activity from local militias. This pentest evaluated people, processes, and technology – including the readiness of advanced military-grade systems deployed to help safeguard the physical premises. The assessment unveiled significant risks across these domains, often very technical in nature, that required a comprehensive approach spanning multiple levels to be adequately addressed.

The essence of storytelling, in this context, lies in the ability to make these abstract risks palpable and somewhat personal for every stakeholder involved. For instance, awareness sessions designed for end users attempted to frame cyber risks in the context of personal identity protection and financial security, the narrative was made relevant and urgent, attempting to reach each of the individuals.

For technical staff, on the other hand, I engaged in a narrative that peeled back the layers of the pentest, delving into the sophisticated methodologies and red-teaming tactics employed. This not only highlighted the potential for privileged asset compromise but did so by drawing on their intrinsic interest in technology, helping them gain a deeper understanding of vulnerabilities and the critical role operations play in defending against them.

For the executives and senior management, the story was simplified and distilled into a strategic overview, emphasizing the risks and the tangible impact on service delivery and safety. This narrative was tailored to convey the urgency of implementing systemic risk mitigations and enhancements, without getting into technical detail. By aligning the storytelling with the priorities and perspectives of the VIP audience, it ensured the message not only resonated but spurred executive action.

> In every narrative crafted and shared, I leveraged storytelling as a strategic tool to bridge the gap between complex cybersecurity challenges and the diverse motivations and understandings of the compound's personnel. This approach didn't just communicate risks; it enlisted each individual into a shared mission of overall security and resilience, demonstrating that when stories are told right, they can drive engagement, and cultivate a collective mindset geared towards proactive cybersecurity best practices.

– Alvaro Soneiro

TRUE STORY – STORYTELLING

Communication and storytelling are an essential part of the CISO role. A good portion of our jobs are to influence the change needed to address a specific risk. However, many of the stakeholders also have their own priorities where they are dedicating time, resources, and energy.

At a previous company, I was getting some political pushback on implementing a pretty common security control. Finance said it cost too much, engineers said it would make their job more difficult, and non-technical leaders questioned why we needed the solution, "don't we have enough security toys already"?

I decided to tie this to one of my efforts which was providing some security capabilities as an employee benefit to all employees and their family members. The project was getting some great traction and there were some parallels, so I thought why not, let's give it a try.

I had several one-on-one sessions with some influential stakeholders and started off with this new employee benefits tool and shared how impactful this had been for my family and keeping them safe online as well as my elderly parents. There are so many bad things on the internet these days that I am constantly paranoid. Everyone had heard the horror stories of someone's identification being stolen, money drained from their bank account, or in my sons' case a bad actor breaking into Fortnite accounts. However, with this tool in place, it gives me some peace of mind as a father, a son, and a security practitioner.

I went through some of the threats that exist online and how these tools' features prevent bad actors from getting into my parents' and sons' devices. The stakeholders were excited and asked to be part of the initial pilot. Each one of them had a parent, child, spouse, or friend they loved very much. They also shared the same anxiety with online threats and loved the fact that now they had a solution to help mitigate some of their concerns.

I ended the conversation with, "It would be great if we had those same controls for our internal systems, especially the crown jewels that house our sensitive data". And that's when the lightbulb finally went on for my stakeholders. If a security capability could keep their family and friends safe, shouldn't we implement something similar for our company? After that, it was a no-brainer we had to have and when could we implement it. They became champions for the cause!

Those interactions taught me a very valuable lesson in my career, my stakeholders aren't disinterested in security; I had just failed in connecting the dots for them. We all have the same goals at the end of the day, I just needed to translate it better for them. Thus, the power of storytelling and effective communication, and the need for it to be an essential tool in the CISO Playbook. Without it, it is impossible to influence the change needed to mitigate risk or increase the maturity of a security program.

– Paul Guerra, CISO at StockX

CRISIS COMMUNICATIONS

A CISO is responsible for the security of an organization's resources. While this includes identifying, assessing, and mitigating risks and threats to the organization's information resources and assets, a large component of the role revolves around the response to events and incidents. These represent moments of crisis. It is in these exact moments that a CISO can make a positive difference to an organization. But this cannot happen in silent isolation, communication during moments of crisis is of paramount importance.

The way crisis communications are handled is as important as the communiqué itself. Regarding the model used for crisis communication, here are some real-world tips:

- Be proactive – don't wait for people to come to you with questions. Get out in front of a crisis and communicate as much information as you can.
- Be clear and concise – during moments of crisis people are often scared and confused. The last thing they want to do is read something long and elaborate. So, it's important to be clear and concise with your communication. Use brevity and simple language that everyone can understand; avoid jargon or technical terms.
- Be candid and transparent – people will be more likely to trust you if you are clearly honest and transparent with them. If you don't know something, state that humbly. And if you make a mistake, own that too.
- Be consistent – during a crisis people will naturally flock toward what makes them feel safe. Consistency on your part starts with all your communication

prior to this moment of crisis. People need to know that you are calm and consistent during a crisis. The CISO needs to be that one person to make others feel safe. People need to know they can count on you to provide accurate and timely information. Make sure your communication is consistent over time and across all channels.

- Be empathetic – people are going through a lot during a crisis, so it's important to be empathetic and understanding. Let them know that you care about their situation and that you are there to help.
- Be patient – during a crisis you will very well deal with people that are afraid, frustrated, or angry. Be patient with them and answer their questions as best you can. More importantly, make sure your demeanor gives off a clear vibe of patience, calm, and confidence.
- Use multiple channels – given the proliferation of data channels, it is fair to assume that people get their information from varying sources. As such, it's important to use multiple channels to communicate during a crisis. This includes social media, email, SMS (text messaging), and traditional media. The goal is to make your communications accessible to the broadest possible audience of relevance.
- Have a designated spokesperson – following up on the earlier point of consistency, it's important to have a designated spokesperson who will be responsible for communication during the crisis. This should be someone already known to a large subset of your target audience. This will help to ensure that the message is consistent and that there is the least possible confusion.
- Be prepared for the unexpected – things can, and will, change quickly during a crisis, so be flexible and prepared for the unexpected. Have a plan in place for how you will adjust communications as situations evolve.
- Be prepared to address tough questions – moments of crisis bring forth tough questions. This is a natural reaction on the part of humans. Be prepared to answer these questions calmly, honestly, and in a way that is sensitive to the audience and situation.
- Monitor social media – social media can be a valuable source of information as well as a powerful tool for communicating during a crisis. Monitor social media for updates, questions from the public, and to read the general temperature of the public as it relates to the given crisis.

12 Be a Vendor Manager/ Negotiator

The reality of the modern-day cybersecurity landscape is that security-focused products play a critical role in operational and protective settings. Gone are the days of building solutions from scratch, even though focusing on solutions, as opposed to point solutions, is an area you want some team members focused on. New security product companies are hitting the market at a rapid rate, some chasing the allure of being acquired by a bigger, more established, player.

Since the cyber and information security industries rely so heavily on products, managing and negotiating with vendors is of great importance. Understanding vendor motivation becomes very important. Some motivating factors for founders are:

- Solving complex problems.
- Building a company.
- Getting rich.
- Getting acquired.

SALESPEOPLE

Salespeople are motivated by different factors but primarily by competition, money, and the drive to close deals. Generally speaking, salespeople are industry agnostic, but there are some commonalities about their tactics and motivations:

- They are adaptable – these folks are being told "no" many times per day. As such, salespeople must be "thick-skinned", adaptable, and resilient. The successful ones are continuously learning, refining pitches and tactics based on different interactions.
- They are competitive – many salespeople are extremely competitive. This spans their personal lives (e.g., they are competitive with themselves by meeting quotas and goals) and their professional lives (e.g., they are competitive with other salespeople). They are often motivated by winning. This can be very subjective, for example, it could mean trying to exceed quotas or outsell other sales teams.
- They are money-motivated – not many people work for free. Salespeople are no different, but they have the challenge that most of them have packages that are heavily dependent on commission. Commission-based sales roles mean income is directly correlated with sales numbers. The potential to earn bigger paychecks by closing more, and larger, deals is a major motivator. Even in salary-based roles, bonuses and other incentives are usually tied to quantifiable objectives.

DOI: 10.1201/9781003477556-12

- They enjoy closing deals – the thrill of the deal close is a great source of enjoyment for some salespeople. Convincing someone to buy something from you seems to activate some pleasure trigger in their brains. Many salespeople pride themselves on being able to extract that coveted agreement to a deal.
- They build relationships – for the most part building relationships leads to closing deals. Good salespeople work hard to establish trust and rapport with customers. This could consist of using positive attitudes, charm, persistence, and appearing as helpful as possible. The goal is to either turn a prospect into a long-term client or solidify an existing relationship and make it a continuous source of business.

While individual motivations do vary, successful salespeople seem to share a competitive drive, ability to influence, and persistence to keep pursuing sales initiatives. The rewards of both financial gain and personal accomplishment keep top performers dedicated to their craft of selling.

The following is a point-in-time observation (e.g., subject to grow or shrink over time) – there is a great disproportion impacting the cybersecurity product producer/consumer ecosystem. There is a reality in that there are thousands of cybersecurity product companies (vendors) in the overall ecosystem. That number of companies implies a number of salespeople that grossly outnumber the number of customers, the CISOs. One hundred percent of those salespeople want the attention of CISOs in the hopes of winning their business. If a CISO considers the number of hours per workday, or week, there simply isn't enough time to speak to them all. Considering that, a CISO must be strategic in managing relations with salespeople. Salespeople vary in terms of approach, aggressiveness, and relationship building. Some of the more successful ones will aim to build a relationship with CISOs. This has proven beneficial as CISOs change jobs but generally remember good and/or positive relationships.

Negotiations

Ultimately a salesperson has tremendous power over the price you pay for the product they are selling. Here are some effective negotiation tactics when dealing with vendors:

- Leverage competition – every cybersecurity product vendor has competition, use this to your advantage. Do your research and identify multiple vendors that could potentially meet your needs. Make it clear that you have other options and could easily take your business elsewhere if you don't get favorable terms. A little healthy competition usually works to bring prices down.
- Push for added value – see if the vendor will include training, customization/professional services, implementation services, or other add-ons at no additional cost if you agree to the deal. Often, they have the flexibility to throw in a little extra value as a closing incentive.
  - Bundled services – try negotiating lower rates if you agree to purchase multiple services. Push for discounts on bundled services or bulk ordering. This increases business for them while saving you money.

- Research their cycles – salespeople often have quotas to meet at quarter or year-end. Negotiating deals toward the end of certain business cycles can give you more leverage. Salespeople may be especially motivated to finalize a deal even if it isn't in their best financial interest.
- Explore payment term options – if a vendor won't budge on price, see if they will agree to longer or more flexible payment terms to help make the deal work for your organization. If you have the means, offering to pay the full amount upfront can also incentivize discounts.

The key is negotiating from a position of strength and leverage. Make it a focal area to emphasize the value of your business and use persuasion techniques to show you have attractive alternatives if their terms aren't favorable enough.

As a leader and professional CISO one of your strongest weapons/qualities is your emotional intelligence. Understanding the perspective of the salesperson is important as it will ultimately make for a positive experience. This is important because the opposite just does not end well for either side. Being empathetic to the reality of the salesperson can, and most likely will, make you a better customer. This also needs to extend out to the other entities that will fight to get your attention, for example, the marketing folks.

EXPERT ADVICE – SALESPEOPLE

Successful Chief Information Security Officers (CISOs) understand that salespeople also strive for success and, to achieve that, they need to establish a human connection and build relationships with their buyers. If a CISO treats their salesperson as a human rather than just a means to an end, they are more likely to form a partnership that benefits both parties. As a result, the CISO gains an empathetic partner who is transparent with pricing, product/service strengths and weaknesses, and the ability to deliver what is needed efficiently and effectively. Establishing a human connection first and foremost means a healthy relationship between the buyer and seller. Trust creates a win-win situation for everyone involved.

– Maria Graham, Director of Business Development, Nuspire

REAL-WORLD PERSPECTIVE – SALESPEOPLE

A salesperson will approach with good intentions to market their next best solution in hopes you have an active project. If you set up a meeting, help them understand your process upfront. They will be grateful and will engage with your team more effectively.

– Douglas Gotay, Experienced Sales Professional

CISOs and vendors should embrace the opportunity to give back to the cybersecurity community because this will, undoubtedly, strengthen the overall field. By sharing knowledge and lessons learned, sponsoring events, supporting nonprofits, and mentoring newcomers, CISOs and vendors demonstrate a collective commitment to the common goal of managing cyber risk in the marketplace and strengthening the overall ecosystem. There is much to be gained from adopting this approach; CISOs are able to stay abreast of the evolving threat landscape and vendors have the opportunity to build credibility with their buyers.

– Carlos Guerrero, Senior Compliance Executive, 360 Advanced

In the realm of sales, it's imperative for us to recognize the pivotal role CISOs play in our interactions. Understanding how to effectively collaborate with these key decision-makers is paramount to achieving our desired outcomes and ensuring overall success. CISOs are instrumental in assessing the security implications of the solutions we offer and determining their suitability for their organization's needs. As sales professionals, it's our responsibility to establish trust, demonstrate our products' value proposition, and align them with the security objectives of our prospective clients. By forging strong partnerships with CISOs, we can leverage their expertise to tailor our offerings, address their concerns, and ultimately drive mutual success. This collaborative approach not only strengthens our relationships with clients but also enhances our ability to deliver impactful solutions in today's competitive market.

– Adam Lahav, Majors Account Executive, Wiz

TRUE STORIES – SALESPEOPLE

STORY 1

Trust and two-way communication are so critical to the vendor and security leader relationship. There are a lot of outside forces that have influence, life is simpler if the two parties who have the most to gain and the most to lose are on the same page. The security leader is buying products or services for a specific outcome and the salesperson gains a commission and, ideally, a relationship they can continue to sell to for years to come. It's in everyone's best interest to produce successful outcomes.

I've seen positive and negative outcomes, and I'd say transparency and teamwork have the largest impact on these. I have had a CISO of a large enterprise tell me, "We will get this deal done by the end of your quarter, but it will be painful. Our procurement will ask for everything you'll give them and more, our legal will take this into the 11th-hour negotiating terms, my name may become a curse word in your company, but we will get this done!" I took this information back to my manager who gave the advice, "Tell him our quarter ends a week early".

If I relayed this message, it would have eliminated trust and made this a bad relationship for everyone. My manager said it because his motivation was to get the deal in at the end of the quarter at all costs.

The Account Manager is the liaison between the customer and the vendor. That relationship matters. If you cannot trust that individual it's a bad sign for the future. On the other hand, if you can trust the Account Manager and they can trust you when you are in need or crisis mode, they are the ones you can count on to get the help you need versus badgering you if you bought their product, upsell or service, this would have never happened to you.

– Neil Saltman, Enterprise Account Executive

STORY 2

One of the most leveraged sales tactics is the reverse timeline for closing deals. Sales reps look at the time when you tell us you need to buy and build out an assumptive timeline with something like "if you need to buy by December then we need to start contracts by November, a proof concept in October, etc.". The flaw is that we look at it from the purchase date.

Early on in my career, I had a vocal security leader tell me, "I don't care about your quarters, my bonuses are paid based on completed projects". If you remind a salesperson of your goals and the timelines (deployment, audits, renewal, or replacement, etc.) that matter to you, it will make for a much smoother process the whole way through for everyone. Communication can prevent so many negative outcomes like the daily calls, "Where's my order"? The constant requests for more meetings and the painful attempts to keep your attention will be reduced most of the time by communicating.

"I'm a big believer that the more people we help the better the world is. Helping salespeople can make your life better in reducing the painful part of procuring the things you need to do your job".

– Neil Saltman, Enterprise Account Executive

DEMAND TRANSPARENCY AND HONESTY FROM
YOUR SALES AND MARKETING VENDORS

During the big conference doldrums between Christmas and RSA Conference, I found myself engaged in a conversation with a pre-revenue stage cybersecurity business focused on a sub-category of Threat Intelligence. We'll call them Threat Mapping Inc.

They believe that there was wide open space to operate in this sub-category before any platform vendors or existing players – of which there were only a few – caught on to their entrance.

Threat Mapping Inc.'s head of marketing was doing what all early-stage hires do: wearing 100 hats, having the time of their life, and doing everything on their own. At the insistence of a mutual acquaintance, she scheduled a meeting with my marketing agency to discuss offloading some of their tactical responsibilities to a firm like ours that specialized in working with cybersecurity companies.

We spoke once. Then a second time. A flurry of emails went back and forth between the conversations.

And by the time we spoke a third time, I realized something: their order of operations for what to offload first, second, and then, third was out of whack.

They deserved radical transparency and honesty from me.

"Listen . . . this isn't in my best interest to say this to you. But what you want – paid ads – isn't what you need right now. And while I could sell you those services, it's not the right thing for your business today".

The contours of their eyes behind their glasses changed. They visibly sat back in their chair. I could tell they were in deep thought.

"You know . . . I've been struggling with this same question. Are paid ads the marketing investment that we need to be making right now? And you just confirmed my own intuition. It's not the right time. And I appreciate you bringing this to me right now".

We could have easily sold them a paid ads package. Made some money on that contract right away.

But we knew it wasn't the right time for their business to make that investment. The confidence wasn't there that it would help them move to the next level.

So, we didn't.

"Demand transparency and honesty from your marketing or sales partners. They owe it to you to act in your best interest at all times. Set that standard and hold them accountable to that standard".

– Mike Krass, Founder, MKG Marketing

VENDORS

When dealing with cybersecurity product vendors a CISO will want to understand, or at least gain insight into, many factors. Some of them are:

- How long has the company existed?
- Who are the founders and key team members?
  - What qualifies them to build such a product?
- Who makes up the advisory tier(s) of the company?
- How mature is the product?
  - Is the product in General Availability (GA)?
- Where is the company in its journey (bootstrapped, pre-seed, seed funded, Series A/B/C, etc.)? Here are some general points that should give you a sense of what each stage could mean:
  - Bootstrapped
    - The founders self-fund the company.
      - This could include the use of personal credit cards and assets.
    - The founders acquire small loans or cash from friends and family.
    - At this stage there is generally no formal investing process in place.
    - At this stage, the company is typically founder-controlled or there is some type of small partnership in place.
  - Pre-Seed/Angel
    - Typically, the stage includes some outside angel investors putting up small amounts of capital, possibly in the $10K – $400K USD range.
    - May or may not involve formal investment paperwork.
  - Seed Funded
    - Typically, this stage sees the first formal VC round in the $250K – $2MM USD range.
    - At this stage, most companies seek to set an externally vetted valuation and capitalization (cap) table.
      - A cap table is a chart used by startups to depict ownership stakes in the business.
    - Preferred shares may be distributed.
  - Series A/B
    - This stage raises the bar of investment with VC-led rounds designed to scale business operations for growth.
    - Series A is typically in the $5MM – $15MM USD range.
    - Series B could be in the $10MM – $50MM USD range.
    - Funds typically go toward growing the team with key resources, scaling product, marketing/sales, and scaling out development teams.
    - This stage typically sees the formalization of a board of directors and the invested VCs may very well want seats (voting and/or observatory) on that board.
    - This stage typically also sees the addition of metrics/KPIs and formal reporting structures.

- Series C/D/E
  - These stages encompass larger funding rounds, $50MM+ USD.
  - These stages should see steady revenue, and this requires focus on supporting growth.
  - A professional executive team is put in place.
  - The path to a potential Initial Public Offering (IPO) starts to form.
- What features exist today and what is on the roadmap?
  - Professional perspective – if a business development or sales professional from any company cannot show you the product roadmap on the spot, that is a red flag and something to consider. Companies that have their act together and run a professional shop can share a roadmap at any given moment.
- Do you perform Proof of Concept (PoC) or Proof of Value (PoV) deployments?
  - Do these cost money?
- Are you looking for us to be part of your customer feedback loop (this gives you the ability to help guide and mold the product)? Or are you just trying to get a sale?
- Provide me copies of your externally validated security maturity.
  - Copies of external pen tests.
    - Get contact information so you can reach out directly to the pen testers.
      - You want to understand the rules of engagement for the pen test. If the vendor (the one being pen tested) was very restrictive then chances are they truly don't want the truth, they just want a nice-sounding report.
  - Copies of compliance or certification reports.
    - ISO-2700X
    - PCI-DSS
    - SOC-2
    - UK Cyber Essentials
- Who are your competitors?
  - A confident company will always give you a real list of competitors.
- If you have the expertise (either you or relevant team members) to get value from the answers to these questions:
  - Explain your software engineering processes.
    - Focus on how thoroughly they test the product(s), especially looking at how they handle edge and/or corner cases.
      - This will give you a sense of how mature the engineering team is, and how stable the product will be.
  - What happens when tests fail?
    - This should impact a release cycle as opposed to the release of a product where there are known bugs.
  - What is the process (automated and/or manual) for code to be scrutinized from a security perspective?
  - Do your software engineers perform security testing (fuzzing, etc.) as part of their standard unit testing?

- Is a Secure Software Development Life Cycle (SSDLC) process/framework followed?
  - If so, please share the documentation for said process/framework.
- Is cryptography supported? If so:
  - Are keys and/or initialization vectors involved?
    - If so, how are those secrets managed?
    - Are they rotated on a regular cadence?
- How are sensitive user data and passwords handled?
  - Please explain for both run-time and for at rest (persistently stored, etc.).
  - Real-world advice: This question is critical because some vendors expose sensitive data at run-time but may secure them well at rest. Anyone with local access to the hosting entity can then see said data elements when the software is running (e.g., via "ps -ef" on a *nix system).
- How do you actively defend against common web app ingress vulnerabilities like SQL injection, cross-site scripting (XSS), cross-site request forgery (CSRF), etc?
  - Do you use input validation?
  - Do you sanitize input?
  - If so (to either or both), how?
    - If this is based on homegrown code, dig into this because there are plenty of validated libraries for this type of functionality.
- How frequently do you install security updates on operating systems, frameworks, libraries, etc.? Is this an automated process?
- Do you have a vulnerability disclosure program?
  - How do you accept/fix security flaw reports from external entities (researchers, etc.)?
- Do you have an SBOM that shows all dependencies and libraries?
  - If so, are you willing to provide me with copies of those lists?
- What security controls are in place around deployments and CI/CD pipelines?

If you are dealing with more reputable and established vendors, then you must make it clear to the relevant personnel that you will not become an account they only check in on when it is renewal time. Unfortunately, this happens. But as a paying customer, you can ensure they pay attention to you by making it clear that you will not accept becoming a number on some spreadsheet. You have buying power, use it. This is negotiating power.

EXPERT ADVICE – VENDORS

The stage a startup is at can greatly influence the experience security leaders are likely to have when working with the company. It's important to keep these differences in mind and make decisions that take them into account. Pre-seed and seed-stage companies are just starting out, so their products are likely to have a high number of gaps, bugs, and performance issues. Subsequently, working with these startups may require a higher investment from the security team. At the same time, early-stage companies are typically very responsive, eager, and ready to work nights and weekends to make sure that their customers have a great experience. More importantly, they are usually happy to get feedback from CISOs and security teams and are quick to act on that feedback. Customers who understand these dynamics can get an opportunity to, not only, negotiate favorable prices but also help shape the product roadmap in the direction most aligned with their needs. As the startup moves toward later stages of development (Series C, D, and beyond), it transforms into a mature company. On one hand, this leads to more robust, stable, and mature products, more comprehensive documentation, and peace of mind that the company is less likely to go out of business a year later. On the other hand, this also often means slower response times, and lower willingness to include feature requests and ideas on the company roadmap. By that point, only the most significant customers can usually get an opportunity to talk to the company CEO – the majority will be interacting with sales and account management teams.

– Ross Haleliuk, Cybersecurity product leader

REAL-WORLD PERSPECTIVE – VENDORS

Unlocking Innovation and Agility: The Strategic Advantage of Partnering with Cybersecurity Startups for CISOs

Engaging with early-stage cybersecurity start-ups as vendors presents a nuanced landscape for CISOs. While concerns about the longevity and stability of these start-ups are valid – given the uncertainty of their survival or potential acquisition – embracing such partnerships can offer unparalleled benefits that often outweigh the perceived risks. Here's a more in-depth look at why the collaboration with these burgeoning entities is worth considering:

1. Innovation at the Forefront: Larger cybersecurity vendors might find themselves encumbered by legacy systems, entrenched technical debts, and a labyrinth of internal bureaucracy, leading to a slower pace of innovation. Start-ups, unshackled by such constraints, operate with agility, embracing cutting-edge technologies and frameworks to address the evolving landscape of cybersecurity threats and requirements. This dynamism often positions start-ups as the go-to source for groundbreaking solutions, enabling CISOs to tackle pressing challenges with novel approaches.

2. Unmatched Flexibility: The scale of operations for larger vendors necessitates substantial deals to justify their extensive sales, engineering, and support efforts. This scenario might sideline entities not among the ranks of the S&P 500, making it challenging to secure tailored engagements. In contrast, start-ups thrive on the opportunity to build trust, brand recognition, and lasting relationships. As such, early-stage start-ups are more inclined to adapt their offerings to meet the unique needs of their clients, regardless of the client's market stature, ensuring a level of service and customization larger vendors may not afford.

3. Access to Premier Talent: The cybersecurity field is notoriously competitive, with a perpetual shortage of skilled professionals. Start-ups often attract top talent by offering opportunities to work on cutting-edge problems with significant autonomy and advanced tools. Partnering with these start-ups allows CISOs indirect access to this pool of talent, providing insights and solutions that might be unattainable internally due to resource constraints or the allure of more prestigious names in the tech industry.

4. Educational Opportunities: The rapid evolution of the cybersecurity domain means that staying abreast of all pertinent challenges and solutions is a formidable task. Start-ups usually concentrate on solving specific issues, making their founders and teams de facto experts in their chosen niches. Collaborating with these entities not only facilitates a deeper understanding of specific challenges but also exposes CISOs and their teams to cutting-edge thinking and methodologies that can enhance their organization's security posture.

5. Cost-Effectiveness: The financial structures of established vendors, necessitating adherence to sales targets and the recovery of significant operational costs, often translate into higher pricing for mature solutions. Start-ups, eager to establish their market presence and validate their solutions, may offer more competitive pricing. This cost advantage, coupled with the potential for negotiated perks in exchange for promotional support, makes start-ups an attractive option for CISOs looking to maximize their security investments.

While the partnership with early-stage cybersecurity start-ups carries inherent risks, the advantages – spanning innovation, flexibility, access to talent, educational benefits, and cost savings – present compelling reasons for CISOs to consider such collaborations. This approach not only enhances an organization's cybersecurity framework but also supports the dynamic ecosystem of innovation within the cybersecurity domain.

– Rubi Arbel, CEO & Co-Founder, Scribe Security

As a serial entrepreneur and the founder of a cybersecurity company whose primary customer is the CISO, I can tell you that it is terrifying to learn how much CISOs dread interactions with vendors. When I started my company, my entire purpose was to make the life of my future CISO customers easier and make them immensely successful at their jobs. To know that these same individuals who are the sole reason for my work to exist, might find it stressful to interact with me, gives me a great pause. CISOs should keep in mind that just like they want to be treated as humans first and "sources of revenue" second, founders also want to be treated as humans first and "vendors" second. My most successful customer relationships have turned into strong friendships because we connected as humans before and independent of the business transaction. Founders are more likely to go out of their way to support CISOs who are respectful, friendly, and genuine, and offer them their best discounts as well as create as many opportunities as they can for CISOs to shine on both a professional and personal level.

Arti Raman, CEO and Founder, Portal26

INVESTORS

The cybersecurity product/vendor landscape does not exclusively consist of the consumer (the CISO, CTO, etc.) and producer (the product vendors). Another integral component in that ecosystem is the investors, particularly professional investors, the Venture Capitalists (VC).

EXPERT ADVICE – VENTURE CAPITALIST

Don't underestimate the value of working with early-stage startups rather than just incumbents. While established vendors may have more mature platforms, younger companies are far more willing to work with you to shape their products to your company's needs, while also bringing new technology approaches that may be more effective than what older solutions can provide. You will likely be able to develop a personal relationship with company leadership, often at the CEO level, ensuring a high level of customer support. Offering to be a design partner to companies at this stage will often get you a product that is tailored to your requirements and at the same time is more affordable than a legacy vendor's solution.

– Seth Spergel, Managing Partner, Merlin Ventures

REAL-WORLD PERSPECTIVE – VENTURE CAPITALIST

How CISOs should evaluate the startup vendor's product innovation: When buying from a startup it is important for a CISO to understand if the company has truly achieved product market fit with a best-of-breed product (i.e., there is a real use case, and the company can address it). Often times this involves two things:

- Validation that the startup has deployed at "real" customers (who are not friends and family).
- Pilot deployment with clear KPIs to validate:
  - Features.
  - Superior performance vis-à-vis competitors.
  - Scalability.
  - Integration with existing security infrastructure.

The first step can be achieved through Q&A during initial meetings and doing some blind checks. The second step requires investing time to clearly define measurable pilot objectives and KPIs to evaluate success. Without clear KPIs the startup runs the risk of ending up in Pilot Purgatory and the CISO runs the risk of having no clear data to determine whether there is sufficient business value to deploy the startup's technology within their enterprise. These two simple steps can go a long way to ensure that CISOs triage startup vendors efficiently to evaluate product innovation.

– Anik Bose, Managing Partner, BGV

As a venture capital firm focused on cybersecurity and related sectors, we work closely with CISOs of enterprise organizations to identify and validate new areas for product innovation not addressed by existing vendors and solution providers. Most cybersecurity innovation is driven by the changing threat landscape and the critical role information security professionals play in addressing these attack vectors.

Cybersecurity is now a business enabler, accelerating digital transformation and the safe and responsible adoption of advanced technologies such as AI while ensuring compliance with increased regulation. Many leading CISOs recognize the critical role they play in driving cybersecurity innovation and business growth. They proactively engage with leading venture capital firms helping entrepreneurs build the next generation of solutions and companies.

At Forgepoint, we closely collaborate with CISOs to:

- Develop and validate new investment theses and opportunities. This includes:

- Identifying unmet needs and emerging vendors building next-generation solutions.
- Mapping the current vendor landscape to uncover market gaps and understand potential competitive dynamics.
- Help our portfolio companies hone and refine their product and go-to-market strategies. This includes:
  - Vetting and verifying early versions of products by testing them in controlled production environments.
  - Shaping product roadmaps including the features and platform capabilities required to effectively address emerging threats.
  - Enabling the adoption and implementation of these new, vetted solutions, by actively using them to address the new attack vectors in their production environments.
  - Sharing direct feedback and opportunities for improvement with the entrepreneur and team.
  - Serving as references to other CISOs interested in evaluating these new vendors and their technology.
- Cultivate meaningful and mutually beneficial long-term relationships. This includes:
  - CISO to CISO, peer-to-peer connections and conversations, catalyzed at curated, in-person private dinners and summits on the latest trends and shared perspectives on what's impacting our industry.
  - Enabling their participation in our portfolio companies' advisory boards to gain additional exposure and professional expertise while further influencing product development, go-to-market, and growth.

Forgepoint has a very active Cybersecurity Advisory Council composed of leading CISOs, experienced entrepreneurs, seasoned executives, information security experts, and government leaders who are the key to our success in protecting the digital future.

"We invite and encourage leading CISOs to actively engage with our global community and ecosystem to help develop future cybersecurity solutions and foster critical innovation".

**– Alberto Yépez, Co-Founder and Managing
Director, Forgepoint Capital**

13 Be an Effective CISO

BEING EFFECTIVE

There is a high level of subjectivity around the notion of effectiveness. For the purposes of this book, a pragmatic stance will be taken with a focus on fundamental skills, such as financial literacy, that can be applied generically to any organization and have proven themselves to be important in the industry.

BASICS

These basic items require an investment in attention, time, and sometimes money yet they are major components that can lead to a high level of effectiveness:

- Remove roadblocks – in order for your security teams and squads to be effective a CISOs job as a leader is to remove roadblocks. Facilitating team success and growth is a success factor all CISOs should strive towards.
- Build and manage relationships – relationship management has a strong and direct impact on your success as a CISO. As a security leader, relationships with key stakeholders (C-Suite, peers, board members) in the business are extremely important. Building and nurturing these relationships takes time and perseverance. How each CISO builds credibility with these relationships will vary, but it is crucial that trust and confidence are built.
  - A major part of building relationships is acknowledging that not everyone will agree with you all the time. This is natural and it's ok. Educating yourself in areas such as negotiation and conflict resolution skills will prove invaluable.
- Exercise patience – resist emotional reactions and the pursuit of quick fixes. When facing a challenge or a major security incident, it is natural to react and seek out a quick fix. Realize that folks above and below will look to you, as a CISO, for a general reaction and act accordingly. Being calm under stress goes a long way to making people confident in your abilities.
- Exercise strategic thinking – there is a reality to the tactical and operational needs placed on a CISO. But, getting stuck solely on the tactical will derail a CISOs strategic focus and diminish the value a CISO has as a senior executive. Invest in qualified personnel to manage the day-to-day operations. Then focus on your own critical and strategic thinking skills in order to become a valuable executive expertly contributing to the overall strategy of the organization.
- Always push – put yourself in a state of mind where things can always be improved, stagnation is simply unacceptable in such a fast-moving and ever-changing digital landscape. As a leader, you set the pace and others will notice it. Hold yourself to a ridiculously high standard while not

DOI: 10.1201/9781003477556-13

imposing it on anyone else. Not everyone will work as hard as you but no one should be outworking you.

- Push for risk acceptance at the right levels – the CIO, CTO, and/or CISO should not be the ones accepting risk at an organizational level. Risk acceptance needs to happen at the C-Suite, senior executive, and board levels. If that is not the case where you work, then it's time to make some noise and push for change.

- Embrace crisis – events and incidents will occur. Accept and embrace these moments of crisis as they can prove beneficial. Most mature organizations want a tried-and-true CISO, not one who has never faced real-world challenges. Battle scars can be a walking resume, especially when it's proof of an approach that is not just about recovery and damage control. If the end result of dealing with a crisis shows a forward-thinking transformative recovery with an aim at preventing similar incidents in the future, this can be seen as very valuable. Some of the most valuable leadership qualities in cybersecurity are developed and proven under the conditions created by dealing with real challenges.

- Stay on track – staying on track with strategic initiatives is essential for a successful security program. Distractions will come, but to be effective a CISO cannot accept large derailments. If strategic initiatives are designed properly, they should work toward prioritized risk management. As tempting as distractions might be, they mostly interfere with work toward the larger risk-related goals. Staying the course requires energy and determination but is important.

- Formalize and implement policy – there is nothing exciting or sexy about policies. Moreover, getting a policy right takes time, but policies are simply a necessity. Having formal policies sets forth the rules of engagement within an enterprise. Policies are an important foundation for nearly everything that a security program pursues.

- Understanding regulations – regulations, and compliance with them, can be time-consuming and seem like nothing more than a time suck. The risk of fines and other legal matters is too high not to make understanding regulations a priority.

- Focus on team skills – properly training staff requires budget and time away from day-to-day tasks. But these are worth the investments as team retention has a direct impact on overall security program success.

- Pursue proper documentation – hardly anyone in the security industry enjoys documentation. It is certainly time-consuming, and it can be tedious. But, when it comes time to understand how to do something, documentation is the natural answer and what people reach for. Beyond the pragmatic aspect, having sufficient and accurate documentation is a clear show of maturity.

- Document lessons learned – aim to document lessons learned in a way that can be leveraged in the future. Your succession and team members will appreciate this as it will prove invaluable. Only by learning from the past can security programs really improve over time.

- Embrace advancements – we are trained to focus on risk. But there is no need to be stuck in that mindset. Balance is achievable, embracing advancements rather than exclusively focusing on the risk they bring with them.

- Architect for the future – a CISO must be forward-thinking, forward-looking. At the same time, a CISO must always pursue a state of anti-fragility. Being reactive is natural but always analyzing future angles can prove invaluable. This is especially so when factoring in systemic risk, the epitome of fragility. Systemic risk in cybersecurity refers to the potential for widespread and significant impact on an entire ecosystem, often resulting from heavy and/or fragile integrations and dependencies. To future-proof environments while factoring in systemic risk, consider the following strategies:
    - Adopt a zero-trust mindset – some say, "Never trust, always verify". Others just say, "Never trust". Whichever works for you as a CISO assumes that threats could come from anywhere, both outside and inside the network.
        - Work toward enforcing strict access controls and segmentation, applying least privilege principles, continuous authentication, and authorization of users, devices, applications, and APIs.
    - Don't limit your purview – attackers don't limit their attack vectors and as a CISO you should consider as many angles of attack as possible. You may not be able to cover them all, but part of being effective is being aware and as ready as possible. Consider things like:
        - Can someone socially engineer their way into our facilities?
        - Are our ID badges clone-able?
        - Can someone get in via remotely administered facility systems (HVAC, Elevator control systems, etc.)?
        - Can someone install rogue WiFi access points in our facilities?
    - Embrace security by design – integrate security into processes as well as development life cycles of products, applications, APIs, and systems from the onset.
        - Work toward the pursuit of an SSDLC that implements secure coding practices and ensures security measures are embedded in code, infrastructure, and application layers.
    - Embrace privacy by design – privacy considerations should be integrated into solutions and services from the onset.
        - Work toward data minimization practices and native data protections (encrypt of data, not volumes, at rest, etc.). Other considerations are tokenization and data masking techniques.
        - Stay compliant with data protection regulations (GDPR, CCPA, etc.) and pursue privacy by design principles.
    - Pursue adaptive security architectures – work toward security architectures that are flexible and can adapt to evolving threat landscapes.
        - Modular architectures allow for quick updates and changes while automation and orchestration tools facilitate dynamic responses to threats.
    - Foster a security-first culture – humans often represent the biggest vulnerability. Empowering them as one of the first lines of defense is a sound layer of security.
    - Pursue comprehensive IAM – the goal is to ensure only authorized individuals and services have access to the appropriate resources.

- While nothing covers 100%, the following are sound measures: implement MFA and granular access policies while actively monitoring for anomalous access patterns.
- Plan for IR and DR – acknowledge that security incidents will occur and prepare with a well-defined incident management program that minimizes impact and facilitates rapid recovery.
- Pursue resilience – while IR and recovery are after the fact, resilience brings forth business continuity in the face of security incidents. Actively pursue solutions that are highly available without having to resort to DR efforts.
  - Test your incident-related plans and resilience via simulations and drills.
- Address the supply chain – securing the supply chain sounds great, but it may not be possible because you may not control what happens within an external entity. Yet, your security is only as strong as the weakest link in that supply chain.
  - Aim to establish security requirements for third parties and vendors by incorporating them into contracts. Then use continuous monitoring for relevant risk management.
- Pursue threat intelligence and sharing – whenever possible it is valuable to participate in threat intelligence sharing platforms. Use threat intelligence services to get real-time information and aim to adapt your defenses accordingly.
- Leverage AI for threat detection and response – seek to leverage advanced capabilities to deploy AI-powered security tools for continuous monitoring, anomaly detection, and automated incident response. On this topic, mastering the use of AI where it is strong is imperative.
  - Embrace the fact that the humans that make up a business will use AI, there is no way around that. Seek out that balance between security and functional use.
  - AI is a large field of study and one where at least knowledge of the basics can go a long way. Here are some basics that can help a CISO:
    - Machine Learning (ML):
      - Neural networks are a type of ML model inspired by the structure and function of the human brain. They are made up of artificial neurons (connected nodes), that are in turn organized into layers, the basic ones being:
        - Input – receives initial input.
        - Hidden – intermediate layers between the input and output layers where computations and transformations are performed.
        - Output – produces final output (predictions, etc.).
      - Supervised learning – this technique involves training algorithms on known and labeled data. The goal is to identify patterns and create predictive output. Relevant examples include intrusion detection, email spam detection, and malware detection.

- Unsupervised learning – this technique involves finding patterns and structures in unknown, unlabeled data. Relevant examples include modeling individual behavioral patterns, anomaly detection, and malware classification.
- Deep Learning – this is a subset of ML that uses neural networks to learn and model complex patterns in data sets. Relevant examples include network flow analysis and identification of APTs.
- Natural Language Processing (NLP) – NLP involves the analysis of human language data. Because it is strong in contextualizing data and performing sentiment analysis, relevant examples include the detection of phishing emails and social engineering attempts.
- Reinforcement Learning (RL) – RL involves decision-making components that can also take automated actions. A relevant example is a series of network-based RL agents that can learn and respond to detected security activity in real-time.
- Federated Learning – this technique enables ML models to be trained on decentralized data sets. A relevant example is collaborative threat detection. In this use case, disparate organizations or divisions can train security models without compromising data or privacy.
- Generative Adversarial Networks (GANs) – GANs are a type of deep learning technology that involves two neural networks playing wargames against each other. A relevant example could be one side generating blue security models and the other red. The game would consist of the blue side detecting adversarial actions from the red side.

- Continuously reflect – scrutinize yourself to continuously improve. Some questions CISOs could periodically ask themselves are:
  - Are we (the security program) adding business value to this organization?
    - Where can we add more value?
  - Are we asking the right questions of the business?
  - Is the business asking the right questions of security?
  - Are we using the budget in the most efficient way possible?
    - Are there products we are not getting value from?
    - Is there a great overlap between some products?
  - Am I asking the hard choices and facing the hard challenges?
  - Are we being transparent enough?
  - Do I have the right talent on my team?
  - Are we keeping the good talent challenged and satisfied with their roles?
  - Do we really need to pursue modern technologies, or can they wait?
  - Are our use cases directly tied to a risk that could be actualized if not better managed?

BALANCE

Regarding the point of being technical or not, becoming a balanced CISO is a controversial notion. There are CISOs who are not technical and do not see the need for this type of knowledge. And then there are CISOs who have come up the technical ranks and see this type of knowledge as a necessity. Then there are those who feel a balance between the two extremes is possible. Ultimately, organizational culture and size will have an impact on which type of CISO you are there at that organization. Personal preference also comes into play.

There is no question that some of the best security leaders have great business acumen and knowledge. The non-technical types feel that it is important to know more about business than security or technology. More importantly, though, the best security leaders know the organization they work for at an intimate level. This inherently brings with it business knowledge. Some of the areas where these leaders have knowledge that leads to efficiency and success are:

- They know how the organization makes money (understanding of the business model).
- They know who the customers are and understand where security can add value to them.
- They know what the organization's strategic objectives are and always aim to link in with those long-term goals.
- They add value in business functions such as M&A exercises, technology transformations, and cost optimizations.

From the technical perspective, it must be acknowledged that a large percentage of the assets a CISO is responsible for are based in technology. For instance, data is a technical artifact that is stored on some medium that is, in turn, technology-based. If a CISO is responsible for protecting data, then logic would imply that technical knowledge can only be beneficial to the role. Another strong point here is that security teams are generally technical in nature. The underlying respect they give a person (not the role or title) is partially earned by showing value in this area.

The ultimate contention in this book is that achieving a balance between business and technical skills and abilities is a good goal to work towards.

BUSINESS TERMS

Here are some basic business terms a CISO may likely encounter:

- Assets – resources owned by the company.
- Liabilities – obligations (debt) that the company must honor.
- Profit and Loss (P&L) statement – this document summarizes a company's revenues and expenses over a specific period of time. It showcases a company's ability to generate profit.
- Earnings Before Interest, Taxes, Depreciation, and Amortization (EBITDA) – this single data point showcases a company's operating profitability and

cash flow by adding back non-operating expenses like interest, taxes, depreciation, and amortization expenses.

- Total Addressable Market (TAM) – this value defines the total potential revenue opportunity for a product or service.
- Annual Recurring Revenue (ARR) – this is the yearly value of recurring revenue from sales, subscriptions, or other recurring revenue sources.
- Cash flow – this is the amount of movement that moves in and out of a business, including income and expenses.
- Accounts receivable – this is the amount of money owed to a company by customers for purchases prior to some point.
- Accounts payable – this is the money owed by a company to its suppliers for goods or services received.
- Gross margin – this is the difference (a percentage of revenue) between a company's revenue and the cost incurred to generate that revenue.
- Burn rate – this is the rate at which a company is spending money.
- Churn rate – this is the percentage of customers lost within a given period of time.
- Cost Volume Profit (CVP) – this is a technique that examines the relationship between costs, sales volume, and profits. Components:
  - Cost – this value refers to the expenses incurred by a business in conducting its operations (producing, selling, etc.). Costs can be divided into:
    - Fixed costs – these are expenses that remain constant.
    - Variable costs – these are expenses that fluctuate.
  - Volume – this value refers to the quantity of products and/or services sold or produced during a period of time.
  - Profit – this value represents the difference between the total revenue generated from sales and the total costs incurred in creating those sales.
    - Profit = Total Revenue – Total Costs
- Break-even – this is the point at which a company's total revenue equals its total expenses.
- Working capital – this is a point in time value representing the difference between a company's assets and its liabilities.
- Customer Acquisition Cost (CAC) – this value represents the cost of acquiring each new customer.
- Basis Points (BIPS) – this unit of measurement represents small percentage changes. But these seemingly small values exist in areas where they can represent significant impact. As an example, consider an interest rate increase from 3% to 3.15%, which has increased by 15 basis points.

FINANCIAL LITERACY

Financial literacy is one of the most important skills for leaders in any field, but especially for those in cybersecurity. This type of knowledge empowers CISOs to make data-driven decisions, ensure alignment of cybersecurity goals with organizational objectives, and effectively communicate the financial impact of risk and cybersecurity initiatives to executive leadership.

Financial Concepts

- Budgeting – budgeting is a fundamental concept that involves allocating financial resources to achieve specific goals. A well-managed and planned budget ensures that cybersecurity teams and initiatives are adequately funded.
- Total Cost of Ownership (TCO) – TCO refers to the comprehensive cost associated with owning and operating assets over their entire lifespan. The calculation is simply adding up all relevant costs for a dollar amount TCO value.
  - An example of TCO is the evaluation between a cloud-based and an on-premise security solution. CISOs must factor in things like power redundancy, hardware failures, maintenance, upgrades, and potential downtime costs. On-premise overheads such as these could create a higher TCO in comparison to cloud-hosted environments.
- Return On Investment (ROI) – ROI analysis measures the financial gain or loss resulting from an investment, relative to what it costs. An example of ROI is a scenario where a company invests in a new WAF. A CISO can compare the WAFs cost against the quantified reduction in potential losses or reduced number of web application security incidents. It is usually expressed as a percentage and is typically used to compare a company's profitability over time or to compare the efficiency of different investments. The general formula for ROI is:
  - ROI = Net Profit/Cost of Investment * 100
  - As an example, a company spends $1,000 USD on email marketing. This generates $1,500 USD in sales directly from that campaign. The net profit is $500 USD ($1,500 – $1,000). The ROI would be: 50% (500/1,000 * 100)
- Opportunity cost – opportunity cost relates to the value and benefits that are not achieved with the solution not chosen in a comparison. Sometimes, security investments may conflict with other business objectives. For example, not choosing a strong zero trust solution so as to not slow down employee productivity.
- Financial Impact Analysis (FIA) – financial impact analysis involves identifying potential vulnerabilities and estimating the likelihood and financial impact of some incident. It aims to quantify both direct and indirect financial consequences. The general components of a FIA are:

  - Revenue impact – analysis of how an event or decision will impact the organization's revenue streams.
  - Cost impact – analysis of changes in costs (services, operational, etc.).
  - Cash flow impact – analysis of how the timing of cash ingress and egress are expected to change.
  - Profitability impact – analysis of the effect of changes on profitability.
  - Risk assessment – analysis of potential financial risks and uncertainties associated with some scenario.

Financial Statements

One of the fundamental skills of financial literacy is understanding financial statements, including the income statement, balance sheet, and cash flow statement. As a cybersecurity leader, you may not be responsible for preparing these documents, but you need to understand how to read and analyze them.

The income statement, or profit and loss statement, shows the company's revenues, expenses, and profits over a specific period, typically quarterly or annually. Reviewing income statements can help a CISO understand the drivers of profitability and set realistic budgets. The key components of an income statement are:

- Revenue – the total income generated from the sale of services and/or products before any expenses are factored in (subtracted).
- Cost of Goods Sold (COGS) – what it costs to produce the services and/or products sold by the company.
- Gross profit – revenue minus COGS.
- Operating expenses – operational costs incurred for a business to function (sales, administration, travel, etc.).
- Operating income – gross profit minus operating expenses.
- Net income – the final profit after all expenses (operating, taxes, external services, etc.) have been deducted from total revenue.

The balance sheet provides a view of a company's assets (what it owns), liabilities (what it owes), and shareholder equity at a specific point in time. Studying the balance sheet can help a CISO assess the financial health of a company and act as a gauge of how hard to push for cybersecurity funding. The key components of a balance sheet are:

- Assets
  - Current assets are short-term in nature and are expected to be sold.
  - Non-current assets are long-term investments (property, facilities, etc.).
- Liabilities
  - Current liabilities are short-term in nature and due within one year.
  - Long-term liabilities are due after more than one year.
- Shareholder equity – the amount the owners of a company have invested in their business after deducting liabilities.

The cash flow statement outlines the actual cash coming into and going out of a business and in turn the cybersecurity function. Monitoring cash flow ensures a CISO knows how much liquidity (cash) is available for operations and investments. The key components of a cash flow statement are:

- Operating activities – these are cash flows related to the company's primary business activities, like selling services and/or products.
- Investing activities – these are cash flows from the purchase and/or sale of company assets.
- Financing activities – these are cash flows related to repaying debt, taking loans, and/or raising funds.

When reading financial statements, it is recommended that you initially treat it like a blurry photograph and slowly bring it into focus. Start with the big picture looking at overall finance data. Then compare those figures with previous time periods to identify trends, such as growing revenue or increasing debt levels. When you have a pattern of growth or shrinkage, use financial models, such as return on equity (derived by dividing net income by shareholder equity), to evaluate the company's financial health and performance relative to some baseline (industry standard, peer levels, etc.).

Cost-Benefit Analysis (CBA)

Most CISOs carry the burden of financial justification regarding security invest-ments. This is sensible as any fiscally responsible organization would want to know their money is being spent responsibly. This is typically provided via a Cost-Benefit Analysis (CBA). CBAs involve calculating and comparing the benefits and costs of a decision, or policy to assess its feasibility or compare the value of alternatives. The key components of a CBA are:

- Costs – all expenses associated with a decision (change, new project, initial investment, recurring operational costs, maintenance, etc.).
- Benefits – all the expected positive outcomes expected from the decision (cost savings, new revenue, increased revenue, and improved productivity).

Generally, this process starts with an identification of all the costs and expected benefits associated with the decision. Then comes a quantification exercise where monetary values are attached to the listed costs and benefits. The aim is to esti-mate their value over a complete lifecycle. If applicable, calculate discounts such as depreciation of the value of money. Then calculate the Net Present Value (NPV) by subtracting the total discounted value from the total discounted benefits. A positive NPV indicates that the benefits outweigh the costs.

As an example, let's work with a company looking to migrate from an on-premise environment to a cloud provider. Part of their goal is to enhance data protection and increase operational efficiencies. Here are some example costs:

- Migration – a one-time cost for migrating infrastructure and data to the cloud environment is estimated at $100,000 USD.
- Service fees – enhanced security services are available as a customer of the cloud provider. In order to take advantage of these services there is a new cost of $120,000 USD annually. This is an increase from the current $80,000 USD spent on the on-premises solutions.
- Training – training on cloud technologies for IT staff is estimated at $20,000 USD.

Example benefits:

- Reduced risk of outage – the company has experienced on-premises sys-tem downtime resulting in losses of $150,000 USD annually. Migrating to a cloud provider with superior redundancy and security measures could reduce this risk by 80%, leading to substantial savings.

- Operational efficiency – the cloud-provided infrastructure enables more efficient operations (storage costs, backups, etc.), expected to save $30,000 USD annually.
- Capital expenses – moving to a cloud environment does away with the need to upgrade hardware, the company avoids a projected expenditure of $250,000 USD over a five-year period.

Example CBA Calculation (all costs imply first-year impact unless otherwise specified):

- Total Costs: $160,000 USD
  - Migration – $100,000 USD
  - Service fees – $40,000 USD ($120,000 – $80,000)
  - Training – $20,000 USD
- Total Benefits: $200,000 USD
  - Reduced risk of outage – $120,000 USD (80% of $150,000)
  - Operational efficiency – $30,000 USD
  - Capital expenses – $50,000 USD ($250,000/5 [years])
- NPV – $40,000 USD ($200,000 – $160,000) or (benefits – costs)

The CBA depicted in this example suggests a positive net benefit of $40,000 USD in the first year. This would mean that the financial benefits of the migration outweigh the costs. Additional elements, such as savings and reduced risk, are further justification for this company's decision to migrate to a cloud provider.

Alignment

Cybersecurity goals need to align with organizational objectives. In order to make that a reality CISOs must understand the organization's business model and objectives. This requires collaboration with key stakeholders to identify business drivers, such as increasing customer trust via protecting their data, meeting regulatory compliance, and protecting intellectual property. By aligning cybersecurity efforts with these objectives, CISOs can demonstrate the value of security initiatives to the overall success of the organization. Sometimes this is not easy to achieve. Sometimes this requires a CISO to be very persistent in their journey of becoming part of that organization. This can be done tactfully but one must believe in the adage that persistence overcomes resistance.

A major part of creating that alignment is understanding where security fits into an organization's strategy and culture. CISOs should be aware of where they initially and overtly add value, the potential financial impact of cybersecurity incidents. Organizational and revenue protection positions a CISO uniquely because these impacts can include direct financial losses (legal and regulatory penalties, costs associated with incident management, and direct losses due to data exfiltration and trust erosion). Understanding and being able to effectively communicate these financial implications help CISOs gain support and prioritize investments but more importantly it empowers them to get the business to acknowledge the cybersecurity function as mission critical.

Budgeting

Creating and managing budgets is an essential activity for any leader, but especially critical in cybersecurity given the ever-changing threat landscape and the fact that it generates frequent requests for additional resources. Building an accurate budget requires analyzing past spending, forecasting future needs, and building buffers to cover unexpected costs. CISOs need to consider both recurring and one-time expenses, including salaries, training costs, tooling, and third-party services. The budget should reflect the organization's risk appetite, operational priorities, and anticipated financial impact of potential incidents.

Areas like understanding vendor contracts and leveraging technology advances can have major impacts on a budget. A CISO needs to be able to scrutinize purchase requests to unearth waste and avoid unnecessary spending. This is especially so for legacy contracts. For example, building on capacity for growth is essential as costs tend to rise on an annual level (unless contractual provisions have prices locked in). Historical context matters when coming into a new role. There may be budget hikes in existing contracts that need to be accounted for in budgets moving forward. Be sure to include portions of a budget for maintenance, training, and support, not just new tooling.

Beyond vendors and contracts, CISOs must accurately assess their team's skills and capacity to factor them into the budget. This involves understanding the costs of recruiting, hiring, onboarding, training new team members, and evaluating the existing workforce and identifying skill gaps. Retaining great people requires knowledge of employee engagement strategies and their related costs. When faced with an open requisition, a CISO needs to be able to financially justify the need for backfilling roles. In some cases, it may be more cost-effective to use outside vendors instead of hiring full-timers. Budgeting also involves identifying productivity gaps, for this, identifying those things the team could not handle but still need attention. Then determine whether additional resources, new staff, or third-party vendors, can cover the needs.

Related to budget and teams, it is wise to research salary ranges when creating new positions so offers are competitive. For existing members, evaluate bonuses, equity, and benefits as motivating factors. For example, profit sharing can be a good incentive for security personnel who meet metrics around risk and availability statistics. Another area where this may come into play is when considering tradeoffs between hiring specialized security staff versus training existing employees. Training some team members to double as other roles can save a lot of money while providing growth for the team members that get trained in new skills.

Strategically an effective budget allocation involves a balanced distribution of financial resources based on business needs. CISOs should consider factors such as risk levels and regulatory requirements when allocating portions of the budget. For example, if an organization has high costs due to user-centric security incidents, proactive measures like security awareness training can possibly help reduce those costs. Along the trajectory of being strategic, exploring cost-effective security solutions (leveraging FOSS, negotiating with vendors for better pricing, or exploring contract consolidations) can go a long way in the business seeing you as a partner and not just a cost center.

Financial literacy equips CISOs with the necessary tools to navigate a cyber-security landscape that is linked to business needs. By making strategic decisions based on financial insights, CISOs can build resilient cybersecurity programs that are aligned with broader business objectives.

CYBER INSURANCE

One area where a CISO needs to add value is in evaluating cyber insurance poli-cies. CISOs need to understand the important areas of a policy and their implica-tions based on the details. For example, if a policy does not cover losses from certain types of attacks this is an important detail with potentially large implica-tions for a business. The better policies cover costs beyond just response and recov-ery, they cover things like legal liabilities, ransom negotiations, ransom payments, and possibly lost revenue due to an incident. Insurance brokers are essential to educate you, secure optimal terms, and provide advice. Irrespective of the details stay clear on the fact that risk transference is of limited protective value, cyber insurance policies complement, but do not replace, active protection and sound security programs.

When a CISO scrutinizes a cyber insurance policy, they play a crucial business role. A thorough review of the policy is necessary to help stakeholders and peers understand what is covered and what is excluded. Here are some key areas a CISO should scrutinize in a policy:

- Scope – first-party coverage should include direct costs to the organization due to an incident. These can be in the form of ransomware-related costs, data recovery, business disruption losses, and crisis management costs. A CISO should ensure these coverages are in alignment with the organiza-tion's risk appetite.
  - Look for any third-party coverage. This coverage should include lia-bilities to third parties caused by a cybersecurity incident in your orga-nization. Any organization that is the custodian of sensitive client or customer data is vulnerable to lawsuits. This coverage is intended to cover relevant legal fees, settlements, and regulatory fines. This part of the policy should cover scenarios that are relevant to the organization's operations and regulatory environment.
- Exclusions – these policies often have specific exclusions and understand-ing what is not covered is as important as understanding what is covered. Exclusions are for the benefit of the insurer and insurance companies are in the business to make money. Common exclusions may involve large events that simply are out of the control of a CISO or organization, these are things like global events or incidents involving outdated but needed technology. A CISO needs to identify exclusions and try to address these gaps through operational practices or additional insurance products.
- Coverage – the total coverage limit must be adequate to cover potential losses from cyber incidents. The CRQ data that gets put together when addressing risk comes into play here. An assessment of the organization's

risk exposures and related CRQ estimates will provide the data points for a coverage analysis to be meaningful.

- Sub-limits and deductibles – many policies have sub-limits for certain types of losses. This value places a maximum on the amount that the insurance provider will pay for a specific type of loss. Deductibles represent the amount the organization must pay before the insurance provider begins coverage. These need to be evaluated to ensure the organization is comfortable with them.
- Retroactive reporting periods – a retroactive coverage provision ensures that incidents occurring before the policy is active, but discovered during the policy period are covered. This is important because in some cases incidents are not discovered until sometime after the actual incident. Similarly, there could be an extended reporting period that allows for claims to be made for a certain time after a policy expires.
- Incident response and claims processing – it is essential to understand the insurer's requirements for incident notification. If a window gets missed the organization may lose the ability to file a claim. Also, pay attention to the claims process and the types of documentation the policy specifies and/or requires.
- Third-party vendor coverage – most organizations rely on third-party vendors in some way. A CISO should verify whether the policy covers events and/or incidents originating at the third-party vendor.

By paying close attention to the details in cyber insurance policies, a CISO can help ensure that the organization is receiving comprehensive and relevant protection. In some cases, there is an opportunity to customize the policy or add clauses to address specific risks unique to an organization. Collaboration with legal, finance, and insurance experts is also key to effectively cover an organization with an insurance policy.

Insurance companies are often modifying their requirements for coverage. It is in the best interest of a CISO to be ahead of changes as much as possible. Staying in tune with industry developments and world events is important because often the hints that will lead to some new insurance requirements are found in those developments and events. As an example, at the time of the writing of this book, public companies in the United States are subject to new cybersecurity disclosure rules (www.sec.gov/files/rules/final/2023/33–11216.pdf) from the SEC. The original rule proposal would have required companies to provide proof of board-level cybersecurity expertise. That provision was not included in the final rules that were made public. But this is the type of event that an insurance company will take note of. This could impact the questionnaire that a customer must fill out, treating the board of directors as a key cybersecurity control and, in turn, impacting coverage and/or rates.

SECURITY-FIRST CULTURE

As a security leader, you set the pace and are the foundation of the security culture. A security-first culture ingrains security in every business process, decision, and action. When most of an organization is in this type of sync, there is a level of inherent protection against threats. A CISO can build such a culture based on these principles:

- Transparency – a CISO builds trust by being transparent. Transparency applies to many different areas, from the organization's security posture to incidents. Irrespective of the area, open communication about challenges and how they are addressed can create a culture of trust and make others realize that they are in this fight with us.
- Leadership – the journey toward a security-first culture requires a clear vision of what a security-first culture looks like. This involves articulating the value of security as a team endeavor, business enabler, and competitive advantage. By actively leading from the front, a CISO can inspire trust and confidence from the entire organization.
- Empowering employees – employees should be inspired and empowered to take an active role in the company's security posture. The message is that security is not just the IT department's responsibility; it's a shared responsibility touching all employees within the organization. This can be achieved by creating clear policies and processes, recognizing, and rewarding positive security behaviors, and providing channels for collaboration. This could involve regular cross-functional meetings, tabletop exercises that include disparate groups, and collaborative risk assessments to ensure that security is front and center in all business processes.
- Continuous awareness – creating a security-first culture requires ongoing education and awareness at all levels. This involves storytelling (real events, etc.), continuous training programs, phishing simulations, security newsletters, and engaging content that fosters a mindset of vigilance.
- Tactfully leverage technology – building a security-first culture is mostly about people and processes. But technology plays a role as well. A CISO needs to seek out solutions that are user-friendly and minimize the impact on employees.
- Incident management – despite best efforts incidents will still take place. A security-first culture will make these events judgment-free experiences and learning experiences. A well-defined incident management program minimizes stress over time, creating a blame-free post-mortem culture that focuses on learning and improvement. This approach ensures that the organization not only responds effectively to incidents but also continuously improves.
- Consider the following strategies:
  - Executive tabletops – include executives so there is engagement leadership.
  - Security champion program – identifying and preparing representatives from different parts of the organization to champion security initiatives within their teams.
  - Gamified learning – implementing engaging, game-like exercises where employees learn effectively through fun activities (CTFs, hackathons, etc.).

Over time, these efforts should lead to a decrease in security incidents, increased reporting of suspicious activities, and a generally positive shift in the organization's security posture. Success in this space makes security a topic across all levels of the organization.

ADVERSARIAL MINDSET

One of the most important things a CISO can do is understand the enemy as best as possible. More importantly, a CISO must try to inspire the team to do this as well. Embracing this adversarial mindset involves thinking like a potential attacker in order to anticipate angles of attack. This anticipation can help proactively prepare for threats. Here's how a CISO and team can begin adopting this mindset:

- Immerse yourself in the culture – in this case, the culture of the adversary (attackers, hackers, etc.) is unique and a CISO may find insights by becoming somewhat intimate with it. As an example, consider attending some conferences or get-togethers that only appeal to this crowd. Go there like a sponge, willing to learn as much as you can. Who knows, you may be physically sitting or standing near one of your actual adversaries. Observing interactions and listening to conversations could prove insightful. Other sources of value could be participation in bug bounty programs or in security forums. Make sure that the people behind these programs are the real deal.
- Stay in tune with up-to-date tactics – keep up to date with the latest cyber threat intelligence with some keen attention on emerging patterns, tactics, techniques, and procedures (TTPs). This knowledge allows for better anticipation of potential attacks.
- Play war games – conduct and participate in war gaming exercises that simulate specific attack scenarios. An example of these is regular red and blue team exercises. Penetration testing could also be helpful if they are conducted by folks with a real attack pedigree. These activities simulate actions from an attacker's perspective. It's a proactive way to find and fix security gaps before malicious actors can exploit them, improve preparatory strategies, and test the effectiveness of post-incident plans (IR and DR).
- Leverage deception technologies – deception technologies, such as honeypots, can mislead attackers and expose their intrusion techniques. This approach can also provide insights into attackers' motivations.
- Threat modeling – implement threat modeling processes based on the identification of potential threats, categorizing them, and assessing their likelihood and potential impact. This can expose how appealing a target is to an adversary.

Some of the benefits of adopting an adversarial mindset (e.g., improved IR and DR) are weaved into the points just covered regarding how the proper mindset can be pursued. Other benefits are:

- Shift toward proactive security – by being better educated in terms of how attackers might target your organization you can make some moves to shift from a reactive to a proactive security stance. Where possible, the goal is to implement protective mechanisms before attacks occur.
- Defensive innovation – along with a shift toward proactivity, thinking like an adversary gives you the ability to exercise innovation in developing protective mechanisms.
- Stronger security culture – embedding an adversarial mindset within an organization creates the foundation of a culture of vigilance and security awareness. This becomes the basis of security as a collective responsibility.
- Deeper risk awareness – understanding attackers' perspectives facilitates prioritization of specific risk areas and security efforts.
- Competitive advantage – a mature security posture, built on a foundation of understanding adversarial mindsets and tactics, can be a competitive differentiator. This can show customers, partners, and stakeholders how serious a CISO you are when it comes to protecting data and assets.

Understanding and adopting an adversarial mindset is a strategic approach that enables CISOs to be as ready as possible for ever-changing attack vectors. From a very real-world perspective, staying N steps ahead of potential attackers is highly unlikely, at least given the current state of technology, even factoring in AI. This is all about understanding that in the ever-changing landscape of cybersecurity, the ability to think like an attacker could help you anticipate what an attacker may do. This could prove to be invaluable.

ENVIRONMENTAL, SOCIAL, AND GOVERNANCE (ESG)

ESG initiatives have become a public way that organizations can show their commitment to sustainability, ethical practices, and good governance. As a CISO you must ensure the security program does its part regarding these areas. The governance component is relatively straightforward, but the other areas have some real-world possibilities as well.

Environmental

A forward-thinking CISO can contribute to the environmental area by:

- Supporting sustainability – the focus would be leveraging holistic sources of data the security programs actively pursue. In particular, asset inventories can support sustainability in IT asset lifecycle management. Ensuring that the lifecycle is properly informed at specific stages, such as disposal, and then processes adhere to environmental best practices can significantly reduce electronic waste and environmental impact. This could involve scrutinizing vendors as sustainable during a TPRM process and working with IT operations to properly dispose of end-of-life hardware.

- Supporting energy efficiency – a CISO can advocate for and implement green computing practices (such as with cloud providers) as part of the organizational infrastructure. This would align with broader organizational environmental goals.

Social

The social aspect of ESG focuses on the organization's relationships with the community, suppliers, customers, and employees. Respectively, a CISO can contribute by:

- Building transparency – by implementing transparent practices related to cybersecurity, a CISO can build trust with many of the entities of interest. This should include clear communication about how data is stored, used, protected, and possibly shared.
- Supporting education – by promoting a culture of cybersecurity awareness the social importance of cyber protection is supported. This should extend beyond just the employees of an organization and should include awareness campaigns for the broader community. These types of public service announcements show the organization's commitment to an informed and protected community.

Governance

The area of governance in ESG pertains to an organization's leadership and internal controls. It's the area where a CISO's work is most relevant, as such contributions can be in the following areas:

- Data privacy – a major focal area for most CISOs is data privacy and protection. A lot of traction and support can be gained by having evidence of the way an organization handles data and the fact that it meets the highest standards of integrity and compliance. This not only supports ESG messaging but also builds trust with the community, customers, stakeholders, and employees. It is a clear showcasing of the organization's commitment to responsible governance.
- Supply chain security – a CISO can extend organizational requirements to the supply chain, ensuring that suppliers adhere to similar security and privacy standards. This approach directly demonstrates the organization's broader commitment to secure and ethical practices across its entire ecosystem.

Through these initiatives, a CISO can elevate an organization's posture while also building community credibility. Significant contributions to ESG objectives demonstrate how integral cybersecurity is to modern-day responsible corporate citizenship.

SELF-PRESERVATION

There are many angles to consider when it comes to protecting yourself once in a CISO role. Mental health issues, burnout, and personal liability, they all add up and can have a negative impact on anyone in this role. The role is undeniably stressful. Managing this stress and safeguarding your mental health is your responsibility. Ignoring the personal well-being of a CISO works against the goals of most organizations that would hire one, so chances are you, CISO, are not alone. Here are some strategies a CISO can employ for personal protection against stress and mental health issues, along with insights into potential legal protections:

- Actively pursue work-life balance – you need outlets to balance the stress. This is a fairly simple concept that unfortunately often gets ignored. Prioritize work-life balance by setting clear boundaries between work and personal time. Practice time management to ensure that breaks and time spent on your outlets are part of your normal routine.
- Regular exercise – physical activity is one of the best neutralizers against stress. To augment regular exercise, a healthy diet is in order as is getting adequate sleep. Stress reduction techniques are also recommended, and they can come in many forms such as breathing techniques, meditation, stretching, and yoga. Consider integrating these practices into your daily routine to manage stress.
- Professional support networks – a network of peers with similar struggles can be priceless as they can relate like no one else can. Build and maintain these networks. Peer support groups or professional cybersecurity associations can offer valuable opportunities and coping techniques.
- If needed, seek professional help – there is no shame in this. Don't hesitate to seek help from mental health professionals if you're experiencing strange thoughts, signs of burnout, or other mental health issues. Addressing these as early as possible is imperative.
- Delegate and empower your team – delegating responsibilities effectively can spread the stress across multiple people and help keep it at manageable levels. Empowering your team not only aids in their development but also distributes this burden more evenly.
- Go out of your way to make sure you have coverage – a CISO needs to be many things (as covered throughout this book) and they must all be pursued while always protecting oneself. Being a CISO is a high-risk endeavor, it is the nature of the job. Regarding things like D&O coverage as part of a corporate policy, if you were not able to get that as part of your package, or if you are already a CISO and never bothered to check if you are covered, you must pursue this. Go about it the right way. The goal is to get a certificate with your name on it to ensure explicit coverage by the insurance provider. You may have to go directly to the insurance company. If you do have your paperwork in order, for instance, bring a copy of the company bylaws. Know the relevant sections, in particular, and look for one named something like "Officers Designated". If your role falls into this category, chances are the insurance provider must cover you. In that section you will find something like:
  - The officers of the corporation shall include, if and when designated by the Board of Directors, the Chair of the Board of Directors (provided

that notwithstanding anything to the contrary contained in these Bylaws, the Chair of the Board of Directors shall not be deemed an officer of the corporation unless so designated by the Board of Directors), the Chief Executive Officer, the President, one or more Vice Presidents, the Secretary, the Chief Financial Officer, and the Treasurer.

- For example, your CISO role may be at a VP or SVP level. This means that in this example your role will fall into the "one or more Vice Presidents" category. Based on that, the corporate bylaws set your role as covered by D&O insurance. Get yourself a certificate with your name on it.

CREDO

As a transparent leader, a recommendation is that you have a credo that:

- Will always keep you grounded and properly guided.
- You can share with others so that they understand your principles and what you place value on.

Here is my own credo as an example, I keep it visible as a constant reminder of my commitment to the cause:

As a cybersecurity leader, my personal mission is grounded in the relentless safeguarding of a secure digital landscape with unwavering integrity, fostering a culture of security that extends beyond technology to empower people and protect their way of life. I dedicate myself to protecting our organization's data, systems, and networks against the ever-evolving threats that jeopardize our security, privacy, and trust. This credo embodies the principles and values that guide my actions and decisions in the dynamic realm of cybersecurity. I am committed to:

Excellence

I pledge to pursue and/or maintain the highest standards of professionalism and excellence in every aspect of my work. I will guide, inspire, and support my team with tenacity, passion, empathy, and a clear vision. Together, we will do everything in our collective power to rise to the challenges of protecting our shared future in the digital age.

Ethical Integrity

Recognizing the profound responsibility that comes with safeguarding data, digital assets, and privacy, I vow to uphold the highest ethical standards, ensuring fairness, transparency, and honesty in all my actions and decisions. My actions will always reflect a deep respect for the trust placed in me by my organization, its stakeholders, and society at large. Leveraging technology to secure our digital landscapes, I pledge to consider the ethical implications of our choices. Tools will be used for protection, not at the expense of individual rights or societal values.

Transparency

I pledge to champion trust and transparency while communicating openly about cybersecurity policies, strategies, events, and incidents. I will do everything within my power to ensure all stakeholders are informed and engaged. Recognizing that not all risks can be eliminated, I will prioritize and manage risks in alignment with organizational goals. I will make informed decisions, balancing the need for security with the organization's mission and objectives. Transparently, I will accept responsibility for cybersecurity outcomes, learn from failures, and celebrate successes.

Leading by Example

I vow to lead by example, embodying the principles of this credo in my actions and decisions. I will inspire confidence and trust through my leadership, setting a high standard for excellence, commitment, and integrity in cybersecurity.

Leading With Compassion and Empathy

Recognizing the human element in cybersecurity and the stress that comes with the responsibility of this field, I vow to lead with compassion, supporting and valuing my team's well-being alongside their professional contributions.

Advocacy for Privacy

I will be an unwavering advocate for privacy rights and the protection of data. My commitment extends beyond organizational boundaries to the broader society at large, promoting practices that respect individual rights and contribute to the greater good.

Proactive Vigilance

Recognizing that threats can and will emerge from anywhere at any time, I vow to remain ever vigilant. To the best of my abilities, I will anticipate risks before they materialize, thinking like an adversary aiming to stay ahead of them. My approach to security is not reactive but anticipatory, guided by foresight, strategic planning, and the fostering of a culture of security awareness to ensure that vigilance extends across every level of the organization.

Resilience in the Face of Adversity

I acknowledge that despite our best efforts, security events and incidents will occur. In such times of adversity, I will lead with a calm, decisive, and clear focus on not only responding effectively but also recovering swiftly and emerging stronger. Resilience is a fundamental tenet of our cybersecurity strategy.

Education, Collaboration, and Empowerment

Acknowledging the principle that cybersecurity is a shared responsibility, I commit to fostering a culture of education, collaboration, and empowerment throughout my organization. I will seek partnerships within and outside the organization, sharing knowledge and strategies to strengthen our defenses collectively. Fostering a culture of continuous learning, curiosity, and critical thinking, we will build a more secure organization. Personally, I pledge to remain a lifelong learner, staying informed of emerging trends, technologies, and tactics to protect our digital landscape.

Service to the Community

As a shared responsibility, cybersecurity extends beyond organizational boundaries. Acknowledging this, I vow to serve the wider community whenever possible. Through outreach, education, and collaboration, I will share our strengths and do my best to protect those most vulnerable to cyber threats.

Innovation and Adaptability

Embracing change as the only constant in cybersecurity, I will embrace change, and encourage my team to grow with me. I will encourage creative solutions to cybersecurity challenges, not for innovation's sake but to enhance our security posture effectively. I will strive to achieve balance between innovation and risk, ensuring the technologies we adopt serve our overarching goal of maturing security.

Building for the Future

I am fully committed, to the best of my abilities, to prepare for a future that will be constantly evolving. I vow to do all I can to develop the next generation of cybersecurity professionals and implement a forward-thinking mindset to pursue long-term resilience.

This credo serves as my guiding light, a personal declaration of my dedication and commitment to lead by example, champion cybersecurity as a foundational tenet of our organization, and protect our digital world ethically, with diligence and unwavering resolve.

FINAL THOUGHT

The CISO role is a complex one that is still evolving. To add to that complexity, organizations structure the role differently and treat the CISO function accordingly. There is no question that CISO will have to "be" many different things at different times. A politician at times, a mediator at others, an operator and responder, a source of direction, and a leader always. Leadership aside, this does not mean one has to be an expert in all these areas, but fundamental knowledge is in order so that respect can be earned, and good decisions can be made. These foundational areas can also be the basis for handling the new and unknown as those seem to be a constant in the industry.

The ultimate qualities a CISO can attain are adaptability and flexibility. Acronyms will come and go, acronyms will evolve, new categories will be invented by analysts, new categories will be created by product companies, new attack patterns will be invented by fresh and innovative minds on the adversarial side, this is an industry where the static seems to be short-lived. Hence, adaptability and flexibility are key qualities so that CISOs can handle anything thrown their way, and "be" what they need to when they need to.

Index

800-171 63
800-30 207

accounts payable 246
accounts receivable 246
adaptability *see* soft skills
adversarial mindset 255, 256
AI *see* artificial intelligence (AI)
annual loss expectancy 203
Annual Recurring Revenue (ARR) 246
antifragility 132, 133, 242
Application Security (AppSec) 31, 53, 69, 75,
 104, 107, 110, 148, 149, 150, 152, 154,
 158, 247
AppSec *see* Application Security (AppSec)
artificial intelligence (AI) 35, 115, 117, 121, 122,
 155, 156, 193, 197, 243
assets 245
asset inventory 40, 49, 50, 51
attack surface 30, 31, 42, 48, 49, 51, 54, 55, 56,
 57, 58, 59, 78, 82, 86, 110, 113, 157,
 196, 202, 209, 215, 216
audit trail 72, 127

balance 8, 9, 17, 46, 59, 64, 73, 87, 106, 114, 154,
 157, 158, 164, 165, 169, 170, 171, 188,
 241, 243, 245, 248, 251, 258, 261
Basis Points (BIPS) 246
blockchain 126, 127
Board (Board of Directors or BoD) 4, 5, 7, 14,
 17, 24, 26, 33, 42, 72, 86, 90, 98, 106,
 114, 167, 176, 186, 187, 188, 190, 191,
 199, 200, 202, 205, 209, 213, 217,
 218, 219, 220, 221, 232, 240, 241, 253,
 258, 259
BoD *see* Board (Board of Directors or BoD)
bonus *see* CISO role
burn rate 246
business continuity 30, 63, 66, 70, 89, 94, 123,
 131, 135, 184, 187, 221, 243
business driver 250
business terms 88, 167, 191, 245

career *see* CISO role
CBA *see* Cost-Benefit Analysis (CBA)
Center for Internet Security (CIS) 52, 62, 64
chaos engineering 77, 125, 132, 134, 135, 136,
 157
churn rate 246
CIS *see* Center for Internet Security (CIS)

CISO role 1, 3, 4, 6, 7–11, 14, 23, 25, 44, 99, 178,
 188, 223, 257, 259, 261; bonus 11, 14,
 17, 24, 226, 230, 251; career 17, 20,
 21, 22, 42, 43, 47, 96, 137, 160, 161,
 168, 174, 178, 224, 230; compensation
 10, 11, 12, 17, 24, 96, 146; Directors
 and Officers (D&O) insurance 13, 14,
 258, 259; equity 11, 14, 17, 24; golden
 parachute 13, 14, 15; non-compete 14,
 18; offer letter 17, 18, 24; package 10;
 right of defense 13; salary 10, 11, 12, 17,
 20, 226, 251; severance 14, 18, 186, 240
CJA *see* Crown Jewel Analysis (CJA)
cloud security 31, 149, 150, 154
Cloud Security Alliance (CSA) 69
communication *see* soft skills
compensation *see* CISO role
compliance 6, 12, 13, 18, 19, 22, 35, 38, 46, 51, 61,
 62, 63, 64, 66, 67, 69, 72, 83, 84, 89, 103,
 104, 107, 110, 119, 125, 146, 149, 155,
 162, 176, 180, 181, 182, 183, 184, 185,
 186, 187, 188, 189, 190, 198, 199, 208,
 214, 221, 222, 229, 233, 238, 241, 257
continuous improvement 2, 49, 76, 78, 79, 98, 99,
 107, 114, 121, 124, 131, 133, 135, 136,
 171, 183, 189, 208
controls 9, 13, 35, 36, 37, 38, 42, 49, 51, 52, 54, 56,
 57, 62, 63, 65, 66, 67, 69, 70, 71, 72, 74,
 75, 77, 78, 79, 89, 91, 92, 94, 95, 98, 103,
 104, 106, 107, 111, 113, 114, 122, 124,
 133, 138, 140, 146, 152, 154, 155, 156,
 157, 174, 176, 177, 181, 182, 183, 184,
 185, 188, 189, 193, 197, 234, 242, 257
corporate governance 90, 185, 186, 187, 188, 189
Cost-Benefit Analysis (CBA) 249, 250
Cost of Goods Sold (COGS) 248
cost saving 46, 192, 193, 236, 249
cost volume profit (CVP) 246
credo 259, 260, 261
crisis management 104, 141, 142, 252
Crown Jewel Analysis (CJA) 30, 129, 201
CRQ *see* Cyber Risk Quantification (CRQ)
culture 2, 3, 7, 10, 15, 19, 26, 27, 29, 33, 38, 42,
 43, 49, 62, 76, 85, 92, 93, 98, 99, 101,
 102, 107, 108, 110, 112, 131, 136, 146,
 147, 148, 158, 159, 160, 162, 163, 164,
 165, 166, 169, 171, 175, 177, 180, 185,
 186, 187, 188, 189, 190, 191, 195, 208,
 209, 222, 242, 245, 250, 253, 254, 255,
 256, 257, 259, 260

Printed in the United States
by Baker & Taylor Publisher Services